Lucky Hitler's
Big Mistakes

Lucky Hitler's Big Mistakes

Paul Ballard-Whyte

Pen & Sword
MILITARY

First published in Great Britain in 2022 by
Pen & Sword Military
An imprint of
Pen & Sword Books Ltd
Yorkshire – Philadelphia

Copyright © Paul Ballard-Whyte 2022

ISBN 978 1 39907 437 7

The right of Paul Ballard-Whyte to be identified as Author of this work
has been asserted by him in accordance with the Copyright, Designs
and Patents Act 1988.

A CIP catalogue record for this book is
available from the British Library.

Typeset by Mac Style
Printed in the UK by CPI Group (UK) Ltd, Croydon, CR0 4YY.

FSC
www.fsc.org

MIX
Paper from
responsible sources
FSC® C013604

Pen & Sword Books Limited incorporates the imprints of Atlas,
Archaeology, Aviation, Discovery, Family History, Fiction, History,
Maritime, Military, Military Classics, Politics, Select, Transport,
True Crime, Air World, Frontline Publishing, Leo Cooper, Remember
When, Seaforth Publishing, The Praetorian Press, Wharncliffe
Local History, Wharncliffe Transport, Wharncliffe True Crime
and White Owl.

For a complete list of Pen & Sword titles please contact

PEN & SWORD BOOKS LIMITED
47 Church Street, Barnsley, South Yorkshire, S70 2AS, England
E-mail: enquiries@pen-and-sword.co.uk
Website: www.pen-and-sword.co.uk

Or

PEN AND SWORD BOOKS
1950 Lawrence Rd, Havertown, PA 19083, USA
E-mail: Uspen-and-sword@casematepublishers.com
Website: www.penandswordbooks.com

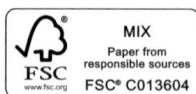

To Philip Fawkes for his resolute support,
to Andrew Roberts for his inspiration,
and to Aza for her unswerving encouragement

Contents

About the Author

Paul Ballard-Whyte

Paul Ballard-Whyte was born in Aberdeen, Scotland and now lives in Oxford, England. He studied British history at Sunderland University and graduated with a First Class Honours Degree. He is married with two adult children; his son is a Major in the British Army and his daughter is Head of Mathematics at an independent school.

Before becoming Head of History and rugby coach at an Oxfordshire Prep School, he was a successful businessman in Travel, Personnel, Restaurant and Hotel businesses, a Parliamentary Candidate at two General Elections, a Formula 2000 racing driver with the JKR Team, a Scottish Superkart Champion and an Epee Bronze medallist.

He has recently published a short story set in Afghanistan titled '*The Three Birthdays*' and has previously written and directed several short films.

Contact Paul via his website: www.luckyhitler.com

'Congratulations to Paul Ballard-Whyte on this well-researched, well-written, and thought-provoking book, which could not have been published at a more apposite time.'

Andrew Roberts, author of *Churchill: Walking with Destiny*

Credits / Acknowledgments

On turning my attention to writing this section, the final manuscript being ready for publication, I began to think more deeply about how I got to be writing a full-sized, non-fiction history book and I realised that the first person to thank was my father, Archie. Sadly for me, he passed away almost 40 years ago, far too young for a man who was loved, respected and admired by all who knew him. My first recollection of being fascinated by history, particularly military history, was when, as a 10-year-old, I would sit with him and watch the documentary, *Victory at Sea*, on a black-and-white TV. He would also tell me of how he had been part of the team in the REME that built and transported the concrete Mulberry Harbours just before D-Day. I was intrigued but the seed of obsession with the subject was not cultivated at school due to the dull and boring teaching methods and the limited history syllabus in the 1960s. Fortunately, the twentieth century, with its two world wars, is a central part of today's curriculum and I have been able to indulge my passion for this period while teaching history at schools over the past two decades. From there grew the ideas developed in the book.

The second person I cannot thank enough is Philip Fawkes. After spending 35 years in a number of different businesses, I decided it was time to go back to school – as a history teacher. Philip had been Headmaster of the Preparatory School attended by my two children, and he was generous enough to offer me a new 'career' in my two favourite subjects at his splendid private school in Oxfordshire, teaching history and, as if that was not enough, coaching rugby. Philip has, since then, proofread each chapter of this book, giving me lots of encouragement over many months while his corrections and suggestions were vital in the production of the first manuscript that I then submitted to agents and publishers.

Andrew Roberts, Britain's' most esteemed historian and author of several best-selling history books including *Churchill: Walking with Destiny* has been a major influence over many years as I enjoyed and absorbed some of his other tremendously informative and captivating books such as *The Storm of War, Masters and Commanders, Hitler & Churchill,* and *Leadership in War.* Andrew was generous in finding time in his busy work schedule to read my manuscript, offering me reassuring compliments and encouraging me to press-on with the writing and the submissions. His guidance and inspiration were immeasurable contributions to my final achievement.

I also have a great deal to thank Henry Wilson for. As the submissions editor at Pen & Sword Books Ltd he was very supportive, showing great confidence in the project by taking it on to publication. Matt Jones, the Production Manager, was always very helpful and understanding of my vision, Olivia Camozzi was fully in-tune with my marketing and advertising ideas and Barnaby Blacker, who sadly passed away before the book was completed, had made invaluable and constructive comments as a copyeditor, in the short time we worked together. Jon Wilkinson turned my basic ideas for the book's jacket design into a superb and professionally finished front and back cover. The original image of Hitler used on the cover had been cleverly re-worked by the artist Julia Koterias at deviantart.com, and I thank her for allowing me to use it on the cover and in all subsequent promotions.

Several people then helped me greatly through the final stages and I am eternally grateful to each of them. Stephanie Hale, Director at Oxford Literary Consultants, gave professional advice and expertise that was very helpful in the final presentation of my manuscript and the ensuing discussions with Pen & Sword Books Ltd. I could never have achieved the Social Media results without Debi at mediamanagerdebs@gmail.com whose enthusiasm, ideas and technical knowledge were irreplaceable. Lewis, my son, as an officer in the British Army, gave me some useful comments on tank tactics; Marcus Ferrar, an author of several books, including *The Fight for Freedom* and an authority on all things Russian, also gave me sound advice; and Michael Timbs at Amera Tech, whose ideas and professional skills assisted me in fulfilling my ambition of having a website (www.luckyhitler.com) that not only complimented the book but promoted it as well.

Most of all, however, I thank my wife, Aza. Not only did she put up with the hours I spent researching, checking, writing, rewriting and editing this book on my computer, but she was, in fact, the instigator of this whole project. In April 2020, the world was presented with what was to turn out to be an international pandemic – COVID-19. When the school where I was teaching moved to online tuition, I decided that this was the moment to retire. Aza promptly told me that I should use the time to write a book – and for that instruction I am most grateful as I have not had a spare minute from that moment onwards, right up to the day of publication.

Without my wife's continuous support, advice and encouragement I could not have reached this point and to her, and to all my friends and those mentioned above, I give my sincere thanks.

Paul Ballard-Whyte
www.luckyhitler.com
Oxford
September 2022

'leaders need to be lucky…Napoleon wanted to know whether his Generals were lucky [before appointing them] and luck undoubtedly does play a large part in war leadership. The role of chance [luck] and contingency in history is worthy of an entire book in itself…'

Leadership in War

By Prof. Andrew Roberts FRSL, RHS, Historian and Author
Page 206, The Leadership Paradigm Chapter,
Penguin Random House, 1745 Broadway, New York,
NY10019 reference #74650

'What luck for rulers that men do not think.'

Adolf Hitler

Prologue

In 1940, many people, ordinary members of the German public, officers and soldiers of the German Wehrmacht and a large number of onlookers around the world, believed that Adolf Hitler, the recently elected, charismatic Dictator of the newly named German Third Reich, was '*the Greatest Commander of all time*'. [15]

This momentous accolade had been publicly declared, and quickly accepted by so many after it was made on 19 July 1940 by Hitler's Chief of Staff, Field Marshal Willem Keitel, soon after the capitulation of France.

It is not surprising so many agreed with him at that moment as Hitler, who all Germans had to refer to as '*Mein Führer*' or 'my leader', had led the German nation from the pit of a world economic depression in 1933

Was Adolf Hitler '*the greatest commander of all time*'? Many people, members of the German public, officers, soldiers and a large number of onlookers thought so. (*Shutterstock*)

to being, without question, the dominant and most powerful country in Europe. Hitler had personally ordered his army, air force and navy to attack and quickly conquer Poland, Czechoslovakia, Holland, Denmark, Norway, Belgium and France. All other countries in Europe such as Hungary, Bulgaria and Romania had quickly complied with his demands and became his allies within what was to be known as the Axis forces, along with the other acquiescent military powers of Benito Mussolini's Fascist Italy and General Franco's Spain.

By any historical standards or comparisons to the accepted great commanders of the past like Julius Caesar, Alexander the Great, Richard the Lionheart, Frederick the Great or Napoleon Bonaparte, Hitler's achievements by the middle of 1940 were unquestionably remarkable and perhaps on a grander scale than had ever been achieved in history, up to that moment.

Keitel's declaration that his Führer was the greatest commander of all time may well have been the ultimate in sycophancy, but he was not alone in believing Germany had found the genius leader it had been longing for and that they had at long last been delivered their Messiah.

This book will consider whether Hitler was worthy of such a magnificent title and look at the skills he possessed, not only as a military commander, but also as a political leader, as well as his qualities as a human being.

'The broad masses of a population are more amenable to the appeal of rhetoric than to any other force.'

Adolf Hitler

Hitler certainly possessed one trait that made him appear a '*genius*' to some and the '*Messiah*' to others, and it was the basis of nearly all the decisions that he either made or were made for him by events. It was a true talent, a gift even – an entrancing, mesmerising power of oratory that displayed a rhetorical skill and eloquence that moved his audiences, large or small, by conveying his deep sincerity and empathy that he blended into his message with a subtle but determined aggression and forcefulness that the often spellbound audience absorbed and with which they became infected.

Every single step towards power happened because of this astonishing ability to capture the attention of an audience from the moment he started to talk, then the almost intangible technique that he used to say words that rang deep into individual souls, rousing the ever more engrossed crowd to emotions of ecstasy and total worship.

For this natural talent, he had neither experience nor training, so it was indeed his greatest piece of luck; it was the foundation of all the successes and further moments of very good luck that he was able to exploit thereafter.

When I was teaching the history of the Second World War to my class of enthusiastic students, I soon noticed that I had been using two phrases on many occasions: '*That was another bit of good luck for Hitler*' and '*That was another mistake made by Hitler.*'

The more I thought about them, the clearer it became that between 1914 and 1941, every step in the rise of Adolf Hitler was due, almost entirely, to his great good luck (Part One), and that every step thereafter, from 1941 to 1945, the decline and fall of Adolf Hitler was due, without exception, to the big mistakes (Part Two) made by him personally.

Without question, the best luck that Adolf Hitler had was the gift of oratory. This turned an otherwise small, unattractive, narrow-minded, and middle-aged man into the charismatic, dazzling, and hypnotizing leader of a nation.

But What is Luck?

According to the Oxford Dictionary definition, luck is '*success that seems to happen by chance, the arbitrary distribution of events or outcomes*'.

Over the centuries many great thinkers and philosophers have tried to explain the phenomenon of 'luck' that can come in two contradictory states: good luck or bad luck. The phenomenon is often also believed by many to happen in 'runs'. Some people argue that 'you make your own' and while that can certainly be true up to a point, can the outcome of your own conscious actions then be described as luck?

British Prime Ministers live in constant fear of the next, arbitrary event – will it be good for them, or bad? When asked what was the most challenging part of being prime minister, Harold Macmillan reputedly replied, '*Events dear boy, events.*' Forty years before that, Winston Churchill, at that time Secretary of State for War, had already declared, '*the difficulties we have to face are only the difficulties of circumstances… and the only opposition we have to encounter is the opposition of events.*'

No matter how much a politician or a minister or even a prime minister likes to believe he or she is 'in charge', events will inevitably conspire against them. How that person deals with those events results in the mark they leave behind them in history.

In 1066, the most famous date in English history, an entirely new era began, and its legacy is the Britain we all know today. But it would probably have been quite different had it not been for the fact that William, Duke of Normandy, just happened to be incredibly lucky. He had his army standing by on the beaches of Normandy waiting for the winds to change so he could sail over to England. He had waited for the whole summer of 1066 and finally, in mid-September, the winds turned favourably. King Harold of England had gathered a larger, well trained, experienced, and well-armed army that was fully prepared to repel any invasion. But luck struck – bad for Harold, good for William, when a huge Viking army in 300 ships attacked the north-east coast of England. This forced Harold to march quickly 200 miles north and there, to defeat the unexpected invaders in the bloody battle of Stamford Bridge. On that very day, the winds in the Channel had changed and William invaded onto an empty beach at Pevensey Bay on the south coast of England.

Only three weeks later, Harold's bloodied, depleted, exhausted and largely now untrained recruits were soundly defeated by the entrenched Normans. The outcome was a consequence of '*the arbitrary distribution of events*', not military genius, changing the history of England forever after.

Five hundred years later, the uncontrollable and unpredictable weather again made its mark on history. In 1588, the Spanish had sent a massive fleet of 350 warships and a huge land army to invade England and displace Queen Elizabeth I. Although the great maritime hero, Sir Francis Drake, undoubtedly played an important part in harassing the Armada, it was in fact, by sheer good luck that a storm in the Channel blew the Spanish fleet a long way off course and the widely dispersed ships were either wrecked or lost at sea. The outcome again was the result of an arbitrary event, not military or naval genius.

One of the greatest military commanders of all time, Napoleon Bonaparte, recognised the value of the luck factor in warfare. He is often quoted as saying that he would much rather have a lucky general than a good one. Napoleon won 53 of the 60 battles in which he fought, and he knew, better than anyone, that even the very best battleplan had to be adapted as soon as contact with the enemy was made, and that no matter how smart the commanders, the unexpected arbitrary event, just that one moment of bad luck or good luck, could so easily determine the outcome.

Adolf Hitler's rise to power fits the dictionary definition perfectly. All of the events looked at in the first eleven chapters of this book did just that – they happened by chance. Each event, some small and seemingly insignificant, others on a much grander scale, was never planned or created by the man who benefited directly from it. Luck can sometimes be 'bad luck', but when such a moment appeared in Hitler's life, it too turned out to be nothing worse than the silver lining of a cloud, with him still ending up the beneficiary.

Was Hitler Just Lucky?

Hitler admitted at a Press Interview:

> *If providence had not guided us I would often never have found these dizzy paths.*

Hitler used the word providence on a number of occasions, but he actually meant good luck, although he never used those two words to describe any of his own successes. Providence means the influence of some unseen or unknown power or a divine intervention but Hitler did not believe in any religion even though he did cynically use the word 'God' in some of his speeches as he understood the strength of Christian beliefs throughout the German population.

Hitler was born in Austria on 20 April 1889. He did not have a privileged or even a comfortable upbringing. His father died when he was only seven years old, and he was forever grateful to the mother he loved more than anyone. He had an older brother and a younger sister, but he was very aware of the incest that had probably caused her mental issues. Hitler showed poor ability at school and was seen as a dreamer and a loner. He possessed a lazy character and it suited him to claim he was an artist as an adolescent, allowing himself to live the life of a drifter and layabout, living off a small inheritance from his father's will, in hostels or dosshouses. He was refused entry to the Munich Art School, and it was only the enforced conscription for the First War that helped to give him some direction and, eventually, a vision for his future.

Hitler's good luck can be seen in the random way he survived four years on the front-line trenches. He was present in many of the great battles like Ypres where his regiment started the battle with 3,600 men and finished with just 611. There can be little doubt that he had an inherently brave attitude to warfare as his records show that he was awarded five medals and decorations, including the Iron Cross, first and second class. Some reports say he was not promoted because he lacked leadership qualities due to his unmilitary bearing, scruffy appearance and odd personality, but others contradict this by claiming Hitler '*refused to be considered for promotion*' [196].

It was only when he found himself involved in post-war politics, due entirely to his astonishing and entirely natural gift of oratory, that his steps to world domination began to emerge before his eyes. Army propagandist Karl Mayr noticed Hitler's gift for public speaking and after describing him as a '*tired stray dog looking for a master*', sent him out to observe political activities in Munich. In September 1919, Hitler came across the German Workers' Party, a tiny fringe faction. He spoke up at one of its meetings and joined its ranks. Within a few months, he had become the leading orator of the group, which was renamed the National Socialist German Workers' Party, or NAZI Party.

The technicalities and theories of leadership skills can be learned, but beneath those is the indefinable X-factor that separates the good leaders from the exceptional throughout history. Individuals like Julius Caesar, Alexander the Great, Richard the Lionheart and Napoleon Bonaparte were the few of the few who seemed to attain, from an early stage, a kind of worshipful status by those who followed them. Numerous other books have been written on this mystery, including some on Adolf Hitler, and despite many words of wise analysis, the X-factor remains the greatest mystery.

The qualities that Hitler did possess have to be acknowledged as a factor in some of his moments of good luck. For example, he deliberately varied his personal timetable and would often not appear at a certain venue, or perhaps leave a meeting much earlier than planned. This habit, which may or not have been deliberate, undoubtedly helped to save him from most of the assassination attempts that had otherwise been well planned (Ch.11).

Hitler trusted few individuals so he also had a habit of giving the same, or similar, orders to more than one individual, thereby creating a kind of competitive chaos among his activists and later his ministers and senior military officers. The confusion this caused had the effect of them pushing innovation and ideas forward at greater speed, as each sought to impress their leader ahead of their rivals.

Hitler had other qualities, not necessarily good but were effective, and became apparent only as he became more powerful. He was single-minded, self-centred, self-confident, duplicitous, dismissive, and impassionate. He certainly had an excellent memory, proved to be a determined negotiator and was an excellent delegator, especially of the 'dirty jobs', an instinct that led to many accusing him of being a 'lazy dictator'. In most matters, he favoured radical solutions, and after he realised that he had the luck, or as he preferred to call it 'providence', he became a gambler, not in cards or horse-racing but in politics and warfare.

Hitler did also have an artistic eye, understanding the importance of icons, images, banners, music, and parades. It was not by chance that the Nazi Party had an aesthetic appeal to the man in the street. The flag was a construct of Hitler's artistic mind – blood-red background, large white circle, and a black swastika. It was powerful and unmistakable.

Nazi Party uniforms were much sharper in design than the clumsy First War one, being black or grey trimmed with white or red and adorned with skull and crossbones insignias. As they marched with a goosestep, the soldiers' calf-length black leather boots stamped emphatically onto the land, and they displayed the visual power in huge gatherings with torch-light parades, triumphal music, and mass rallies at which they chanted *Sieg Heil*. Add to that the click of heels, the straight arm salute, and the shout of *Heil Hitler*. No spectator was left in any doubt as to who the leader was. Hitler had created his own very personal image. Even today, no-one can mistake the 'Hitler-look'. He wanted and created the short, straight black hair, swept to one side, and the trimmed, square 'toothbrush' moustache balanced under his nose; none of this was a mistake – it was masterminded iconography.

Finally, Hitler had one other inherent trait that made him charismatic to his followers, a resolutely stubborn, undebatable belief and blind faith in an ideology that he had created in his mind and that he absolutely believed was right, and from which he could not, or would not, ever move away. By the time he had become party leader, his own ideas on almost everything political, social, military, and philosophical were considered sublime, especially in his own head.

These were, and they remain, important elements of good leadership, but they can only be recognised in hindsight, and only if they have resulted in victory.

For Hitler, however, all of these were his secondary qualities and none of them would have had any effect or influence had it not been for the one truly great attribute with which he had been born, his power of public speaking and his ability to rouse an audience to fever-pitch.

Many years before, in 1897, a 23 year-old Winston S. Churchill had ominously written:

> *'Of all the talents bestowed upon men, none is so precious as the gift of oratory. He who enjoys it wields a power more durable than that of a great king.'*

Hitler soon recognised that within his natural public speaking style, some techniques worked better than others, and by a very early stage in his beer-hall speeches he had already identified and honed the structure of every speech to a format along the lines of:

1. Do not start immediately, stand silent, wait, increase expectancy.
2. Begin slowly by giving credit to the audience for their strength in suffering the shortcomings of the times.
3. Tell them they are being cheated, lied-to, betrayed by authorities and others hidden within society. Gradually increase the speed, use shortened words and sentences and raise the voice pitch.
4. Get louder, use hand signals like finger-wagging and point out those who are causing the pain; name groups in society – bankers, ministers, businessmen, then identify them as Jews and Bolsheviks, all living within their own society.
5. Offer himself as a saviour, one man who is uncorrupted by it all, who has the simple answers to resolving their problems.
6. Then ask the audience if they agree – do they want the same, and do they believe he is the man to do it?

The one truly great attribute with which Hitler had been born was his power of public speaking and his ability to rouse an audience to fever-pitch. Hitler honed the structure of every speech to a perfect format.

As early as 4 May 1923, the 34-year-old rabble-rousing and beer-hall agitator, Adolf Hitler, recently made leader of the National Socialist German Workers' Party, ended his speech with these words:

> '*Germany can be saved only by the dictatorship of the national will and determination to take action. People ask: is there someone fit to be our leader? Our task is not to search for that person. Either God will give him to us or he will not come. Our task is to shape the sword that he will need when he comes. Our task is to provide the leader with a nation which is ready for him when he comes! My fellow Germans, awaken! The new day is dawning!*' [197]

Together, all of these characteristics, oratory skills and presentation tricks produced the man that the people of Germany saw as their *saviour*. At

last, the *volk* believed, a man who had
the vision and the determination to take
them out of the condition that the whole
nation was in after Germany's defeat in
the First World War and its humiliating
treatment thereafter and onwards to a
new and better place.

This could only have happened at a
certain moment in history when a number
of events, not controlled or guided by any
one factor, just happened to create the
need for a new leader in Germany with
those qualities. In other words, Hitler
was the right man in the right place at
the right time.

At any one of countless moments, any
one of these events could just as easily
have turned only slightly another way
and Hitler would never have become the

Adolf Hitler became more and more
convinced that he was somehow
pre-ordained to attain his ideological
vision that he had laid out in *Mein
Kampf.*

great dictator who ruled most of mainland Europe, caused the death of
more than fifty million people and so nearly created a massive German
empire, the Third Reich, that would have included Great Britain and the
Soviet Union.

However, the more those events around Hitler led him, without any
planned strategy, onto and into the next success, the more his followers
grew ever more convinced by his charisma. His audience cried out for
more, and his self-belief grew with every new triumph. Hitler soon began
to recognise how good luck seemed to be helping him out of near misses,
dangerous situations and sex scandals and then leading him on and, after
one of the many times he avoided the assassin's bullet, to finally admit,

'This is proof to me that Providence wants me to reach my goal.'

What makes Hitler's run of good luck so remarkable, however, is not that
it happened once or twice but that it followed him, led him on step after
step for the next twenty years, sweeping aside obstacles he often did not
even see and opening new doors before he got there.

Adolf Hitler became more and more convinced that he was somehow pre-ordained to attain his ideological vision that he had taken from the First War and laid out in *Mein Kampf*; no matter the difficulties, the obstacles or the indirect events, luck was on his side and luck would take him to the summit of his dream.

Just as his dream was realised, however, Hitler made his first big mistake. He now believed what his worshippers were telling him – that he was '*the greatest commander of all time*', that he was the true saviour of the German people, that he was infallible, that he was always right, and that his word was God.

The one impediment to his extra-terrestrial luck was his ever-growing belief that he was not only the '*Messiah*' to the German people but also that he was infallible in his judgement of all things.

Hitler's chain of good luck was interrupted only when he chose to make military decisions based on his own judgement, for Hitler never was the '*greatest Commander of all time*' as laughably described by the sycophantic Keitel.

Adolf Hitler had huge plans for his Third Reich and nothing short of total domination over Europe and Great Britain would satisfy him. But while he was able to occupy some countries, including Poland and France, he did not get his 'hands on' Great Britain or the greater part of the Soviet Union. In fact, Hitler made such profound errors in judgment that even his own generals and tacticians knew he was wrong. They were many times frustrated, even angry, but they were too afraid of him to say so.

Hitler was no military mastermind, and this book will reveal the many occasions when he was the very antithesis of being the '*greatest Commander*'. Whatever successes he enjoyed at the war's outset had more to do with the sheer force of his geographical ambitions and the brutality of his ideology than his strategic or tactical skills as a field commander.

Hitler had been a mere Lance Corporal, a *Gefreiter* and a regimental *Radfahrer* (bicycle) messenger in the First War. He had no experience whatsoever of command in action, had shown no recorded leadership skills in battle, and had certainly never been to staff college, where officers are trained in war craft.

He made many mistakes in the Second World War, partly because his ideological dreams greatly outweighed his abilities, but also because he refused to listen to those men around him who had genuine acumen and training and who he had hired to plan the war he so desperately wanted to win. If he had listened, who knows what might have happened? The war might have dragged on even longer, or even had a different outcome. We can be thankful that his ego prevented him from heeding wise counsel.

This book 'Lucky Hitler's Big Mistakes' will show how Hitler's personal qualities of blind ideology, racist hatred and single-mindedness, played only an early part in his rise to success and that it was chance events and good luck that played a disproportionate part in his early achievements, in his string of successes and, most remarkably, in his avoidance of the numerous assassination attempts; and that his downfall was entirely attributable to the string of big military mistakes that he alone made.

Adolf Hitler was, without doubt, not the greatest commander of all time; not by a very, very long way.

Paul Ballard-Whyte
Oxford, 2022
www.luckyhitler.com

Part One

Lucky Hitler

'I go the way that Providence dictates with the assurance of a sleepwalker.'

Adolf Hitler, Munich, 1936 [160]

Chapter 1

The First World War 1914–1918

'If I should come out of this war alive, I will have more luck than brains.'

Manfred von Richthofen [The Red Baron]

Twelve million soldiers were killed during the bleak trench warfare on the Western Front between 1914 and 1918. Adolf Hitler served there with the 16 Bavarian Reserve Regiment over those four years, being involved in all the bloodiest of battles such as Ypres, Loos, Fromelles, Arras, Passchendale and the Somme where the casualty rate was 50 per cent.

He was certainly lucky right from the start. During the first Battle of Ypres in October 1914, 40,000 men were killed in the first few days; the 16 Bavarian Regiment started the battle with 3,600 men and ended with only 611, one of whom was Hitler [14]. Later that year Hitler's main duties were as a bicycle messenger or *Radfahrer*, a dangerous job where he was often exposed to the enemy while carrying orders or instructions from one side of the battlefield to the other.

In November 1914, a French bomb exploded in the regimental forward command post minutes after he had just gone out, leaving almost the entire staff dead or wounded, including his commanding officer who had just recommended Hitler for the Iron Cross for saving his life a few days earlier [15].

Perhaps his luckiest moment in the Great War was when a British soldier named Henry Tandy claimed – and his story was later substantiated by Hitler himself – that he had had the wounded corporal in his rifle sights on the battlefield in September 1918. Tandy says he hesitated as he felt unease at firing at a wounded soldier and recalled that the German looked over towards him and nodded his thanks for not being shot. Hitler later had a painting of the moment made by an Italian artist named *Fortunino Matania* and had it hung on his *Berghof* wall.

Hitler (far left) fought in all the bloodiest of battles the First World War; Ypres, Loos, Fromelles, Arras, Passchendaele and the Somme but 'Lucky Hitler' came through it all alive and in one piece. (*Shutterstock*)

When the British prime minister, Neville Chamberlain, visited him there in 1938, he saw the painting and asked Hitler why he had a picture of a British soldier on his wall. Hitler pointed at the painting and said *'That man came so near to killing me that I thought I should never see Germany again; providence saved me from the devilishly accurate fire that those British boys were aiming at us.'* [66]

Hitler then specifically asked Chamberlain to personally thank Tandy for sparing his life – and he did.

Despite the massive artillery bombardments, machine-gun attacks and poison gas explosions, the monumental casualty toll, being wounded in the thigh in 1916, and then hospitalised in October 1918 when he was temporarily blinded from a mustard gas attack, 'Lucky Hitler' came through it all alive and in one piece!

But this was just the start of the most incredible run of good luck over the next 25 years that would save his life many more times and would also take him, by events well beyond his influence or control, to a position of absolute power as the ruler of most of the European mainland.

Chapter 2

The Munich Beer Hall Putsch 1923

'No barrier to success is so secure that it could not be opened by a lucky opportunity.'

Democritus, 470–370 BC

A dolf Hitler's good luck continued in 1919 when Dietrich Eckart, the founder of the German Workers Party that was to become the NAZI Party, heard Hitler speak in a beer hall and instantly convinced himself that he had found the *'Messiah'* he had been hoping would appear to save Germany. Eckart generously sponsored the penniless ex-soldier and soon large numbers of people were being introduced to and taken in by Hitler's remarkable public-speaking talent.

In 1921 his passionate, engrossing oratory skills ensured his election, by an overwhelming majority, as the undisputed leader of the re-named National Socialist German Workers' (Nazi) Party. Under Hitler, the party membership and public support grew rapidly, particularly in the southern Germany state of Bavaria.

By 1923, Hitler was expressing the frustrations of the party over the fledgling German Republic government's apparent submission to what many Germans saw as the erroneous and draconian terms of the Treaty of Versailles. The Chancellor and the President of the Weimar government had agreed to co-operate with the French in the Ruhr Valley, and to pay the massive reparations demanded by the Treaty of Versailles. This was, in the eyes of Nazis, a sell-out and thereby an acceptance of guilt that Germany had started the war, an admission that was implacably opposed by Hitler and his many nationalist followers. Remarkably, Hitler had even convinced the former wartime national hero of the German victory at the Battle of Tannenberg, General Erich Ludendorff to join his party. This gave the relatively small Nazi party great prestige and also added confidence to Hitler's plot to seize power from the Bavarian state government in Munich.

Inspired by Benito Mussolini's successful march on Rome one year earlier, Hitler planned to follow up his local *coup d'etat* with a huge revolutionary march against the Weimar government in Berlin.

In November 1923, Hitler and hundreds of his supporters crashed a large public meeting being held by Gustav von Kahr, the Bavarian State Minister in the *Bürgerbräukeller*, one of the biggest beer halls in Munich. Hitler's followers surrounded the hall while he and a gang of his henchmen burst in; Hitler fired a shot into the ceiling and as the crowd silenced, he spoke.

One witness, Professor Karl von Müller, later recalled:

'When he spoke it was a rhetorical masterpiece. In fact, in a few sentences he totally transformed the mood of the audience. I have rarely experienced anything like it'. [15]

Hitler had declared a '*national revolution*'.

The minister and two other politicians were pushed into a back room where Ludendorff was able to convince the three men to give in to Hitler's demands for the march on Berlin. Ludendorff, however, was then persuaded by von Kahr to allow them to leave, promising he would not report the matter to the local police.

But that is precisely what he did. Hitler was furious when he realised what Ludendorff had done and soon chaos and indecision took over and reigned all night. As reality dawned with the new day, failure of the planned putsch seemed imminent.

Next morning, it was agreed that they should march on to the Munich City Hall in the hope that the police and the citizens would support them. So Hitler, carrying a Browning pistol, was at the front alongside Ludendorff and Rudolf Hess, Herman Göring and Max Erwin von Scheubner-Richter, leading around 2,000 of his followers, many armed, through the streets of Munich.

Some bystanders cheered, but when they reached the narrow street that approached the *Feldherrnhalle*, they were confronted by a large police cordon. Hitler had linked arms with Göring, on one side, and Richter on the other. Göring was shot in the leg and Richter was shot dead. Hitler was very lucky and received only a dislocated shoulder. Had the bullet that hit either men been only a few centimetres to the right or the

As the Munich *putschists* approached the *Feldherrnhalle*, Hitler linked arms with Göring and Richter. Goring was shot in the leg and Richter was shot dead. Fifteen others were also shot dead but with the luck of the devil, Hitler escaped the carnage once again.

left, history would have been very different. Fifteen other *putschists* and four police were also shot dead. [90] Ludendorff emerged unscathed and immediately gave himself up.

With the luck of the devil, Hitler had managed to escape the carnage once again. [15]

The Nazi putsch received wide coverage in the press and so at his trial for treason against the state, Hitler was given the perfect opportunity to grandstand his views. This he did in spectacular style by declaring himself guilty when asked to plead, but then going on to do what only he could do, which was to capture the court and the whole wide audience of the German public by his astonishing oratory talent. Dressed in a smart suit and wearing his war medals, Hitler was given the floor by the very sympathetic Judge who was later heard to remark about Hitler '*what a tremendous chap*'. [15]

Although Hitler was given a five-year prison sentence, a number of questionable rules were either ignored or over-turned, including what should have been a statutory deportation to Austria. The Judge stated that '*it cannot apply to a man who thinks and feels as German as Hitler and who voluntarily served in the German army, who attained high military honours, showed great bravery in the face of the enemy, was wounded and suffered damage to his health.*' [15]

Hitler's astonishing good luck followed him into Landsberg am Lech prison where, having been found guilty of Treason against the State, he was given a lenient sentence of five years but he had made such an impact with his addresses to the court, in which he declared, '*I alone bear responsibility… I sought nothing bad… I will shoulder all the consequences*' [4] that he served only nine months and was treated very well, receiving gifts and food parcels from his many admirers.

Hitler's prison cell had a large window with a fine view of the countryside and was comfortably furnished with an armchair and a large desk. He had so many visitors that he himself had to put a limit on the number of his supporters who wanted to come to see him. He also had access to a large library from which he read a wide range of books that he said helped him to '*recognize the correctness of my views*' by reinforcing his beliefs on Jewish Bolshevism and the concept of *lebensraum* (living space). He later described his nine months in Landsberg as '*his university paid for by the state*'.

But most of all, Hitler was extremely lucky that his greatest admirer, a man who literally worshipped him, his *Party Deputy Führer* Rudolf Hess was also imprisoned alongside him. This was lucky because Hess, the son of a wealthy German merchant and a graduate of a Swiss business school, encouraged Hitler to dictate his ideas while Hess wrote them down.

At first Hitler had a very negative reaction to the failed putsch, contemplating even giving it all up, but Hess stimulated his thoughts and encouraged him to talk while Hess wrote. Hitler found speaking his thoughts easy, but he had no skills as a writer.

Without Hess, Hitler would never have been able to write in his first volume of *Mein Kampf,* and affirmed in his later second volume, that the blame for all the ills of Germany were to be laid at the feet of his two great enemies, Marxism and Jewry. *Mein Kampf* elucidated the mission of the Nazi movement, which was to destroy '*Jewish Bolshevism*' [15] and presented Hitler's simple vision of a new German empire – it foretold everything that was about to happen and would go on to sell millions of copies, establishing Hitler as a man with a clear vision for the German people, and eventually making him very rich.

Hitler never wavered from these beliefs and aims. Most importantly of all was that Hess had convinced Hitler that the way to power had to be through the electoral system. Nazis had to be elected in large numbers to the Reichstag.

During his time in Landsberg Prison, Hitler also realised he did not have the executive control over his party that he needed and so, in a public statement to the press in July 1924, he announced he was standing aside as the leader of his party, appointing the widely disliked Alfred Rosenberg as his successor. Hitler probably felt that, on the one hand, being associated with the strong-arm behaviour of Ernst Röhm's unruly Brownshirts, or SA, on the streets of German cities could only harm his chance of an early release from prison.

This may have been a tremendous piece of political planning but was much more likely to have been another bit of good luck, as the party then started to fall apart through internecine fighting. As others challenged to fill the gap, the support for National Socialism across Germany lost widespread support. In the two General Elections of 1924, the National

Landsberg Prison staff gathered in an astonishing 'guard of honour' to applaud, salute and be photographed with their now famous prisoner as he stepped back into a world that he was about to rally to his cause.

Socialists won only 32 seats in May, and that dropped even further, to only 14, in December.

The Judiciary in Bavaria, for reasons likely to have been the consequence of tacit political sympathy, released Hitler on 20 December 1924, after he had served only a small part of his sentence.

Prison staff gathered in an astonishing 'guard of honour' to applaud, salute and be photographed with their now famous prisoner as he stepped back into a world that he was about to rally to his cause. [15]

Hitler's long discussions with Hess had also brought about a radical change of tactics from armed revolution to the legitimate, democratic way to power through the ballot box. This crucial change was the key to Hitler's march to power over the next few years.

Had it not been for the lucky juxtaposition of these events of 1924, it is very probable that Hitler would have become just another failed revolutionary, confined to the footnotes of history.

Hitler's next stroke of luck came literally 'out of the blue', all the way from the USA.

Chapter 3

The Wall Street Crash – 1929

'Luck is what happens when preparation meets opportunity.'

Seneca AD 60

It can be strongly argued that the world event known today as the 'Great Depression' was the de facto cause of the most devastating event of the twentieth century; the Second World War.

Hitler's condition of release from prison on 20 December 1924 had included a ban on making public speeches, and by the time this was lifted by the Bavarian authorities, his magic seemed no longer to be working and public interest in the Nationalist Socialist movement had waned. By 1928 Hitler and his *'Führer cult'* movement no longer seemed a threat in Germany's new democracy. But this decline in broad support had effectively forced the more extreme right-wing supporters to rally behind the one person who never failed to put their aims and ideals over in dramatic prose: their enigmatic leader, Adolf Hitler.

Hitler had used the ensuing years to build and reinforce loyalties within the movement, establishing a new personal relationship with the vast paramilitary army of Nazi supporters, the *Sturmabteilung* (meaning Storm Detachment), better known as the SA or 'Brownshirts'. He had been meeting with businessmen in the industrial Ruhr and sympathising in speeches with small business owners. Then, aided with the ideological fanaticism of his most ruthless disciple, Heinrich Himmler, he targeted the vast number of low paid agricultural workers in the rural stretches of Germany, and a much wider variety of social groups not previously addressed by the party, winning them over from Marxism to National unity. [18] He was also lucky to have found a great organiser in Gregor Strasser, who was a master at the physical mobilizing of the masses, a very important skill not suited to Hitler whose instinct was more for oratory and propaganda.

Despite all these measures, however, the election in May 1928 resulted in only twelve members being elected to the Reichstag. Germany had been enjoying a few 'golden years' of recovery and even relative prosperity, so National Socialism had lost its sharp appeal. Nevertheless, the Nazi party now had returned some notables as deputies in the Reichstag including Strasser, Frick, Feder, von Epp, the recently returned front-man Hermann Göring, and the soon to be master of propaganda, Joseph Goebbels, who told the readers of his Berlin newspaper *Angriff* (Attack) '*We are going into the Reichstag… like the wolf into the sheep-pen.*'

But these twelve were just enough for Hitler to demand the ministries of the Interior and of Education as his price for co-operation. Hitler said, '*He who controls both these ministries and ruthlessly and persistently exploits his power in them can achieve extraordinary things.*' [18] Hitler had shown his brilliance as a politician and as a negotiator, always his two finest talents, and they would take him eventually to controlling most of Europe. It was not, however, the successful use of the political power that the National Socialists had acquired that carried them to further success, but the chaotic failings of the other parties which led to the imminent demise of the Weimar Republic. Once again luck was with Hitler. The coalition partnership of the SDP and the DVP fell out, the other parties in the Reichstag, in response to the declining economy, moved to the right, and the President dissolved Parliament.

Hitler understood very well that his party's current advantage was precarious, that it could go either way, and what he now hoped for was that his good luck would bring about events to his advantage; and that is exactly what happened. It is unlikely Hitler ever considered himself lucky. He was told by his supporters that he was gifted, a '*messiah*', their undisputed 'genius' Führer; for certain, Hitler believed them.

World events, however, were well beyond Hitler's influence, so it was most opportune for him that economies across the western world were in decline at that moment in history. Within a few months Germany was to feel the utterly devastating shockwaves of the catastrophic crash of the world's economy that culminated in the Wall Street crash in the USA.

Unemployment in Germany rose sharply to almost 3 million by January 1929 and the ruling party, the governing SDP, was reeling from attacks from all sides and from mass public unrest. The Social Democrats and Communists were bitterly divided and unable to formulate an effective solution: this gave the Nazis their opportunity and Hitler's message – blaming the crisis on the Jewish financiers and the Bolshevik traitors – resonated with wide sections of the electorate. It was not long before the hated issue of reparations, the millions of marks being sucked out of the German economy that had been inflicted by the Treaty of Versailles, loomed again at the top of public concerns.

The effect on Hitler's party was extraordinary; the seeds had been sown since 1924 and now they reaped the harvest. Membership soared, and throughout vast areas of the countryside disaffected workers rallied in their tens of thousands to hear Hitler's speeches and absorb his propaganda offensive.

Hitler concentrated on the suffering of the ordinary people, the economic failings of democratic rule, and the need that the *entire system must be altered... and for people to restore their belief in leadership*. [18]

Hitler joined the former director of the massive Krupp Company to call for the rejection of a revised American plan to re-structure reparation payments, and the publicity he gained from this put him up as a national leader who was prepared to stand up to the hated blood-letting of the country's economy. The bi-annual Nazi Party rally at Nuremberg was a massive propaganda success as huge crowds flocked to hear the Führer, including many honoured industrialists, thousands of the Hitler Youth, the SA, and the SS. Hitler was at his most vociferous as he hammered home the same messages and exploited every opportunity for agitation. If things had got bad in Germany earlier that year, they were about to get a whole lot worse, and Hitler was now in pole position to exploit the political fall-out to its absolute limit.

Unemployment soared to over four million as industrial output, prices rose and wages dropped, exacerbating the existing agricultural crisis, and people were quick to take on Hitler's message that democracy had failed them. What Hitler wanted now was another general election – and he got it in that September of 1930. Hitler was now in his element; his good luck had led to this opportunity, but it was his very effective skills as a campaigner that were to bring the result for which he had long been looking.

Firstly, Hitler sacked his rather too leftish-leaning Strasser and replaced him with the gifted idealist Joseph Goebbels as the party's propaganda chief. Goebbels was totally loyal to Hitler and worked only to improve Hitler's image.

Hitler offered a positive, clear vision, a utopia, an ideal – an end to moribund coalitions and instead a national government through strength and unity. His positive National Socialist message was that the new Reich 'had to be built on racial values…re-establishing Germany's power and strength as a nation.' The result in September 1930 surprised Hitler and his gifted idealist propaganda chief, Joseph Goebbels; 107 seats won made the Nazi Party the second largest party in the Reichstag.

(*Shutterstock*)

(*Shutterstock*)

Now the years of ground work done by the Nazi party paid off as they conducted an election campaign that would leave all others in its wake, using all the modern resources available to them at that time in a way that had never been done before. Hitler used his speeches, not as a tirade against the Jews, as he had in the decade before, but instead speaking more of 'living space' or *lebensraum,* the unfair imposition of reparations and promising their abolition, the failings of the democratic system, and the idea of national unity under a party that transcended class, land and profession. It was, he propounded, time to *'clear out the rot'.*

He offered a positive, clear vision, a utopia, an ideal – an end to moribund coalitions and instead a national government through strength and unity. His positive National Socialist message was, he said, one of *'national redemption'* as the new Reich *'had to be built on racial values… freeing the genius of the individual and re-establishing Germany's power and strength as a nation'.*

The result in September 1930 surprised even Hitler and Goebbels; 107 seats won, a nine-fold increase making them the second largest party in the Reichstag.

This was the moment that began Hitler's inexorable rise to absolute power. Hitler now came to be seen as de facto leader of the opposition and donations poured into the Nazi Party's coffers. Some major businesses gave generously, but many other businessmen remained suspicious of the extreme nationalist tendencies of the Nazis. His supporters, however, were ecstatic and even more convinced now that Hitler was the *'chosen one'.*

Over the next two years, Germany's political crisis deepened, but Hitler's personal popularity only grew as he applied Goebbels' tactics of flying to all corners of the country (courtesy of Lufthansa, who gave him free use of one its planes), showing his unique personal image and engrossing his new worshippers in passionate speeches that concentrated on nationalist ideals. Goebbels named this brilliant, captivating campaign *'Hitler over Germany'.* This benign, hand-shaking, god-like descending-from-the-sky style was combined with terror tactics on the ground as the 400,000 strong SA Brownshirtss clashed in running street battles with the SPD and Communist paramilitaries, who were also fighting each other. Hitler even managed to twist these clashes into good reasons why the frightened and demoralised middle class should support his promise to *'restore law and order'.*

The political signs were now very promising, and Hitler built on his nation-wide popularity that identified him as the most realistic challenger to the incumbent president, Paul von Hindenburg. In the May election, Hitler won almost 37 per cent of the vote to Hindenburg's narrow victory with 53 per cent.

Germans had voted for Hitler primarily because of his promises to revive the economy (without explaining exactly how), to restore German pride and honour, to scrap the Treaty of Versailles and to save Germany from the communists. Hitler's wide popularity was now on public display and was realised in the next Reichstag election on 20 July. The Nazis made another huge leap forward, winning 230 seats and becoming the largest party in parliament by a wide margin. The Communists and Social Democrats remained enemies and civil war was threatening Germany, so the door was now open to real power for Hitler and the Nazi Party. Hitler, however, consistent with his inbuilt character, refused to compromise; for him, it was the chancellorship or nothing, he stood firm, immovable. His greatest inborn skills shone through in a blend of sheer obstinacy and instinctive political manoeuvrings.

Even when Hindenburg would not agree, Hitler held his ground so that a fifth election in that year was forced upon the German public.

Possibly as a result of voter exhaustion, the turnout in November was well down and the Nazis actually dropped their share of the vote by 5 per cent so Hitler was very lucky that the leftist opposition parties still continued to refuse to work together.

After two more months of wrangling, in which Hitler displayed his inherent political instincts, the former Chancellor, Franz von Papen, finally agreed to Hitler becoming chancellor, so long as he could remain vice-chancellor and 'tame' Hitler for a short time. As von Papen said, 'We've only hired him'. [18]

The 83-year-old Hindenburg's health was weakening, and it was a strained but relieved president who was left with little option but to agree to the appointment of Hitler as chancellor on 30 January 1933.

On the same day, the new cabinet was sworn in and Hitler's first act as chancellor was to ask Hindenburg to dissolve the Reichstag. He did this so that the Nazis and the DNVP could win an outright majority. This would give him crucial authority to pass the Enabling Act that would give

Hitler being sworn in as Chancellor.

the chancellor power to pass laws by decree that could not be cancelled by a vote in the *Reichstag*.

The Nazi Party supporters were euphoric and great celebrations took place immediately. Thousands of SA and Hitler youth carried burning torches in a mass parade through Berlin and many other cities of the Reich.

In the ten years since the Wall Street crash, Hitler had ridden his luck all the way. Events beyond his control had repeatedly given him one lucky turn after another to climb closer and closer to power. He took each one as it came along, using his intoxicating skills as a rousing orator, his instinctive politician's feel and, as a dogmatically determined negotiator, to finally reach the position for which he had sought so long. The former Chancellor Bruning had ominously stated Hitler's basic principles were always *'Power first, politics second'*. [15]

It would not be long before Hitler's astonishing run of good luck gifted him his next step towards absolute dictatorial powers.

Chapter 4

The Reichstag Fire – 1933

'If you want to shine like the sun first you have to burn like it.'

Adolf Hitler

The timing of the Reichstag Fire could not have been luckier for Hitler if he had planned it himself.

In the 1930 general election Hitler's party, the NSDAP or the National Socialist German Workers Party (Nazi Party), had increased its number of seats in the Reichstag from 12 to 107. This still only represented 18 per cent of the popular vote, but it did make them the second largest party. Hitler then ran a brilliant campaign in the 1932 presidential election, finishing second to Hindenburg but with a remarkable 37 per cent of the vote. From this position of public popularity, Hitler was able to persuade President von Hindenburg to have him sworn in as Chancellor of Germany.

Exactly four weeks later, at 9pm on 27 February 1933, the Berlin Fire Service was called out to an already well-established fire that was engulfing the main Chamber of Deputies in the Reichstag building, the seat of the German government. Five Communists were immediately arrested nearby, and one of them, a 24-year-old Dutch man named Marinus van der Lubbe, a lifelong Communist activist, was blamed and tried; and freely admitted his guilt. He was promptly executed by guillotine, the terror weapon of the French Revolution 140 years before.

Hitler used the incident to his great advantage by immediately persuading the conservative President von Hindenburg to pass an emergency decree condemning the Communist Party of Germany, and shortly after hold a new general election. The NSDAP won 44 per cent of the vote, making it the largest party in the Reichstag with 288 Deputies, though not with an overall majority. To achieve full political control, Hitler immediately brought forward the Enabling Act to give himself 'plenary' powers: the

Only four weeks after Hitler is sworn in as Chancellor by President Hindenburg the mysterious Reichstag fire gave him the lucky opportunity to pass the Enabling Act that gave him plenary powers. Soon after Hindenburg died, Hitler assumed absolute control and declared himself Führer of the Third Reich. (*Shutterstock*)

authority to enact laws without the Reichstag's consent for the next four years. Not everyone agreed, but on 23 March 1933, Hitler addressed the Reichstag which was assembled in its temporary venue, the Kroll Opera House, and despite crowds outside shouting threats at members of parliament as they arrived, the Act was passed by a vote of 441 to 84. Only the Social Democrats voted against, as the Communist Party members had been arrested under the earlier emergency Reichstag Fire Decree, the real consequence of which had, by a series of lucky events, transformed Hitler's minority government into a de facto dictatorship. [16]

The Enabling Act had given Hitler and his Cabinet full legislative power to rule by emergency decree, but Hindenburg remained president, the head of state and commander-in-chief of the military. Hitler, as ever in politics, moved very fast, and by July had already abolished all non-Nazi political parties and taken away the independent power of each state. Hitler showed his commitment to his promise to deal quickly with the hated Treaty of Versailles and its reparations by withdrawing from the newly formed League of Nations. He immediately tested public opinion and his popularity by holding a referendum in July in which 95 per cent of voters backed his judgement and actions.

The last piece of good luck that completed the jigsaw of Hitler's rise to absolute political power happened the following year.

President Hindenburg's failing health resulted in his demise on 2 August 1934. Hitler was hovering like a falcon over a dying lamb, and on the day of Hindenburg's death, Defence Minister Werner von Blomberg ordered all members of the *Reichswehr* (armed forces) to take the new 'Hitler Oath', swearing unconditional obedience to Hitler personally, not to the nation state.

The day before, Hitler's cabinet had passed a law merging the office of chancellor with that of president, *Führer und Reichskanzler,* and a campaign was already on standby for an immediate plebiscite asking the public to agree. Not that many Germans would find the courage to disagree as SA Stormtroopers were outside every polling station where many 'no' votes were destroyed and 'yes' votes counted twice.

The outcome was never in doubt and the official result elevated Hitler to the effective position of Dictator of Germany with an 89 per cent approval. In other words, over forty-three million citizens voted for, and just over four million against. Goebbels was said to be '*disappointed*' with the 10 per cent, but there can be little doubt that, even with adjustments for fraud, Hitler '*had the backing, much of it fervently enthusiastic, of the great majority of the German people*'. [15]

Incredible good luck had given Hitler opportunity after opportunity to reach this position of absolute power and total control of the German Empire. It was not about to desert him at this moment and he would certainly need a lot more of it from now on.

Chapter 5

Röhm and the Night of the Long Knives 1934

'Be certain that he who has betrayed thee once will betray thee again.'

Johann Caspar Lavater, poet 1780

Ernst Röhm was an early member of the NSDAP or Nazi Party. When Hitler became leader in 1921, Röhm organised and headed the SA, the *Sturmabteilung*, soon to be better known as the 'Brownshirts'. The paramilitary organisation was created to protect and guard at Party meetings and to disrupt those of its opponents, usually by violence and thuggery.

Röhm had previously linked arms with Hitler at the Munich Putsch in 1923 and was one of only a few to be appointed to Hitler's cabinet in 1933. Röhm's ambition, however, was to merge the massive SA with the *Reichswehr* (the German Army up to 1935) with him in overall command. The SA had grown in membership to around four million and was acting as a state within a state, running prisons of torture and murdering Jews, Communists and Socialists with impunity. There was mounting widespread abhorrence of their actions and public offence from industry, commerce and local government about the unpunishable actions of the brown-shirted stormtroopers. Hitler felt Röhm was becoming far too powerful and possibly even a challenger for the leadership and so, with the compliance of Göring, Himmler and the Gestapo, evidence of 'treason' was accumulated. Hitler was only too aware of the huge risk it would be to remove the founder and leader of what were his most militant and aggressive supporters, who by this time, were feeling they were still waiting for their just reward for the years of support that they had given Hitler and the Party.

Hitler was chancellor but had his eye on the presidency, the head of state, and for that he knew he would need the support of the establishment – the generals and admirals of the *Reichswehr,* all of whom resented the SA and in particular its cult-leader, Röhm. Hitler brought Defence Minister and devotee Werner von Blomberg and Ernst Röhm together in mid-

1934 forcing an agreement between the two that allowed the SA certain responsibilities such as border protection.

In the end Röhm seemed to accept that the newly formed Wehrmacht would be *'the sole bearer of weapons of the nation.'* But one SA officer, *Obergruppenführer* Lutze reported to Hitler that Röhm had said privately, *'what that ridiculous corporal declared does not apply to us.'* Lutze reaped his reward when Hitler appointed him the new head of the SA a few weeks later.

Hitler meanwhile, apart from ordering the Gestapo to record any excesses of the SA, deferred any action, hoping events would develop to help him out of his quandary. While the SA continued to intensify their military exercises, holding bigger parades and building up extensive weapon caches, the Gestapo and Reinhard Heydrich's (see Ch.8) *Sicherheitsdienst* (security service of the SS), known usually as the SD, stoked up rumours that Röhm's SA was planning a putsch for state control. In June, a fake 'order' was uncovered saying that SA action was imminent so Hitler summoned the leaders to a conference south of Munich. At the same time as Hitler was having to deal with a highly critical speech from the vice-chancellor, Franz von Papen, he received another call that spoke of *'the SA rebels being on the point of striking at Berlin'.*

Hitler ordered two SS companies of his *Leibstandarte*, his personal bodyguard, to meet him in Munich where the SA was shouting protests on the streets. Hitler was near hysterical with anger as he interpreted all the Gestapo reports as betrayal by Röhm. He immediately drove with his SS troops to the Hotel Hanselbaur in Tegernsee where he knew Röhm and other SA leaders were staying.

Pistol in hand, Hitler personally arrested Röhm and had six others shot without trial.

This action, on 30 June 1934, to be known thereafter as *The Night of the Long Knives* was ratified as legal on Hitler's return to Berlin and this effectively gave him the right to commit murder in the interest of the state. Hitler then went on to gain the support of the whole Reichstag with a speech in which he said he was guilty of ordering the shooting but that it was justified. *'I further gave the order to shoot those most guilty of treason…and to burn out, down to the raw flesh, the ulcers of this poisoning of the wells in our domestic life and of the poisoning of the outside world'.* Hitler was cheered to the rafters.

The public asked no questions as they were relieved to see the removal of the immoral and corrupt scourge of the SA from their midst. Instead the press acclaimed *'the swift and resolute actions of their Führer'.*

But for Hitler, to be without the support of the SA was dangerous. It even meant that his future as chancellor or as leader of the Nazi Party could be in jeopardy. But these events coincided with yet another bit of unplanned luck, at precisely the right moment.

Just over one week later, Hitler was told that President Hindenburg's death was imminent and his position so solid that all his ministers had quickly signed a new law stating that the office of Reich President would be combined with that of Reich Chancellor, thereby making Hitler Chief Minister of the Government, defender of the German Constitution, and supreme commander of the armed forces.

In one fell swoop, the good luck of Hitler had resulted in him now being the absolute ruler and dictator of Germany. So great now was his popularity that Blomberg and Reichenau, the leaders of the *Reichswehr*, devised, with no input from Hitler, the oath to be sworn by every member of each of the armed forces of Germany, giving their personal loyalty to the actual person of the Führer, Adolf Hitler.

In the Night of the Long Knives Hitler ordered the murder of the SA leader, and the *Reichswehr* devised the Führer Oath to be sworn by every member of each of the armed forces of Germany, giving their personal loyalty to the Führer, Adolf Hitler.

Chapter 6

The Sex Scandals 1926–38

Maria Reiter, Geli Raubal, Renate Müller, Unity Mitford, Eva Braun

'A man must be able to put his mark on every girl…a girl of eighteen or twenty is as pliable as wax.'

Adolf Hitler [188]

Throughout political history, the one setback that leaders have always had the most difficulty surviving was a sex scandal. Whether true, false or half-true, scandal always sticks, invariably becoming the first tag people attach to the name when they hear or see it.

Caligula was assassinated in AD 41 after less than four years as Roman Emperor because of his eccentric behaviour and perverse sexual practices. Edward II, King of England, was despised for his homosexual relations with several of his court favourites and in 1327 was imprisoned by his wife and murdered by some of his barons, allegedly suffering the ignominy of having a red-hot poker strategically inserted into his innards. In 1961, British Secretary of State for War, John Profumo MP, was exposed for having an extramarital relationship with a prostitute, Christine Keeler, who was at the same time providing her services to an officer of the Soviet Navy, Captain Yevgeny Ivanov. Profumo was disgraced and the scandal tainted his prime minister, Harold Macmillan, whose government was defeated at the subsequent General Election.

In the USA it was no different. Eight years after the assassination of President John F Kennedy, his youngest brother, Edward, was held responsible for the death of a 22-year-old single female, Mary Jo Kopechne. Late at night, after a party, while his pregnant wife, Joan, was at home, Kennedy, with Mary Jo beside him, drove his car down a country lane and it slid into a river near the ferry on Chappaquiddick

Sex scandals cost the career of many politicians like US Senator Edward Kennedy, Jeremy Thorpe MP and US President Bill Clinton, but Hitler was able to get through several potential personal scandals involving nubile teenage girls without his worshipping public ever knowing any of it.

Island. Mary Jo drowned, but he swam away and did not report it until the next day. His presidential ambitions were subsequently dashed, and he carried the inferences with him for the rest of his life.

Another US President, Bill Clinton, was impeached in 1998 after his extramarital affair with a 23-year-old White House intern called Monica Lewinsky was exposed. Although he was then acquitted by his supporters in the senate, he too has had to live with the scandal hanging over him and his wife, Hilary.

In British politics, another scandal in 1979 involved the leader of the Liberal Party, Jeremy Thorpe. He stood trial for conspiracy and incitement to murder of a former homosexual lover, Norman Scott. Thorpe had to resign as leader and disappeared from public life.

Hitler

Adolf Hitler was much luckier, very much luckier in fact. Scandals that involved him and others close to him did not have the end result of any of the aforementioned.

In the eyes of his adoring public, Hitler was a man with no overtly sexual inclinations. He enjoyed the company of women, particularly younger, pretty ones, but he restrained any outwardly flirtatious behaviour to nothing more than polite manners. That at least was the deliberate image Hitler wanted to portray. He understood the importance of appearing morally pure, untainted by the base elements of life as conveyed to him in his younger days and generally held as accepted standards by the largely Catholic, or certainly Christian and conservative, population of Germany. Yet it was all a lie, a false image, but one that had to be preserved as the rising star was increasingly seen as a *Messiah* by his worshipping followers, many of whom were young females, and, just like Jesus Christ, a man so perfect he could not be tainted by anything so base or be distracted from his great mission by a mere woman. Hitler believed his image to be that of the pure, infallible, perfect man; one that had to be preserved at all costs or the price would surely be political destruction. It was an image propounded by his sharp-brained propaganda maestro, Joseph Goebbels.

Hitler liked, indeed preferred, to be seen wearing a uniform with long leather riding boots, as he believed it made him look more masculine. He also liked to carry a leather bullwhip around with him that he would

smack against his thigh as he strode around
a room or crack it as he made some point
that he needed to emphasis. When talking
to unknown young girls he liked to call
himself Herr Wolf.

He knew that some had questioned his
sexuality with many believing him to be
homosexual. After his meeting with Neville
Chamberlain, an American journalist
reported that he had a *'very curious walk
indeed – very ladylike with dainty little steps'*.
[175] And a British diplomat recorded Hitler
as being the *'most profoundly feminine man
that I had ever met, almost effeminate'*. [176]

Even Hermann Göring (Ch.8), one of his
closest followers, often referred to him as
'that womanish fool' and when Hitler had a
tantrum he would behave *'like a hysterical
woman… in high, shrill notes'*. [177]

Herr Wolf in macho gear

But Hitler was not a homosexual. He was heterosexual, but not in the
generally regarded way; he was a sado-masochist. [180] In other words,
Hitler got sexual gratification from inflicting physical pain or humiliation
either on another person or having it inflicted upon him. This peculiarity
did not just apply to his sexual preferences but was ingrained in his
ideological beliefs (Ch.12). Nazism was synonymous with sadistic methods
of control and rule entirely by the abuse of the weak and helpless. It
entailed top-down bullying and the infliction of pain and humiliation
through every layer of authority to the lowest ranking soldier and on
to the unarmed, weakest civilian, even if it was a female or a child. All
citizens, just like the females in Hitler's own private life, were required to
subordinate themselves entirely to the will of their leader, a view he had
incontrovertibly stated in *Mein Kampf*.

Hitler once told an SA officer's wife, *'A woman must be soft, sweet and
stupid and a man must be able to put his mark on every girl as women would
not want it any other way. Women think of nothing else but men and there is
nothing more enjoyable than educating a young thing – a girl of eighteen or
twenty is as pliable as wax.'* [189]

Hitler had shown a fetish interest in erotic art. He liked to walk among nude models posing in the art academy and he kept a collection of such books in his flat. The commander of the SA, Ernst Röhm, knew Hitler well and said that he liked to watch peasant girls working in the fields as he could see their bare buttocks when they bent over working. [181]

As he became more powerful and wealthy, and his fame grew, so he found himself on the receiving end of 'fan mail', with endless offers of romance, sex and even marriage from his many thousands of adoring supporters. Hitler enjoyed the ego-boosting fame, and although he had no problem spending much of the vast sums of money he was making through the sale of his books, the two volumes of *Mein Kampf,* he did not indulge in costly romantic affairs, preferring to fund his luxurious new Alpine mansion, the *Berghof,* his large apartment in Munich, and his fleet of Mercedes limousines.

Hitler's chauffeur, Emil Maurice, was able to observe many aspects of Hitler's private moments and records that there were times when teenage girls deliberately tried to be knocked down by his car so that they could be comforted by him, and that he had also seen some girls of the Young Nazi group turn up at his house, naked under their uniform, offering their virginity to the Führer. [182]

The opportunity was certainly there for him to exploit females, but he was always formally polite to those he met in public life. However, in his intimate relations, of whom he had only a few, he was quite different.

Maria Reiter (Mitzi)

The first was recorded in 1926 when the 37-year-old Adolf was living in the *Deutsches Haus* Hotel in Berchtesgaden. This suited his busy political lifestyle as he usually spent the other half of his time in Munich on Party business. One day, as he walked his Alsatian dog Prinz in the local park he spied the nubile blonde Maria Reiter walking her dog. This made opening a conversation easy and he soon discovered that Maria was 16-years-old, had just left the convent school and had recently started working in the local dress shop that was being run by her sister following the demise of her mother.

He was always more relaxed speaking to teenage girls than to more mature women as he could talk to them as he would to a child. He soon

How was Hitler able to escape public scandal having a sexual relationship with a 16-year-old shop-worker, have his live-in niece shoot herself dead, have another 20-year-old lover shoot herself in the first of two suicide attempts, avoid a scandalous relationship with a Jewish Princess and another with an actress who finally threw herself out of a window? If Hitler's perverted sexual demands had been exposed to his adoring public, he would surely have been finished.

Maria Reiter (Mitzi)

invited her to go with him to a concert in the town, but she said that she would have to ask her sister first. They both went together to the shop, but her sister, Anni, said that she was too young to go out with an older man. Undaunted, he immediately invited both to come and hear him speak at a political meeting to be held in the hotel, knowing that he could impress them with his oratory skills. The naïve Fraulein Maria was certainly impressed by his public speaking, but was to be less enthusiastic over his attempt to display to her his masculinity, when next out for a walk together, by whipping his dog for its disobedience.

Indeed, she expressed horror at his cruelty and any possibility of a romantic moment had been squandered. It was a measure of his misunderstanding of females that he then asked her for a kiss; and a perfect example of his complete inability to interpret feelings when, having been refused, he stuck out his arm in a Nazi salute and gruffly shouted, 'Heil Hitler'.

The relationship did not end there, however. On another day, soon after, they were both standing together at her mother's gravestone. He took her hand and, gripping the ever-present whip in the other, he attempted to be romantic by saying that she was his woodland spirit and that, as an artist, he would love to paint her standing in front of the trees. This made her laugh, but Hitler was so insecure with women that he made her stop. He told her never to laugh at him again, and then he kissed her passionately and squeezed her tightly. They were soon lovers, and by July 1927 he was talking of renting a flat in Obersalzberg and living with her. Maria, or as

Hitler now called her, Mitzi, had certainly fallen for him as shortly after he received a gift from her. Perhaps this was what caused him to think again as he sent her a reply that was polite but not encouraging for the infatuated and, for him, dangerously naive teenager. Or maybe it was that he now had an eye on another!

Geli Raubal

Three years before, Hitler's stepsister, Angela Raubal, had visited him while he was serving his much-shortened sentence in Landsberg Prison (Ch.2). She had brought along her son, Leo, and her 16-year-old daughter, Hitler's step-niece, also called Angela. He was captivated immediately by the winsome teenager in that short encounter.

Since then, Hitler had become wealthy from the sale of more than a million copies of his book, *Mein Kampf*, and was now scheming a plan that would appear as if he was being generous to his poor stepsister by employing her as housekeeper in his new *Haus Wachenfeld* in Obersalzberg. Angela of course agreed, glad to be out of the dreadful poverty in which she had been struggling to survive, and she moved in as housekeeper and cook in March 1927. A short time later, as soon as her daughter, Angela, had passed her school leaving exam, Hitler personally drove his Mercedes to her Convent school in Vienna and took her back to live with him and her mother in *Haus Wachenfeld*. For young Angela Maria Raubal, it was all very exciting and looked like a wonderful new life alongside her now famous Uncle Adolf. Uncle Alf, as she called him, was already obsessed by his youthful, energetic, and comely niece.

This time he did not have the worry he had had with the teenage Mitzi, over whom he had no authority; this time he had another young, impressionable girl right where he wanted her – directly under his unaccountable and total control.

Strictly speaking, young Angela, or 'Geli' as Hitler always called her, was niece to her 36-year-old uncle Adolf, but not directly. She was born in Linz, Austria, in 1908, her deceased father was Leo Raubal and her widowed mother, also called Angela, was the daughter of the father of Adolf Hitler's first wife, Franni, who had died in 1884 of tuberculosis, aged 24. Hitler's father, whose name was Alois Schicklgruber, then married Klara and changed his family name to Hitler. They had six children; Adolf was the fourth and the only remaining son. Adolf's father died in 1903 and Klara died when Adolf was nineteen years old.

It was clear that Hitler had become very attached to Geli, and only a few weeks after they had arrived at *Haus Wachenfeld* he moved her into a flat in the

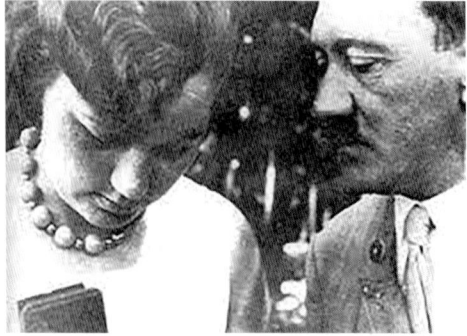

Geli Raubal.

centre of Munich as he was having to spend more and more time there. He also enrolled Geli as a medical student at Munich University, but made sure her mother remained as housekeeper in his Obersalzberg home.

To Hitler, she was the perfect young Germanic woman. She was quite tall, charming, free-spirited, and well-built with dark wavy hair and big brown eyes. Hitler watched and gloated over her, taking her shopping, to the opera, the theatre and on picnics in the countryside.

Everyone noticed how much happier Hitler seemed as Geli walked proudly by his side with her hand in his arm or even accompanied him to meetings where no women had ever been allowed before. She was popular with all who knew her as she seemed always to be smiling and laughing and helped to put everyone in a good mood. The 38-year-old Hitler fell more and more in love with her, but the 19-year-old Geli, despite her outgoing and jolly persona, never was in love with Hitler. Hitler became more possessive, more demanding, and more controlling. She was not allowed out with another man, and she had to account for any time the two were apart. Hitler then rented a large apartment in Prinzregentenplatz and insisted Geli move into the room next to his. She did not have any real option.

Now Hitler had full control and, if their relationship had not been consummated before, it certainly was from then on. Throughout 1929, Hitler hardly left Geli alone.

He started to make unusual demands of her. She had to allow him to make drawings of her private parts and, according to what Otto Strasser, a political rival to Hitler who had escaped to America, told an official of the US Office of Strategic Studies in 1943, Hitler was a sado-masochist. He explained -

'Hitler made her [Geli] undress… he would then lie down on the floor. She would have to remove her underwear and squat over his face… so he could examine her at close range… this made him very excited. After he peaked he demanded she urinate on him as it gave him sexual pleasure… but she said it was extremely disgusting to her.' [179]

Earlier in the year, Hitler had written letters to Geli in which he fantasised about playing sex games with her that included some of the masochistic behaviour to which Strasser was referring. One letter had somehow ended up in the hands of a Doctor Rudolph who then attempted to blackmail Hitler. Hitler knew an anti-Semitic and corrupt priest who was able, by devious means, to retrieve the letter for a suitable reward paid by Franz Schwarz, the Nazi Party treasurer.

Scandal had been avoided – the priest and the doctor were eliminated shortly afterwards.

The following year, Hitler was again lucky to avoid a scandal. He had created a portfolio of the intimate drawings made as part of their sex games but he had kept them in his private desk and somehow they got into the wrong hands. Schwartz again paid the blackmailer and wanted to destroy them, but Hitler, rather than destroy them, insisted that they now be kept in a safe in the Brown House, the Nazi Party headquarters in Munich. The building was later destroyed by Allied bombs and none of the evidence was ever seen again, but at that moment in 1930, Adolf Hitler was incredibly lucky to have avoided another sex scandal that would surely have finished his public career.

Geli probably knew nothing of the blackmails and Hitler certainly did not desist from his perversions. Geli was compliant as she had only the choice between enjoying the lifestyle that rewarded her with luxury and privilege or returning to the poor life of domestic service with her mother. She must have needed to talk about her dichotomy as she confided in one of her girlfriends that she could not love him because he was *'a monster'* and she added, *'You'd never believe the things he makes me do.'* [187]

It did not take Geli long to lose interest in her medical studies, but as she had a pleasant singing voice, she soon began to have ideas of a career in opera. Hitler gave her everything she asked for, including paying for singing lessons from the best teacher in town, but even he knew that was well beyond her. Despite Hitler's close watch, Geli was able to have brief, if secret, liaisons with a few different men.

As she was a healthy, attractive 20-year-old it is not surprising that Geli was looking past her 41-year-old '*Uncle Alf*' for fun and romance. One SA officer, on regular guard duty outside Hitler's Munich flat later recalled, '*Many times when Hitler was away for several days at a political rally or tending to party matters in Berlin or elsewhere, Geli would associate with other men. I liked the girl myself, so I never told anyone what she did or where she went on these free nights. Hitler would have been furious if he had known that she was out with such men as a violin player from Augsburg or a ski instructor from Innsbruck.*' [189]

The first time Joseph Goebbels met Geli in Munich he did not realise who she was and, being the lothario he was, and despite having two lovers and a wife at that time, he immediately offered her a chance to meet him in Berlin.

She accepted and he records her being '*a darling thing*'! [190] He soon found out about his Führer's interest, and nothing further came of it.

The closest affair Geli had was with Hitler's driver, Emil Maurice, an SS officer with whom Geli genuinely believed she was in love. Maurice had fallen for her when he had first met her and as soon as he had the chance, he asked her to marry him. She agreed and told him she would be '*unconditionally faithful to you*' but that Hitler, who she had clearly told, demanded that their love had to be '*kept completely secret*' – Geli then told her close friend Henny that she no longer wanted to be loved by Hitler and preferred her relationship with Maurice saying, '*Being loved is boring, but to love a man, you know, to love him – that's what life is about. And when you can love and be loved at the same time, its paradise.*' [184]

When Hitler found out, or was told by Geli, he seemed at first understanding and tolerant of the relationship so long as it remained platonic. It may just have been another element of his masochism as he derived vicarious satisfaction from Geli's frustration, but just for a short time. In the end, Hitler was prepared to share Geli with no-one, so Maurice was then sacked and sent back to his position in the SS.

Maurice claimed many years later that he was still deeply in love with Geli despite her peculiar relationship with Hitler, and Maurice even remembered the time he had walked into her room to find her making love with another student who he promptly grabbed by the neck and threw out the door. [187]

Geli may also have been in love with another man whose name is unknown but who, according to the memoirs of Hitler's private secretary, Christa Schroeder, was a Jewish violin teacher in Linz. He had written to Geli in 1931, expressing his concerns about '*your uncle's behaviour towards you...he is hoping to change your mind, but how little he knows your soul*'. [191] There is no mention of it in the letter, but some accounts of events claim he was the father of her unborn child, if indeed Geli was pregnant.

Geli's mother was still based in Obersalzberg and remained sure that Hitler and Geli would shortly be married and that the Pope would grant them special dispensation. Perhaps if Hitler had asked her, Geli may have accepted a proposal of marriage, but Hitler was not prepared to go that far, despite telling his personal photographer, Heinrich Hoffmann, '*You know, Hoffmann, I'm so concerned about Geli's future that I feel I have to watch over her. I love Geli and could marry her. Good! But you know what my viewpoint is. I want to remain single. So, I retain the right to exert an influence on her circle of friends until such a time as she finds the right man. What Geli sees as compulsion is simply prudence. I want to stop her from falling into the hands of someone unsuitable.*' [189]

For a young, naturally affectionate and outgoing country girl, the effect on her of moving from the lonely, boring, and remote Alpine life of the past to the non-stop, busy society life and her celebrity status in Munich, must have been difficult to cope with. Add in the constant attention she was receiving from men, many of them in senior positions of power and the wealth she could enjoy, just for the asking – it was all so wonderful – and yet – she had to pay a personal price to the very person who had made this new lifestyle possible, her half-uncle Adolf Hitler.

The more she revelled in it, the more uncomfortable Hitler became. By the summer of 1931, 23-year-old Geli had been living with Hitler for nearly three years. For her, it was like being a prisoner. She had little freedom of movement or choice and could no longer foresee how she was going to find a good husband. Hitler was increasingly possessive and demanding.

There are a number of different and conflicting accounts, none of which are absolute, of the events of the evening of Friday, 18 September 1931. Geli was with Hitler in his luxury nine-room apartment at 16 Prinzregentenplatz, central Munich. The two of them may have discussed her wish to go to Vienna or she may have said she was pregnant.

It is possible that they may have had a heated argument. According to Hoffmann, his driver, Hitler left on Friday evening to be driven to a meeting in Nuremberg where he stayed overnight in a hotel. Just after he left the next morning to drive to another meeting in Hamburg, he received word that Geli was dead. Hitler was then driven back to Munich at full speed. Halfway back they were stopped by local police for speeding at twice the legal limit.

By the time Hitler got to the flat, the police had been there. Geli's body was lying on the floor in a pool of blood and *rigor mortis* had set in. Hitler's pistol, normally kept in the flat, was by her body on the floor.

The four big questions that remain to this day were, did Angela Raubal, known as Geli,

1. Commit suicide by shooting herself with Hitler's pistol?
2. Shoot herself by accident with Hitler's pistol?
3. Was she murdered by a person unknown? or
4. Was she murdered by Hitler himself?

The first cause of death is the most obvious and was the official version of the events that went along the lines that Geli was frustrated and angry with Hitler for controlling her private life, for preventing her from going to Vienna, and for demanding sexual perversions from her. The flaw in this theory is that the bullet had entered her body from a high point and travelled down to her left hip, which would have required her to hold the gun in a very awkward and unnatural way that was not consistent with a suicide attempt.

The second is plausible except that Geli had received full weapons training and would have been unlikely to have made such a mistake.

The third could have been done by any of Hitler's associates who had wanted Geli out of the way in case of any possible scandals regarding Hitler's peculiar behaviours or if she had been pregnant. However, this begs the question as to why they would create a scandal by doing it in Hitler's flat – and with his gun!

The fourth would only have been done impulsively in the heat of a serious argument, before he left for Nuremberg.

A full and clear account of all the known facts, statements and witnesses is made in Ronald Hayman's book, *Hitler & Geli* [174] but the conclusive truth has never been resolved. There were many witnesses, some of whom may have been more credible than others, as nothing within a Nazi police state can ever be guaranteed to be untainted by the authorities.

Whatever the truth, Geli Raubal, the known and widely liked female companion and half-niece to Adolf Hitler, had been shot, with his gun and in his flat. This was a scandal that would surely have ruined anyone else but Hitler.

Renate Müller

There is little doubt that Hitler was deeply in love with Geli and that he genuinely wished to retain the best memories of their years together. In as much as he was capable, he did appear to be truly sad, mourning her death for a long time afterwards. Nevertheless, about a year after Geli's death, Hitler was watching an actress call Renate Müller making a film on location near the coast of Denmark. Hitler was an avid filmgoer with a penchant for Hollywood 'westerns' and at this moment he had spotted and become infatuated with a beautiful, blonde, blue-eyed German actress called Renate Müller.

Unlike his previous affairs with girls just out of school, Renate was experienced in the way of the world. She had already been pursued by other men in power, so she had no problem when approached by Hitler in the autumn of 1932. Although Hitler was by then aged 43, he was still very awkward with women, and it was only after several meetings that he presented her with a diamond bracelet, for which he expected to be rewarded.

That night, at the Chancellery, his idea of foreplay was to talk, in detail, about the ghastly torture techniques of the Gestapo, comparing them with the grisly methods used in medieval times. He then took his clothes off, as did Renate, and proceeded to lie on the floor. He then begged her to hit him and to kick him. She refused at first, but Hitler became excited and was calling himself her slave and unworthy of her. She finally joined in and began kicking him and abusing him with obscene words. He insisted she whip him with his leather bullwhip which she did while he masturbated and had an orgasm. Then he stood up, got dressed, kissed her hand, thanked her for a pleasant evening, and rang for a servant to show her out. [178]

Renate then went on holiday to London where she stayed with a Jewish lover. On her return to Berlin, she was put on trial for 'race defamation'. Her acting career was ruined, and she consequently became addicted to morphine. She went into a sanatorium from where she sent a message to Hitler, asking to see him. Shortly afterwards four SS men visited her and she jumped (or maybe was pushed) out of a window and was killed when she hit the road below. [183] Hitler did not go to her funeral.

Renate Muller.

Hitler knew that if she had gone to the press with her story about his sexual perversions, it could have spelled disaster for him. By his good luck, or perhaps by the hands of the SS, another sex scandal had been avoided. He made sure he learned from previous experiences and thereafter only one woman, only Eva Braun, would be seen as the companion of the rising star in German politics, but she would have to comply in every way to be tolerated!

Unity Mitford

Unity Mitford was the fourth of five daughters of Baron Redesdale, an English aristocrat. That alone was the perfect reason why Hitler should have had nothing to do with her, but he succumbed to his same weaknesses as with all his other teenage mistresses; he could not resist them.

The Mitford sisters were a rebellious bunch. All were part of the notorious 'Bright Young Things' group of Bohemian aristocrats in 1920s London society. Unity's older sister, Diana, divorced an heir to the Guinness family to have an affair with Sir Oswald Mosley, leader of the British Union of Fascists, whom she later married at Goebbels house, with Hitler as guest of honour. Her younger sister, Jessica was a dedicated communist, decorating her half of their bedroom walls with pictures of Lenin and hammer & sickle flags, while Unity's walls had images of swastikas and Hitler. Unity and Diana set off to Germany in 1933 in pursuit of Hitler and eventually became a part of his 'in-crowd'. Hitler then became intoxicated by Unity's provocative, extrovert youthfulness, even playing her off against his other mistress, Eva Braun. Hitler should have seen past her tantalizing behaviour and, for no better reason than she was part of the English establishment, would have been wise to keep her at a fair distance. Hitler revelled, however, in the company of excitable young girls, and was again extremely lucky to avoid a public scandal when, on the declaration of war between Britain and Germany, Unity pleaded for the right to remain in Germany

Unity Mitford (youngest daughter of Earl Beresford).

alongside her beloved idol. When the request was refused she decided to shoot herself with a pistol in an attempt to get the Führer's attention. She did not kill herself but instead ended up in a hospital in Bern, with a bullet lodged in her brain, unable to talk or walk. Hitler made sure she was shipped back to England immediately, thereby avoiding yet another scandal. In a strange kind of pre-destiny, Unity was conceived in a place called Swastika and her middle name was Valkyrie.

Eva Braun

Two years after he had rushed down to 18-year-old Geli's Convent school to drive her back in his Mercedes to Berchtesgaden and, soon after that, to stay near him in Munich, Hitler's eyes were again drawn to another teenager.

While Geli was still confined to Hitler's luxury apartment in the centre of Munich in the late summer of 1929, Hitler was visiting his private photographer's shop on Amalienstrasse, less than two miles along Prinzregentenstrasse, on the west bank of the River Isar. The shop was owned by one of Hitler's closest acquaintances, Heinrich Hoffmann, and just as he and Hitler were entering the front door, Hitler's eyes were instantly drawn to the long legs of the 17-year-old, slim, blonde girl who was on the top step of a ladder, reaching up to some files on a high shelf.

Eva Braun was Hoffmann's new assistant, and she recounted the moment in great detail later to her sister, saying that she didn't recognise Hitler at that moment as she thought he was just an older man wearing a large hat and an overcoat, but that she did feel his eyes were on her legs and felt a little embarrassed as she had shortened her skirt only the day before. After her boss introduced him as '*Herr Wolf*' she was sent out to

Eva Braun. (*Shutterstock*)

buy sausages and beer that the two men ate soon afterwards in the shop. '*He was devouring me with his eyes*', Eva recalled, adding that when she was about to leave, '*I refused his offer of a lift in his Mercedes. Just think what Papa's reaction would have been.*' [193]

Hitler probably saw Eva as another easily impressionable teenager, like Mitzi who had been '*as pliable as wax*', but that she would also be a lot less demanding than Geli. He was wrong – at least in the beginning.

Hitler returned to the shop the following week carrying a bunch of flowers and inviting Eva to a matinee at the opera. She accepted, and her boss, Hoffmann advised her to stuff hankies in her bra before going out with Hitler as Geli had a fuller figure. [174] Eva fitted the bill for Hitler and he took her out occasionally, but always during the day as Geli was reserved for his own personal entertainment after dark. With his inbuilt narcissistic and dispassionate attitude to sex, he probably had it in mind to keep Eva interested, but not too involved, for a future occasion, should the need arise. The need arose after September 1931.

Hitler was undoubtedly deeply affected by the death of Geli, his step-niece and live-in lover. He was affected emotionally, for one of the very few times in his life, as he was seen to have tears well up in his eyes whenever her name was mentioned, and he also felt the need to keep her room unchanged as a shrine thereafter. These reactions were sincere, as he no doubt felt for her in a way he never felt for any other woman at any time in his life. Her tragic suicide, as he believed it was, did not, however, override his sexual needs.

This was the time for which he had held Eva Braun in waiting. And this also was the time for which Eva Braun had been waiting.

Albert Speer (Ch.8), one of Hitler's closest confidants, noted in his post-war memoir that Eva was *'a pretty, empty-headed blonde, with a round face and blue eyes, who worked as a shop girl in Hoffmann's photographer's shop. Hitler met her there, paid her a few casual compliments, gave her flowers, and occasionally invited her to be one of his party on an outing. The initiative was all on Eva's side: she told her friends that Hitler was in love with her and that she would make him marry her.'* [194].

Geli had confronted Eva on the only occasion they met. Both girls were at the *Oktoberfest* in 1930. Hitler refused to go because apart from the fact that he didn't drink alcohol, it was definitely not his scene at all. Geli had been allowed to go but only because she was taken and supervised by Julius Schaub, Hitler's closest adjutant and a founding member of the SS, along with his wife and that of Franz Schwarz, the Party Treasurer and confidant of Hitler. They were all having a good time drinking beer and eating roast chicken to the sound of the local music when Hoffmann suddenly appeared with Eva Braun, his assistant. In what was unquestionably bad taste Hoffmann introduced Eva as his *'niece'*. The joke, if it was meant to be funny, fell flat. Geli took it as an offensive slight and retorted by insulting Eva's fur trimmed coat, saying she looked like a monkey. It is clear from this exchange that Geli knew only too well that Hitler was entertaining Eva at the same time as he was treating her as a captive, possibly even as his sex-slave.

Not content with having two young women in tow, Hitler had found a new self-confidence with young girls and was simultaneously flirting with Hoffmann's daughter, Henriette. Known as Henny, she was most attractive, and her father used her as a model as well as his shop assistant. The man she would later marry, Baldurvon Schirach, described her as, *'worldly... fashionable... with short, narrow skirts, silk stockings and high heeled shoes... I took her for a French girl... she was the most beautiful girl in Munich'.* [193]

Hitler would not have disagreed, and one evening after dinner the two men left Hoffmann's house, only for Hitler to return saying he had forgotten his whip. He was wearing a long leather coat and standing in the middle of the room, whip in one hand, his large hat in the other, when he asked the 17-year-old to kiss him. She was flattered but said it was not possible for her. Hitler left without further ado.

Henny told her father, but his reaction was to tell her that she was not to mention it to anyone, to forget the whole thing and to go straight to bed. Hoffmann knew what Hitler was like. Henny probably did tell her best friend Geli who then began to notice that her uncle no longer seemed quite so obsessed by her thereafter. [195]

Hitler was stacking up potential scandals, but he just couldn't help himself when he had these young girls so close by and was so powerful. Not that he did not

Henny Hoffman (daughter of Hitler's personal photographer).

understand or see the high risk of scandal he was creating for himself. He was well aware that as party leader he had to look like a model of moral behaviour. He had talked disparagingly of Napoleon's affairs, of Ludwig of Bavaria's scandal with the dancer, Lola Montez, but it didn't stop Hitler, and he didn't have too long to wait for the inevitable. [174]

On 19 September 1931, Geli was dead. Hitler was distraught and, for a long while, almost inconsolable. For Eva Braun, however, this was the moment she knew she had to act. Any other young and attractive girl would probably have moved on, but Eva was dedicated to Hitler. She was utterly determined to marry who she later described as '*the most powerful man in Europe*'. She undoubtedly believed that she was in love with him, but he showed none of the natural reciprocation or fawning that he had done with Geli.

Eva was frustrated. She was now twenty years old and was beginning to feel her aim of trapping Hitler into marriage was not moving along at the pace she would have liked. Desperate action was needed and this is why she got hold of her father's pistol and shot herself. She didn't try to kill herself but it was a big risk and the shot wounded her in the neck. Hitler's main concern was that another shooting of a woman known to be close to him would be a certain scandal. The opposition newspapers had tried to make capital out of Geli's death, questioning whether it was a suicide, an accident or even murder, but Nazi influence in many different places was able to put a lid on the rumours, always just in time.

Hitler had been very lucky over Geli's death but another such incident would be impossible to play down, and he was sure it would lead to the ruin of his political ambitions. So, he acted quickly. He went straight to the clinic with a bunch of flowers and sweet-talked Eva by reassuring her of his devotion and promising better things for the future. It worked to the extent that the press was kept out of it, but Hitler did not change his ways. Over the next couple of years, he continued as before; he would turn up at unplanned times and in unpredictable moods that went from gushing charm to seeming indifference. Eva accompanied him to the usual places such as restaurants and theatres, but she was never shown to be Hitler's girlfriend, even less his lover; indeed, it is not absolutely certain that she was the latter. Hoffmann, his official photographer, was not at all sure that Hitler and Eva had a sexual relationship as he saw no perceptible change in his attitude towards Eva that might have been consistent with intimacy, [182] while 'Putzi' (Ernst Hanfstaengl), always close to Hitler, observed that he lived in a sexual no-man's land in which he found, only once with Geli, a woman who might have brought relief. [187]

Hitler enjoyed having the sweet young Eva on call, but he had no notion of being faithful at that time and continued to have relationships with other women, despite the constant risk of scandal. Hitler was especially fond of film-stars and, as well as his deviant sexual encounter with the actress Renate Mueller in the autumn of 1932, he was later hotly pursued by the British Nazi sympathiser and Hitler worshipper – Unity Mitford. He also became infatuated with the Princess Stephanie von Hohenlohe. The glamorous, sophisticated, and English-school-educated princess had already had extensive experience of seducing powerful men throughout European high society. She fascinated Hitler and flattered him, often in close and intimate occasions, and Hitler took her twice to the Nuremberg rallies about which she wrote so admiringly. Even when he was told the princess was from Jewish stock, he still could not resist her and was so enchanted that he was prepared to take the risk of yet another scandal that would have been hard to argue against.

Hitler loved the company of many adoring females so long as they never challenged his views and did not discuss politics. He had a simple view – a woman, he declared, should be '*a nice, cuddly thing, soft, sweet and stupid*'. [188] He enjoyed greatly the aesthetic beauty of females, but he had no doubt that men were superior beings. His misogyny was absolute and irrefutable.

Eva's relationship with Hitler continued to confuse and depress her. They had spent many times together since Geli's death, and Hitler had even allowed them to be photographed together in public. At these rare times, it all seemed hopeful for Eva. Their relationship was consummated, and she felt happy about that. With Geli, Hitler had willingly gone shopping, buying her anything she wanted in clothes and shoes, but he was mean to Eva and did not try to woo her with gifts; for her previous birthday she had received only cheap earrings that had been bought by his adjutant.

Hitler would go off, often for many days at a time, on political business. This was a period of so many election campaigns, of his appointment as Chancellor of Germany, and ultimately to the top job, President of the Reich. Eva would sit by the telephone, day after day when Hitler was away, waiting for him to call her, but he seldom did. In February 1935, she was sure he would call on this, her twenty-third birthday. Surely, he would remember? She waited, and when he did not call she turned again to the one thing she knew would bring him to heel, the scandal of another lover's suicide. She swallowed about twenty Vanadom tablets, a muscle relaxant and painkiller. Her sister Ilse came into her bedroom to find her unconscious and soon she was in the clinic. Hitler again rushed to her side, fearful as ever of a scandal and desperate to please her. To aid her recovery, he promised this time to give her her own private apartment, next to his in the Reich Chancellery in Berlin. Later he would add one condition – she had to enter through the servants' door at the back.

Hitler had got away with yet another certain scandal. No middle-aged politician could ever have survived having a sexual relationship with a 16-year-old shop-worker; have his live-in niece shoot herself dead; have a teenager from the British aristocracy captivate his interest and shoot herself in the head; have another 20-year-old lover shoot herself in a first suicide attempt, only to fail for a second time two years following an overdose. But Hitler did survive. Not only that but during the same period he had managed to avoid another scandalous connection to a Jewish princess, by whom he had been beguiled, and a glamorous actress who had ended matters by throwing herself out of a window. If the press had not been compliant, or perhaps terrified, then Hitler's perverted sexual demands would have been exposed to his adoring public, and he would surely have been finished.

There can be no doubt that the thuggish reputation and widespread fear already created by his Nazi supporters in the SA, the recently created SS, and the Gestapo, would have had a real effect on keeping Hitler's litany of scandals out of the public eye, but when all circumstances are considered, good luck clearly played a massive part in the great sex scandals escapes, too.

Blomberg-Fritsch Scandals 1937–38

'You never can tell when bad luck may turn out to be good luck after all.'

Winston Churchill

Good luck is often a result of what seems at first bad luck. *Every cloud has a silver lining* is a pertinent saying when looking at how so many of Hitler's problems washed out to his unplanned advantage. At a critical moment in 1937, the Minister for War, Field Marshal Werner von Blomberg, was involved in a scandal that could have seriously harmed the Nazi Party and by implication, Hitler himself.

Blomberg was a lonely type, a 59-year-old widower, with five children, when he became obsessed with Fraulein Margarethe Grün, a working class 'typist', thirty-five years younger than him. As supreme commander of the Wehrmacht, the armed forces of Germany, he was in a very high-profile position and so he needed Hitler's permission to marry Fraulein Grün. Blomberg was well aware of the difference in social status, and he shared his concern openly with his Führer. Hitler, feeling in a most positive mood, buoyed by his successful occupation of the Rhineland and the international success of the recent Berlin Olympic Games, wanted to show full support for his erstwhile, and very loyal, friend. Hitler also enjoyed poking derision at what he saw as outmoded class snobbery and he even offered to be a witness at the wedding, along with *Reichsmarschall* Göring.

The quiet wedding took place on 12 January 1937 but within a week the truth about the new Mrs Blomberg was about to be exposed. She had been investigated by the Gestapo as a matter of course and as a result *Reichsmarschall* Hermann Göring now found himself standing opposite the Führer, waiting for the right moment to tell him that Bloomberg's new wife had been a pornographic model when aged 18 and then registered as a prostitute and a thief by the police in the years thereafter. Hitler's utter shock was compounded by the additional information that she had also been co-habiting in her younger days with a Jewish photographer.

Hitler was nearly physically sick, and he took a bath seven times to rid himself of the taint of having kissed the hand of Frau Bloomberg.

The next day, Hitler considered what to do for the best, as he was sure that such a scandal would certainly make him a laughing stock in the eyes of the world. Goebbels said that Blomberg should do the only honourable thing and shoot himself, but Hitler calmed down a bit and decided to exile Blomberg to Italy with 50,000 Marks in his pocket and on his full pension as Field Marshal.

This may have been enough, but now Hitler had to find a replacement for Blomberg. His first choice would have been Blomberg's deputy Supreme Commander of the Army, Werner von Fritsch. However, the Gestapo had a file on him too. Four years before, Hitler had been told of an accusation made by a homosexual rent-boy in Berlin, named Otto Schmidt that had implicated Fritsch. Hitler always dismissed the story as false and in a military court case one year later, Fritsch's innocence was established as a matter of mistaken identity. He continued to serve as a General but died in the first year of the war in Poland when a bullet tore the artery of his leg, killing him almost instantly.

Hitler did not personally believe the allegation, but he could not risk another scandal becoming public and so, on the advice of Goebbels and with the reluctant support of Göring, he announced a major re-organisation of the Wehrmacht and twelve further generals were sacked, including six from the Luftwaffe. Fritsch was replaced as Head of OKH by Walter von Brauchitsch and Hitler appointed himself as Head of the Wehrmacht. [15]

Four major events – the Reichstag fire, the Röhm scandal, the Blomberg scandal, and the Fritsch 'scandal', had all been well beyond Hitler's creation, but each had made up the silver lining to what could have been a very large black cloud over Hitler's political progress.

Instead, Hitler now found himself in an even stronger position. These unplanned events had each been yet another stroke of good luck with each one cementing further his complete control over all aspects of the state by 1938.

The effects of Hitler's reorganisation of the Wehrmacht went deep and sent huge ripples of alarm, not only through the German press and public but right across Europe. Fears spread rumours, and alarm bells were ringing everywhere, including in Britain where Churchill's forewarnings were now being heard and understood. Prime Minister Neville Chamberlain was finally shaken from his inertia and set off on a mission to prevent the seemingly unstoppable juggernaut of Hitler's ideological vision – another terrible war in Europe.

Chapter 7

Appeasement – Good Luck or Negotiating Genius? 1933–39

'An appeaser is a man who feeds his friend to a crocodile hoping it will eat him last.'

Winston Churchill

Hitler was a hard-headed negotiator, or maybe negotiator isn't even the right word. Once his naturally uncompromising and determined style of leadership was pointed out to him by Dietrich Eckart back in the early days of the beer-hall, Hitler was never interested in debating his ideas, only getting others to follow them. This was how his good luck in politics had started.

He quickly realised that most people were much happier doing what they were told rather than being asked what they thought, and he inevitably found that the more he demanded, the more respect and obedience he got. Hitler put it in his own words:

'I use emotion for the many and reserve reason for the few.'

There has always been a part of the human mind that desires, even needs, to be led. There have been only a few real leaders out of the billions of human beings that have ever lived on planet earth. Some have emerged from the masses, some have inherited their position through a line of leaders, some have taken it from opportunities laid before them. All real leaders have had the dedication and blind loyalty of followers, most of whom have never met or spoken to that leader.

In some cases, it is expressed through religion; a need by the people to have a super-human who can show them the way, and who can give them truth, answers, hope, and reasons for all events – good or bad. Depending upon prevailing circumstances, the exceptional 'man of the time' will rise up out of the crowd.

In times of crisis, great men (rarely women) seemed to be there, to offer the answers to the problems of the time, just when they were needed most. And so it was in Germany during the years of depression after the First World War when there was political turmoil and a financial crisis. Similar events occurred around the same time in Italy, with Mussolini; in Spain, with Franco; and in Russia, with Stalin. Not so much a coincidence but a parallel of each country's national turmoil and Europe's political instability.

The German people wanted a strong leader in the 1930s, as the indecisive, multi-party democratic government, known as the Weimar Republic, was spinning in a mess of disagreements, distrust and endless elections. Adolf Hitler was the man of the moment, an uncompromising leader of an uncompromising party. Hitler had laid out his simple ideology and clear aims in *Mein Kampf.* The masses were keen to follow, and the more employment and personal wealth improved, the more convinced they became. Hitler became more convinced too, and began to believe his disciples. He was the 'Messiah', so if he had listened to others at all in the past, he was certain he had no need to in the future.

Everything he demanded from his band of worshippers, he got. He did not need to be specific, as everyone wanted to please their infallible and ever more despotic deliverer. They all were dedicated to '*working towards the Führer*'. [7]

The League of Nations 1933

By January 1933, Hitler's good luck had taken him on a journey from obscurity in 1919 to the chancellorship of Germany. A few weeks later, the timely Reichstag fire (Ch.4) effectively removed the communist opposition, and the resulting Enabling Act gave him plenipotentiary powers.

Success had come as a surprise to Hitler, however much he had dreamed of it in the past, but now he began to realise that luck was an intangible with which he seemed to be touched, and so he began to push it to see how far it would go. Straight away, as he had promised his electorate, Hitler stepped forward at the gathering of all the great powers, and many of the lesser powers, at a general assembly of the League of Nations. On 14 October 1933, he announced to the world, without the slightest hint of self-doubt, that the German people had given him the authority as chancellor, that Germany would no longer be paying reparations of millions of dollars to the victors of the war, and that he was, in protest, withdrawing Germany from the League of Nations. The Treaty of Versailles was, he declared, forthwith obsolete. Within a month, 94 per cent of the adult population in Germany had supported his actions in a national referendum, or 'plebiscite'.

Hitler knew it was a big risk. He knew that Britain and France could have threatened military consequences to this blatant dismissal of Germany's sworn obligations made in 1919. But nothing happened. The USA, the creator of the League of Nations, had never actually joined it, because some of their own congressmen had objected as they had preferred America to keep its isolationist position in the world and not be drawn into international affairs unnecessarily. The Russians were too busy creating the communist regime dominated by Joseph Stalin, the British were pre-occupied with rebuilding their economy and prosperity with their colonies, and the French just didn't have the public heart for any further trouble with their neighbour. The German people cheered, most now convinced that here, at last, was the new *Messiah*.

Hitler saw it, understood it, and decided he was going to push his luck every step of the way from that moment on. This first but crucial display of appeasement by the great powers opened Hitler's eyes. He had done something highly provocative, but luck was on his side and no-one challenged him. He could now see that the road to his long-held desires, the aims he had written so clearly about a decade earlier in *Mein Kampf*, and the new German Empire, the Third Reich, ruled by him alone, were now destined to be. Not every German agreed with Hitler, or his methods, but those who stuck their head above the parapet, soon lost it. The great majority said nothing and did nothing. Hitler was being appeased by his own people as well as by the international community.

After the '*night of the long knives*' in 1934 (Ch.5), not only did Hitler receive no sign of disapproval from the Reichstag for his blatant murder of around 200 people that he had deemed to be a threat to his position, but he was instead totally absolved. Appeasement, coloured by his astonishing rhetoric, turned into popular, national approval, which was demonstrated weeks later when Hitler became President on the death of Hindenburg.

His new position as Head of State, as well as chief minister of the government, meant Hitler could now pursue, in earnest, his military ambitions that he called his Four-Year Plan in which the German army was to be made operational and the economy made ready for war. The latter would lack any scientific or technical detail, but would be based, as ever, on Hitler's inflexible ideological vision of Jewish liabilities, the rewards from the defeat of Bolshevism, and the economic sacrifices the 'true' German would be willing to make.

Hitler only liked his lieutenants to assure him his wishes would be fulfilled – how they did it was to be their own personal responsibility.

Economic and Military Expansion

Making the army operational was much clearer. Now that Hitler had made himself Minister for War, following the Blomsberg scandal (Ch.6), he would start with conscription. Over the previous couple of years, and in contravention of the Treaty of Versailles, Germany had found clandestine ways of building its military strength.

By 1935, Germany already had 2,500 war planes in its Luftwaffe and an army of 300,000; 200,000 above the treaty limit. It would now grow rapidly to over half a million.

The French preferred to develop a defensive strategy, extending and strengthening their massive Maginot Line, huge forts of concrete with gun emplacements and even an underground railway system, along the entire length of the Franco-German border.

Britain had taken a more conciliatory stance. Believing Nazi Germany would develop its navy regardless of the clause limiting this to no submarines and a maximum of six warships, the British signed the Anglo-German Naval Agreement in June 1935, allowing Germany to build a surface fleet up to one third the size of the Royal Navy and, almost incredibly, an equal number of submarines. [21]

All this on the basis, reasoned the British government, that it would build trust between the two countries. There was also an unconfessed feeling of 'guilt' that the Treaty of Versailles had been too harsh and was only inciting hatred and envy and that it would, as a result, be in Britain's better interest to know just what navy the Germans actually had. Only Churchill, supported as ever by a handful of anti-appeaser members of parliament such as Alfred Duff Cooper, Duncan Sandys, Leopold Amery, Bob Boothby, Brendan Bracken, Anthony Eden, and a few others, spoke up strongly against Chamberlain and his Cabinet's constant appeasement of Hitler's actions and its naive granting of this expansion of German naval power.

The massive re-armament programme that followed took the German economy out of its deep depression and by the mid-30s the country enjoyed almost full employment. The shipyards and aircraft factories provided opportunities galore for the advancement of individuals, increased personal wealth, revolutionary research, and development in technology, aeronautics and new weapons.

Rhineland March 1936

'The broad masses of a population are more amenable to the appeal of rhetoric than to any other force.'

Adolf Hitler

It is hardly surprising that the German people raised no objections, but it is remarkable that Britain and France did nothing to stop Hitler's military expansionism. The opportunity to act arose almost immediately when Hitler took his first chance and sent 3,000 Wehrmacht troops into the large area of western Germany known as the Rhineland.

This action was in direct contravention of the Treaty of Versailles and Hitler had ordered his generals to retreat immediately if the French showed the slightest hint of making a military stand against him. France however, lacked political leadership, and the British were sympathetic to the argument that Germany was only *'going into her own backyard'*.

While France and Britain appeased Hitler, the local population cheered in celebration.

Hitler could not believe his luck and later remarked that the march into the Rhineland had been the most nerve-racking 48 hours of his life. He said, *'If France had then marched into the Rhineland, we would have had to withdraw with our tails between our legs.'* [22]

Winter Olympics and Olympic Games August 1936

Germany had been awarded the Olympic Games before Hitler came to power, so it was a propaganda gift to him and the Nazi Party as it gave them the chance to present a benign and progressive face to the rest of the world. Hitler had purposely kept his anti-Semitic rhetoric on a lower level with the Games in mind as he knew this great international event offered him the perfect shop window to the world, and he deliberately created the image of a united, modern, prosperous country of culture and sporting prowess. To the world's eyes, it all added up to an aesthetic form of appeasement.

Following so closely after the retaking of the Rhineland, the Games should have offered the Allies an ideal moment to show their strong objection to Hitler's actions, but not one country boycotted the event, nor did any world leader even mention it. Hitler was riding his luck; not that he called it luck, nor did his followers or any of the German public. Instead, he was now seen as the great leader who had brought prosperity back to the people and, perhaps more than anything, had restored international respect and national pride in the Fatherland. Germany, it seemed, was back and was better than ever. Its leader was determined to drive forward and fulfil his dreams, and as events, largely beyond his making, were unfolding so he knew that this was, without doubt, the time to push that good luck as far as it would go.

Spanish Civil War 1936–39

The Spanish Civil War was a lucky event for Hitler. Although he had nothing whatsoever to do with it starting, it gave him the ideal 'live-ammunition' training ground for his new army and air forces. In January 1936, political unrest in Spain, caused by the election of a far-left wing government, was the grounds for the Spanish generals to attempt a military *coup de gras*. By September, the Nationalists, headed by Generalissimo Franco, were victorious at the siege of Alcazar, but accusations of civilian atrocities were spread by both the Nationalists and the Republicans, and civil war followed. Although Britain and France supported a non-interventionist stance, along with most other neighbouring countries, Germany and Italy committed increasing support for their fellow fascists, while communist Russia backed the Republicans.

After three years of bloody civil war, Franco finally took control of Madrid, the Republicans surrendered, and on 1 April 1939, the war was over. For Hitler and Mussolini the war had given both countries the perfect opportunity to 'blood' their troops, giving them invaluable combat experience, test their weapons and develop their aircraft.

By the end of 1936, Hitler had delivered a massive amount of materiel to Franco, including 40 Panzer Tanks, 6,000 rifles, 500 machine guns, 10,000 grenades and more than a hundred aircraft, known as the Condor Legion, organised by Herman Göring (Ch.8). Naval support was also sent into Spanish waters, including some U-boats. Spain was to prove an invaluable practice ground for Hitler's forces, giving them experience of battle both on the ground and in the air, where his fighter pilots had to learn the hard way against the often-superior tactics and skills of the Russians. [43]

Not only had Hitler's blatant intervention in the Spanish Civil War, his use of new weapons and armed forces and their involvement in the deaths of thousands of civilians, gone on for four years without any attempt by Britain or France to prevent it, but he had also been allowed a level of wartime experience from which none of the Allies would be able to benefit when hostilities began with the German invasion of Poland on 1 September 1939.

Unplanned events and astonishing good luck continued to favour Hitler along his road to European domination.

Winston Churchill

Up to this point, Hitler's luck was solid. Britain, France and the USA had stood back – watching, concerned but silent; somehow complacent or just blind to the step-by-step progress Hitler was making in Europe.

Britain continued to be governed by the National Government; a coalition of the main parties aiming to re-build the British economy after the near-bankrupting First World War. It had been led by the Labour leader, Ramsay MacDonald, until he lost his seat in the 1931 General Election. The new prime minister was Stanley Baldwin, the leader of the Conservative group which made up the great majority of the 615 MPs in the House of Commons. In 1935, the electorate re-elected the National coalition in what was to be the last General Election in Britain until 1945.

Throughout the 1930s, almost no-one in the British government advocated criticising or confronting the actions of the new Chancellor of Germany. Despite the clear limitations placed on a defeated Germany in the Treaty of Versailles in 1919, it was clear to the Allies that Hitler was pushing the interpretation of these agreed limits beyond the original aims and intentions. There was an overall feeling among MPs that Adolf Hitler was trying to rebuild the economy of Germany and there was considerable sympathy for the more extreme punishments that the Germans had had to endure, particularly following the years of the Great Depression after the Wall Street crash in 1929 (Ch.3). However, a few MPs had been raising their voices for some years; the leader of this small group was Winston Churchill.

Churchill knew better than most of what he was warning. He had been in Germany in 1930, three years before Hitler became chancellor, researching for his book on his great predecessor, John Churchill, Duke of Marlborough, whose victory at the Battle of Blenheim in 1704 had effectively marked the rise of the power of Britain, and her Empire, at the expense of both France and Spain. [44]

When Churchill was dining at the Regina Palace Hotel in Munich, in company with his wife Clemmie and his son Randolph, a German friend of Randolph's, Ernst Hanfstaengl, known as 'Putzi', had invited Hitler to join them but according to 'Putzi', Hitler made excuses about not being shaved and added *'what on earth would I have to talk to him about?'* [45]

It was during this stay in Germany that Churchill saw, first hand, the Nazi propaganda, the parades, the 'Brownshirts', the anti-Semitism, and the gathering storm that was happening in Germany.

As early as October 1930, after Churchill met with Prince Bismarck at the German Embassy, he warned that Hitler and his followers would start a war as soon as possible, and in 1932 he strongly opposed the idea of giving Germany the right to military parity with France, speaking ominously of the dangers of German rearmament. In 1934, Churchill stressed the need to rebuild the Royal Air Force and to create a Ministry of Defence. He also urged a renewed role for the League of Nations. These warnings were repeated constantly thereafter. Few listened.

During the latter half of the decade, the 'Churchill Group' in the House of Commons consisted of only a handful of anti-appeaser MPs. The rest of the Conservative Party dismissed or ignored the group's calling for faster rearmament and a stronger foreign policy. Most MPs remembered Churchill from his First World War experiences as both a front-line fficer in the trenches of Flanders and as secretary of state for the Navy. It was too easy to tag him a 'warmonger', as many did, and to dismiss his warnings as 'scaremongering'.

Churchill was, of course, a long way ahead of those MPs, as he was to be proved astonishingly accurate in his predictions by the events that made Hitler's intentions crystal clear in 1938.

Austrian Anschluss March 1938

Hitler had announced his Four-Year Plan in 1936 which aimed at speedy rearmament and for German self-sufficiency in preparation for war by 1940. Hitler was in a hurry to succeed and recognised that considerable material resources within Austria were needed for this programme. Austria also sat in a strategic geographical position in relation to Russia, so it was logical to him to target Austria for *'Anschluss'* or unification with Germany. After the First War, the Austro-Hungarian Empire was broken up and although the Austrian people seemed to want to be in a union with Germany, this was strictly forbidden under the terms of the Treaty of Versailles. Hitler legitimised his claim to incorporate Austria into Germany by a plebiscite in April 1938 that returned support of 99.75 per cent. When German troops crossed over the border and marched through Vienna, thousands of Austrians crowded the streets, waving flags, giving Nazi salutes and cheering for Hitler.

The reaction in Britain was along the lines of, *'Well it's what the Austrians want, and they are Germanic, so let's not interfere.'*

But Hitler could hardly believe his luck, and this was when he realised he could use the appeasement of others way beyond what he had hoped. Within weeks, he claimed that the people of north-west Czechoslovakia, known as the Sudetenland, were Germanic and that this land should also be part of the new, greater Germany.

Although it was not an unjustified claim based on that fact, Hitler's real motive was the massive number of arms factories in that area. This time, Hitler could see it was not going to be a walk-over, as in the past, and in June, he signed a secret directive for the rapid construction of more capital ships and U-boats in anticipation of the likely British reaction. He also gave the order to prepare for war against Czechoslovakia, setting a date of no later than 1 October. To this end, Hitler's propaganda machine went into full flight against the Czech government, falsely accusing them of atrocities against the people of the Sudetenland and of threatening Germany by conspiring with France.

Neville Chamberlain

'Given a choice of war or shame, he chose shame, but he will get war.'

Churchill

For the British government, however, the penny was beginning to drop. On 13 September, Chamberlain asked Hitler for a personal meeting to find a solution in an effort to avert a war. Chamberlain flew by plane to Germany on 15 September and was driven to Hitler's residence in Berchtesgaden. There, Hitler insisted that the Sudeten Germans must be allowed to exercise the right of national self-determination and be able to join Sudetenland with Germany, adding that if Chamberlain was willing to accept this, he would be willing to discuss the matter further. Chamberlain flew back to Britain and immediately met with his cabinet.

The day after, the Czech government asked France for support, saying that Poland was also prepared and willing to stand up to Germany. Shamefully, Britain and France advised Czechoslovakia, a democratic country, to accede to Germany's demands, in exchange for which they would guarantee the independence of the rest of Czechoslovakia. The proposed solution was rejected by both Czechoslovakia and opponents of it in Britain and France.

On 22 September, Chamberlain again flew out for further talks at Bad Godesberg, near Bonn, telling the press, *'My objective is peace in Europe; I trust this trip is the way to that peace.'* On arrival, he received a lavish grand welcome with a German band playing *'God Save the King'* and Germans giving Chamberlain flowers and gifts. This time, Hitler told Chamberlain that he wanted Czechoslovakia to be completely dissolved, its territories redistributed to Germany, Poland, and Hungary. Chamberlain was left shaken by this and the *'take it or leave it'* option given him. One of Hitler's aides entered the room in a pre-arranged ruse to inform Hitler of more Germans being killed in Czechoslovakia, to which Hitler screamed in response, *'I will avenge every one of them. The Czechs must be destroyed.'*

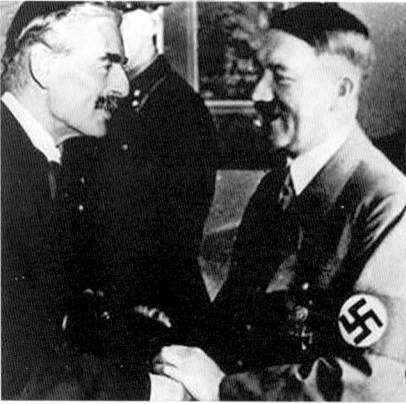

Neville Chamberlain, the British Prime Minister was easy prey for Hitler's determined and devious negotiating skills. In London Chamberlain declared 'there will be peace' but Churchill prophesied in the House of Commons that Chamberlain had been 'given a choice of war or shame, he chose shame, but he will get war.'

Hitler then said to Chamberlain that there was only one concession that he was willing to make to the Prime Minister as a *'gift'* out of respect for the fact that Chamberlain had been willing to back down somewhat on his earlier position; if he agreed to the annexing of the Sudetenland, then Germany would hold no further territorial claims upon Czechoslovakia and would enter into a collective agreement to guarantee the borders of Germany and Czechoslovakia.

Chamberlain returned to Britain, waving a signed agreement with Hitler in his hand and declaring he had achieved *'peace in our time'*, but Churchill purportedly told Chamberlain *'you were given a choice of war or shame, you chose shame, but you will get war.'*

Hitler was now convinced that the democratic nations would never put up any effective opposition to him, and he expressed his contempt for them in a speech he delivered to his top military commanders that same day: *'Our enemies have leaders who are below the average. No personalities. No masters, no men of action…our enemies are small fry. I saw them in Munich.'*

Shortly after, on 5 October 1938, Winston Churchill told the House of Commons that the German dictator was being appeased over every demand made, one after the other and he warned that *'the maintenance of peace depends upon the accumulation of deterrents against the aggressor…'* and then ominously predicted *'You will find that in a period of time… measured only by months, Czechoslovakia will be engulfed by the Nazi regime'*. [46]

Public opinion at that time is often thought of as being pro-appeasement, but a Gallup poll in October 1938 showed this was clearly not the case as it recorded 86 per cent of the British public believing Hitler was lying about his future territorial ambitions. This news was suppressed by Chamberlain who also replied to a journalist's question about the abuse of Jews and minorities in Germany by denouncing the reports as 'Jewish-Communist propaganda'. [48] Chamberlain clearly was bending over backwards to appease Hitler in every way, denying the public mood and ignoring the reality of a Germany being driven towards Armageddon by an enigmatic, ideological extremist.

Despite this, and Churchill's vociferous attempts to oppose both the acceptance of the Munich Agreement and Britain's appeasement policies, the House of Commons voted 366 to 144 in favour of both, thereby shamefully affirming the occupation of a democratic country by a belligerent dictator whose self-belief, self-confidence and dismissal of all opposition was now, it seemed, unstoppable. Chamberlain had shown himself to be inept, naive, weak, and trusting and had been completely fooled by Hitler's adroit deceptions and hard-headed skill. It was incredibly good luck for Hitler that he had to face Chamberlain and not Churchill at that moment.

But that day was soon to come because of it.

Czechoslovakia – March 1939

In January 1939, when Hitler's head of the Luftwaffe, Herman Göring, threatened to bomb Prague, the recently elected President of Czechoslovakia, Emil Hácha, immediately suffered a heart attack and promptly signed his country over to German control. Soon after, German troops entered the remaining parts of Czechoslovakia, meeting practically no resistance.

Czechoslovakia was in reality, a gift to Hitler as it was a major manufacturer of machine guns, tanks, and artillery. Czechoslovakia also had other major manufacturing companies, including steel and chemical factories. Hitler well understood the military importance of the occupation, telling his generals that Germany had gained a huge cache of weaponry which included 469 tanks, 500 anti-aircraft artillery pieces, 43,000 machine guns, and over one million rifles; sufficient to arm about half of the Wehrmacht of the time. [47]

Hitler had never previously mentioned annexing Czechoslovakia in *Mein Kampf* but now, in March 1939, without one shot being fired in anger and without any real protest from any other European democracy, he not only ruled Germany and Austria but had, by the most astonishing combination of lucky events, also conquered seven million Czechs.

Ribbentrop – Molotov Pakt – August 1939

Although the pre-First War Triple Entente no longer existed, Britain and France still held the unconfirmed understanding that the Soviet Union, formerly Russia, would naturally look for support from the western powers in the event of renewed German aggression. Hitler had, after all, made it clear in *Mein Kampf* that his main expansionist aims were towards the east, to acquire vast areas of *lebensraum* and the subjugation of the Slavs living there.

This was a mistaken belief by Britain and France, as Russia was now ruled by the suspicious and suspecting tyrant, Joseph Stalin, of whom nothing could be assumed, least of all any allegiance that may be owed to the west for the defeat of Germany in the First World War. Stalin, it seemed, trusted absolutely no-one. Since taking power in 1925, he had wiped out tens of thousands of individual Russians based on the flimsiest of suspicions.

Stalin's suspicious nature had reached the point where he could not tell whether the information or military intelligence that he was receiving was true or false; this he determined himself. So, it was most remarkable that he preferred to believe Hitler's offer of a deal to the one that his grim and obstinately suspicious foreign minister, Vyacheslav Molotov was prevaricating and dragging out over the whole summer of 1939 with the British and French. [21]

This would prove a monumental mistake by Stalin, but not his last. Based on the spurious belief that the West wanted to encourage German aggression in the East, Stalin was susceptible to overtures from Hitler's diplomats. Instead of the bullying tactics used in the past, Hitler's instructions to Ribbentrop were to flatter and deceive. Stalin, it seems, was taken in.

Hitler, on the other hand, saw that the British-Polish alliance was looking towards Soviet co-operation, and so he had no problem setting aside his rabid ideology of Slavish *untermensch* by telling his diplomats, '*When Germany's life is at stake, even a temporary alliance with Moscow must be contemplated.*' After watching a newsreel of Stalin, his sworn ideological and political enemy, overseeing a military parade, Ribbentrop recalled Hitler saying that Stalin '*looked like a man he could do business with*' [49] – it was all very convenient!

The outcome was a new deal or '*Pakt*' between Hitler and Stalin named after the two foreign ministers who signed it on 23 August 1939; Joachim von Ribbentrop and Vyacheslav Molotov.

Hitler was intent on taking Poland by force, and his biggest fear was a Russian offensive from the east. This was now negated by offering Stalin the eastern half of Poland. Soviet troops should invade two weeks after Germany attacks and they would then divide the spoils; for Stalin this not only gave him a big prize at a cheap price, it also gave him, he thought, the security of having an ally and a valuable trading partner for the technology and industrial equipment needed for the development of his own 'Five Year Plan'.

So, for Hitler, his great plan of creating a German Empire was taking shape. Great good luck had taken him so far, so relatively easily. The next step was to be real war and in this the difference between his luck and his judgement would have much greater significance than hitherto.

End of Appeasement

'When diplomacy ends, war begins.'

Adolf Hitler

Britain and Poland signed an Agreement of Mutual Assistance on 25 August 1939 just two days after the Ribbentrop – Molotov Pakt was signed. Although this made Hitler postpone his planned invasion of Poland from 26 August, he need not have worried for even at this point, Hitler was in luck.

The agreement, which was supported by France, was aimed at curbing further German aggression but any perceived threat to Germany was, in fact, hollow. The Polish government could not have been aware of how unprepared both France and Britain were for war or they would surely never have felt any comfort in the agreement. One British diplomat wrote in his diary, *'Naturally our guarantee does not give any help to Poland… it was cruel… even cynical.'* [50]

On 1 September 1939, Germany attacked Poland abrogating the 1934 German-Polish Treaty by faking a Polish attack organised by the Gestapo in *'Operation Himmler'*. The Poles had been given only nine million pounds of the requested sixty million needed to make realistic defensive plans, so despite being alerted by an aborted attack one week before, they were unable to make any meaningful defence of their borders. The Germans had more than 3,000 aircraft to support 1.2 million troops in 60 divisions, 5 of which had 300 tanks each. In defence, Poland fielded 30 divisions that included horse cavalry, 300 dated tanks and 400 aircraft.

Hitler's biggest fear was a joint Allied attack from the west where France had 85 divisions facing 49 German divisions at the Siegfried Line. Instead, Britain and France could do no more at that moment than declare war on Germany.

The French did nothing, even though the German border was vulnerable to attack through Belgium and Holland, preferring to sit tight in the Maginot Line. The only action the British took was to drop 12 million leaflets from bombers, urging the overthrow of the Führer.

So, Hitler's good luck continued into the war and by mid-September 1939 Russia had complied with the Ribbentrop – Molotov deal and attacked East Poland. In only 27 days, Poland had been conquered with only the lightest of German casualties, and Stalin's Russia had been duped by Hitler into believing they had become Allies.

Chapter 8

Hitler's Henchmen –
Working Towards the Führer

Goebbels, Göring, Himmler, Heydrich,
Keitel, Bormann, Hess, Speer

Hitler could not have been luckier than he was with the band of his closest disciples, each of whom had been pulled in towards him, like a nail to a magnet, desperate to do his bidding. One by one, over the previous two decades, Hitler's henchmen had arrived; self-selected and offering themselves, their skills, their loyalty, and their very souls to the bright-eyed mystic that each believed needed them to fulfil his mission to save the Fatherland.

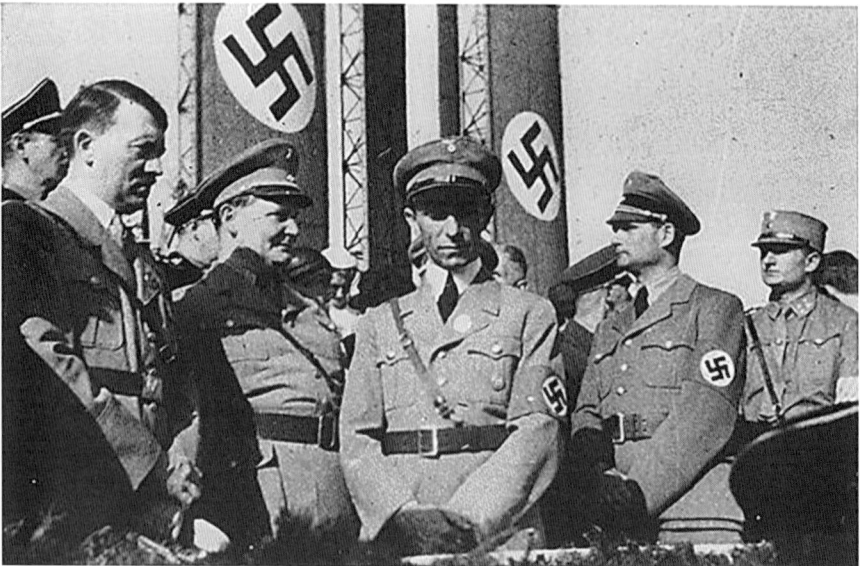

Hermann Göring, Joseph Goebbels and Rudolf Hess had been pulled in towards Hitler, like a nail to a magnet, desperate to do his bidding and offering their very souls to their *Messiah*.

Hitler did not ask for their service, they simply gave it, unquestioningly, and that suited Hitler's personality perfectly as he was an inherently lazy individual. [90] He had been a languorous school pupil then a feckless, unemployed youth who tried to avoid proper work and then the draft and when he had to join the army he looked for the softest job he could get away with. After 1918 he had to return to civilian life and he immediately resumed his shiftless, itinerant 'arty' type lifestyle in Munich. He wandered around looking for the easy life until a writer, twenty years his senior, Dietrich Eckart, took him under his wing and led him into a life of politics. So he was very lucky that his new 'disciples' or henchmen were each inspired only by their master's orations and ideological visions, and they went forth eager to carry out his most extreme ideas. They did not have to be given detailed orders or told how to carry them out. Never at any time, did Hitler give any written order that could have proved he was directly responsible for the killing of around six million Jews.

Instead, he made speeches that contained sweeping statements of his ideology on races that he deemed were inferior to the Germanic, Aryan race. Thereafter, he instructed his henchmen to remove all Jews from Germany and all new territories won throughout the war. The methods, the planning, the ghettos, the construction of camps, gas chambers and ovens were all the initiative of one or another of Hitler's inner-circle of henchmen.

Hitler's inbuilt political shrewdness made sure that, at all times, he was able to maintain control by ensuring there was constant rivalry, jealousy and even, at times, hatred between individuals. This was Hitler's great skill; it may have come naturally, as Hitler had shown on many past occasions that he was either a master delegator or was just a lazy dictator, who talked well but who left all the work to others.

Joseph Goebbels found new and creative ways to get Hitler's various messages over to the German people; Hermann Göring made Hitler's ideas acceptable to the upper levels of German society; Heinrich Himmler interpreted Hitler's ideals to their limits; Reinhard Heydrich carried out the extremes of Hitler's orders; Martin Bormann kept Hitler sheltered from any criticism; Wilhelm Keitel continually reassured his '*Messiah*' of his genius; Rudolf Hess worshipped Hitler's every move; and Albert Speer amused Hitler by sharing his boyhood dreams.

Whatever his motives, each henchman was constantly desperate for Hitler's praise and each fervently believed that, whatever actions they took, they were always justified as '*working towards the Führer*'. [7]

Paul Joseph Goebbels 1897–1945

The most fervent, the most loyal, the most devoted henchman was a clever university graduate who made himself available at the right opportunities, and who rose to power through the Nazi Party by impressing Hitler with his understanding of the potential of National Socialism, with his skills as a writer and with his broad-minded use of the relatively new media of radio and film for propaganda purposes on topics such as rabid anti-Semitism, attacks on the Christian churches and the shaping of public morale.

Goebbels would revolutionise election campaigning, in particular with his use of the plane and the train for the successful political strategy he named as '*Hitler over Germany*'.

It cannot be exaggerated just how dedicated Goebbels was to the aims, philosophies and ideologies set out by Adolf Hitler. When Hitler had been in prison in 1923, Goebbels was in Berlin, but the story of the Munich Putsch (Ch.2) and the subsequent trial that included Hitler's speeches made in the courtroom, were printed in the national press, and read and absorbed with glowing admiration by Goebbels.

Goebbels had not done military service during the First World War as he had a club-foot. This affliction, along with his small physique, was probably a consequence of his having polio as a child. Later, his enemies took pleasure in saying that he had a cloven hoof and the limp of the devil. Despite these physical impediments, he was known as being very charming towards women, and was, of course, very powerful and influential, a recognised aphrodisiac for many females. In 1931, he married a beautiful woman named Magda, but he soon became known as a 'womaniser', having many affairs thereafter.

By 1936, Goebbels had been *Reichsminister* of Public Enlightenment and Propaganda for three years, which had given him unlimited access to all forms of media, including film making, and thus to the beautiful actresses therein.

Goebbels had a number of relationships with them, but he seems to have fallen for a glamorous 22-year-old Czech actress called Ludmila

Babková. Goebbels did not try to hide the relationship and he wanted to make it permanent. This almost marked the sudden end to his career as his wife, Magda went straight to Hitler on hearing of the affair. Hitler was very fond of Magda and she was a most devoted admirer of the Führer. Furious, he called Goebbels to account and issued an ultimatum. Ludmila was promptly dropped, in fact prevented from doing any further acting in Germany, and Goebbels had just saved himself by the tightest of margins.

Goebbels was not instinctively anti-Jewish. He had admired his Jewish teachers and had even been engaged to a half-Jewish girl in his youth, but he listened to Hitler's early rants and became the classic 'convert', more rabidly anti-Semitic than even his teacher. Goebbels was in effect, the instigator of the notorious *Kristallnacht* in 1937, when Jewish businesses were sacked, synagogues burned and Jewish citizens murdered on the streets.

Goebbels and Göring were bitter rivals within the circle of henchmen, and the extensive damage done to property throughout Germany was used by Göring as an excuse to get rid of Goebbels, asking why the German people should have to pay the estimated one billion *Reichmarks* for all the damage done. But Goebbels outwitted them all by declaring that all costs to properties should be paid for by the Jews themselves. Hitler liked that and supported Goebbels, leaving Göring somewhat isolated, and more than a little miffed for a time. Goebbels developed his public speaking skills to a very high level, based on his Führer's example, and as Hitler's public speeches became rarer as the war progressed, so Goebbels more or less took over in that role of expressing Nazi propaganda.

Joseph, as he preferred to be called, was probably Hitler's greatest admirer and most loyal minister, and was appointed by Hitler in his last will and testament to be his successor as Reich Chancellor. Hitler had been very lucky to have had the unusual talents of Goebbels come to his services, just when he needed them most. Nazi propaganda was very successful and without Goebbels, Hitler would not have had the wide reach and massive popularity he had by 1940. Hitler understood that *All propaganda has to be popular and has to accommodate itself to the comprehension of the least intelligent of those whom it seeks to reach.* [162]

On 1 May 1945, the day after Hitler took his own life in the Berlin Bunker, Goebbels and Magda committed suicide, and gave cyanide pills to each of their six children.

Hermann Göring 1893–1946

From a very different background came the celebrity, flying-ace war-hero Hermann Göring who would go on to hold many important positions and at times enormous power in the Nazi regime. He was never really a deeply committed National Socialist, much more an opportunist looking for position, status and especially wealth.

But Hitler was very fortunate to have such a henchman as he was by nature a sociable and affable character, who always exuded a 'larger than life' *bonhomie* personality.

This meant Göring could go into classes of society where Hitler would feel most uncomfortable, but where he revelled, desiring to be accepted as an aristocrat. He was able to have Hitler make him into a grand and powerful figure with whom all people of status would want to be seen.

Before the First World War, Göring was brought up by his wealthy Jewish godfather, a doctor and businessman in his castle home near Nuremberg. His parents lived abroad in Haiti, where his father was the consul-general. His mother eventually returned home and became the mistress of his knighted godfather, now titled von Epenstein.

As a boy, Göring always enjoyed dressing up in uniforms (a pleasure he was to indulge to excess throughout his time in power) and aged sixteen, was very happy to go to military academy, from where he graduated with distinction.

During the First World War, Göring became an ace pilot and ended with awards for seventeen 'air victories', which while impressive was a long way short of the legendary German pilot Baron von Richthofen, better known as the Red Baron, who flew eighty 'victories'; or the British ace, James McCudden, who shot-down fifty-seven enemy aircraft.

Nevertheless, Göring was hailed as a national celebrity for a time, and he took over command of von Richthofen's squadron when the 'Red Baron' was killed in July 1918. As the war ended, Göring felt, like many veterans, that Germany had somehow been betrayed and wanted to find someone to blame for its humiliating surrender.

Göring was instantly impressed by Hitler when he heard him speak in a beer cellar in Munich in 1922 and the impression was mutual when he introduced himself shortly afterwards.

Hitler, despite his verbal disparaging of all aristocracy, was it seems taken in by the inbuilt self-assurance and immodesty of this former

As a boy, Göring always enjoyed dressing up in in uniforms – a pleasure he was to indulge in to excess throughout his time in power.

pilot-ace and apparent member of the upper classes. Hitler soon appointed Göring to take command of the *Sturmabteilung* or SA, later complimenting him by writing, '*I liked him. I made him the head of my SA. He is the only one of its heads that ran the SA properly. I gave him a dishevelled rabble. In a very short time he had organised a division of 11,000 men.*' [51]

In 1923, he was in the front row alongside Hitler as they marched

through Munich on the Beer Hall Putsch (Ch.2) when the police opened fire and Göring was shot in the thigh. While Hitler was imprisoned, Göring had to receive morphine for his injury and soon became addicted. Despite other personal problems, he was elected to the Reichstag as one of only twelve Nazi members in 1928, but in 1931 his beloved wife died from tuberculosis. Following the Great Depression the Nazis popularity soared and in the next election they won 230 seats and Göring was elected President of the Reichstag. When Hitler became Chancellor of Germany in 1933, he made Göring minister for the dominant state of Prussia. Göring set about creating the secret police known as the Gestapo.

Meanwhile, Göring had found a new love, Emmy, and life took on a new meaning for him when they married in 1935; Hitler was best man and made Göring Supreme Commander of the Luftwaffe.

In 1936 Hitler also put Göring in charge of his sacred 'Four Year Plan' and Germany's foreign exchange reserves, telling the Economy Minister to *'trust this man I have selected, he is the best man I have for the job.'* This privileged position eventually made Göring the richest man in Germany. Göring and Hitler worked very closely together over the period that included the Rhineland demilitarisation, the Anschluss of Austria and the occupation of Czechoslovakia. Hitler continued to be blinded by Göring's air of self-confidence, his colourful character, his apparent high level of intelligence (claimed to have been 183) and, it seems, his bluster.

Göring was happy to take on more and more responsibilities, which he rather saw as positions of prestige and authority, each one of which would also allow him to wear yet another grand uniform, carry an ornate field marshal's baton and wear even more medals on his chest.

On the day Germany invaded Poland and the Luftwaffe had virtually free rein in the airspace over Warsaw, Hitler announced that Göring would be his appointed successor as Chancellor of Germany, and after the fall of France in June 1940 he awarded Göring the Grand Cross of the Iron Cross, promoting him even higher to *Reichsmarschall des Grossdeutschen Reiches,* a new rank specially created to make him senior to all field marshals in the military, a status he maintained till Germany surrendered in May 1945.

Göring's many shortcomings, mostly derivations of his own self-importance, were clear to Hitler's other henchmen, to the media and to most of the public, but would take a long time to become evident to the Führer himself. Perhaps Hitler, surrounded as he was by yes-men and strict formalities, simply enjoyed the seemingly carefree, ebullient, overweight, larger than life character who enjoyed everything Hitler apparently abhorred; good food, fine wine, cigars, fine art, fancy clothes, country living, hunting, and all the other trappings of decadence. He also loved big Mercedes cars (as did Hitler), owned a massive motor yacht named *Carin II* and had pet lions on his huge estate in Schorfheide Forest, named *Carin Hall* after his first wife.

Although Göring was often ridiculed by cartoonists and foreigners as a buffoon, nicknamed *der dicke Hermann* or Fat Herman, he had in fact been a very lucky asset to Hitler during the earlier years as Hitler had been able to use him as a counter-balance, able to mix with and influence those elements of German society in which Hitler never felt comfortable. Göring had used all his natural skills, his charm, his guile and his ruthlessness to rise from being a penniless drug addict to the second most powerful and richest man in Europe, albeit for a relatively short time and at the expense of countless lives of innocent people.

Heinrich Luitpold Himmler 1900–45

Himmler became one of the most powerful men in Nazi Germany. From Hitler's point of view he was indeed very lucky to have a man who was to show himself to be a natural organiser and who, with absolutely no military experience, saw a road to power by taking control of the small group of Hitler's personal bodyguards known as the *Schutzstaffel*, or SS (Ch.5) that he turned into the most widely feared army of over a million elite troops called the *Waffen SS*. Among these forces he also created the 'task force', or *Einsatzgruppen*, that was to be responsible for building and running all the extermination camps in which six million Jews, Roma, Slavs, homosexuals, disabled and others deemed *untermensch* would be killed by one terrible means or another.

To bring Hitler's ideological dream to reality needed a unique individual, as putting his ideas into practice by dirtying his own hands was definitely not part of Hitler's character. He needed men who, for their own bizarre reasons, felt the calling to his side and the urge to make those dreams a reality. Himmler emerged from the shadows to do just that.

The young Himmler could be described in modern terminology as a bit of a 'wimp'. In his head, he imagined himself as a fighting soldier, but in reality he was a small, dull, short-sighted weakling. Perhaps this partly explains the merciless way he was to behave when he held the power of life or death over so many others in his own fair hands.

Himmler resented not having been active in the First War, and when he first joined the National Socialist (NSDPA) movement he was happy to see himself as part of a paramilitary organisation, able to wear a uniform but be safely surrounded and protected by the big bully-boys of the 'Brownshirts', as the *Sturmabteilung* or SA was soon to be called.

This way he could safely be part of a gang that attacked and beat up anyone the Nazi thugs disliked, or considered to be communists or Bolsheviks or just non-supporters, including old men and women.

Young Himmler could be described as a bit of a 'wimp' but he was an ambitious visionary and soon saw the potential of the SS. He transformed it into a fanatically loyal, powerful and racially pure elite *Waffen* SS.

Himmler was an ambitious visionary and he soon saw the potential of the SS when it was a small part of the SA. Himmler began his meteoric rise to power when Hitler gave him his first leadership position in the SS as District Leader or *Gauführer* in Lower Bavaria in 1926; only three years later, aged 29, he was appointed *Reichsführer-SS, Head of the SS,* progress that was remarkable by any standard; a clear reflection of the usefulness Hitler saw in Himmler.

Fortunately for Hitler, Himmler loved the minutiae of administration and bureaucracy, something Hitler avoided at all costs, so it was no surprise when Himmler began to collect statistics on the number of Jews living in Bavaria. These lists were soon extended to include all factions hated by the Nazis, including the secretive Freemasons, the mentally inferior, the handicapped, the homosexuals, the gypsies, the Roma, and anyone else seen as an enemy of the party. In September 1927, Himmler impressed Hitler with his vision to transform the SS into a

loyal, powerful, racially pure elite and the subsequent period of the Great Depression gave him the perfect circumstances to build this up with thousands of specially selected men of Aryan race.

Both men loved uniforms and together created the striking black design that the SS wore until 1939 when they became too obvious a target for snipers.

They then had the uniforms manufactured to a sharp couture by a man who was not a tailor, but was a stalwart member of the Nazi Party; a businessman whose small clothes manufacturing enterprise in Metzingen, near Stuttgart, had become bankrupt during the period of the Great Depression (Ch.3).

Himmler's rise from *Gauführer* to *Reichsführer*-SS, in three years was remarkable by any standards.

SS OFFICER
*RENDERED IN POSER 10 TANNENBAUM

Himmler loved uniforms and created, together with Hitler, the striking black uniform design that identified the SS and were then produced by Hugo Boss.

Hugo Boss was a loyal party activist and Himmler gave him the order to produce uniforms for the SA, the SS and the Hitler Youth. His name is still synonymous internationally today with the finest gentlemen's couture.

As a loyal party activist he was given an order to produce uniforms for the SA, the SS and the Hitler Youth. At that moment his business had been reduced to only six sewing machines, but that situation soon changed as demand for his work grew exponentially thereafter.

Many years after the war was over, his name would become synonymous internationally with the finest gentlemen's couture, Hugo Boss.

Himmler moved fast and efficiently. He could see that real power came from knowledge, and he next created the intelligence and security department called the *Sicherheitsdienst* or SD. He needed a very special person to run this organisation in his mould, and as if by some hidden force, a tall, fair-haired, blue-eyed young man, in the shape of Reinhard Heydrich, walked in through Himmler's door at that moment; a man who would soon exceed even Himmler's cold-blooded disregard for humanity.

Himmler was a dedicated bureaucrat, and he created many new departments and rules within the SS. Any man wishing to join his elite force had to prove their purity by producing family trees that showed both parents were of Aryan descent and when he married he would be expected to produce at least four children, thereby creating a pool of genetically superior prospective SS members.

Himmler also had the first recognised concentration camp built at Dachau, where uniforms were issued for prisoners and the guards' uniforms had a special *Totenkopf* (skull and crossbones) insignia on their collars (Ch.10).

Right to the very last day of the war, Himmler continued to carry out the despicable acts of the *'Final Solution'*. Even when it was clear that Germany had lost the war, Himmler pressed his camp commanders harder and harder to eliminate as many Jews as possible. It is estimated that another million men, women and children were executed under his orders between D-Day and the time the Allies were finally able to reach those left behind in the Nazi extermination camps.

From Hitler's perspective, he was very lucky to have such a man as Himmler fulfilling his most extreme ideologies without ever needing to give Himmler clear orders or instructions. Hitler had made his mind clear when he told him: *I do not see why man should not be just as cruel as nature.* [162]

All Himmler needed was acknowledgement through praise and promotion for applying his creations, innovations and ideas that were, for him, *'working towards the Führer'.*

Three weeks after Hitler's suicide, Himmler took his own life while being interrogated by the British.

Himmler had been the perfect inhuman, cold-blooded psychopath that Hitler had been lucky enough to have so willingly carry out his ideology as broadly stated in *Mein Kampf,* and all without Hitler himself having to get his own hands covered in blood.

Reinhard Heydrich 1904–42

Although Heydrich loved music, was the son of the man who founded the now famous Halle Music Conservatory and was himself a gifted violinist, he rejected the option of a career in music and the day after his eighteenth birthday in 1922, he joined the German Navy as an officer cadet. Nine years later, while he was engaged to the daughter of a more senior officer, Heydrich went off with another woman, Lina von Osten. This was considered scandalous by the standards expected of Reich officers, and Heydrich was compelled to resign for '*behaviour unbecoming a Naval officer'.*

Heydrich then married Lina, a woman who was a fanatical National Socialist and who, through family connections, arranged a job interview for him with Himmler. The meeting in 1931 was one of providence; at least, that was how both men saw it, for Himmler had before him a man so cold, calculating, and dispassionate that he would make his new boss look relatively gentle.

During a long discussion about Himmler's new plan for a secret police force within the SS, Heydrich impressed him with his dynamic ideas,

Reinhard Heydrich was directly responsible for creating *Einsatzgruppen*, a 'special task force' that travelled in the wake of the German armies and murdered more than two million Slavs, Jews and other *untermensch* by mass shooting, gassing and starvation.

Heindrich Himmler and Reinhard Heydrich

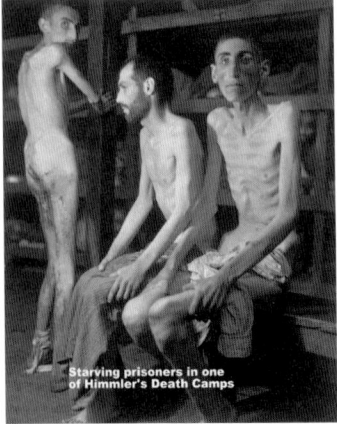

Starving prisoners in one of Himmler's Death Camps

(*Shutterstock*)

(*Shutterstock*)

enthusiasm and apparent knowledge and grasp of such an organisation. What Himmler did not know was that Heydrich had read many spy-thriller books and was using that flimsy knowledge to fool Himmler. But Himmler was convinced and immediately offered Heydrich the task of setting up and running the new secret police organisation he called the *Sicherheitsdienst,* the SD. For such a task, Himmler had chosen the perfect monster.

As Head of the SD, Heydrich's purpose was to seek out any form of resistance to the Nazi aims and to deal with them by threats, arrest, deportation and murder. So impressed was Himmler with his new protégé's drive, organisation and results that within three years Heydrich had control of all the Nazi security, including the Gestapo, Kripo and the SD and was, at Hitler's personal appointment, named Chief of Reich Security.

Hitler quickly realised how valuable Heydrich was to him, how lucky he had been to be presented with a man who fully understood his darkest ideological needs, and who would carry them out without the need for any detailed or specific orders. Hitler described Heydrich as '*the man with the iron heart*'. [52]

In 1941, before Operation Barbarossa, the German invasion of Russia (Ch.10), Heydrich was directly responsible for creating the *Einsatzgruppen,* a 'special task' force that travelled in the wake of the German armies and murdered more than two million Slavs, Jews and other *untermensch* by mass shooting, gassing and starvation.

By 1942, Himmler had identified such a vast number of Jews in the territories already occupied that the task of dealing with them meant that on 20 January Heydrich, as Chief of Reich Security, called a special meeting of senior Nazis at the country house of Wannsee, just south of Berlin. There was to be only one item on the agenda: the '*Final Solution to the Jewish question*'. The outcome of the meeting was the notorious decision to industrialise the extermination of the six million Jews already known to be living in Eastern Europe.

Special camps were to be built that could be linked directly to the main rail network so that large numbers could be transported from the already overcrowded ghettos to purpose-built death-camps.

Buildings would be specially designed to look like large shower rooms but which would, in fact, be gas chambers. The poison gas identified as most effective, killing a human being within a few minutes, was the hydrogen-cyanide based fumigant Zyklon B.

Large ovens would be incorporated within the site to dispose of the estimated 6,000 corpses every day, and all property salvaged from the victims would be recycled to the benefit of the Reich.

As if Heydrich had not already been promoted and exploited fast enough, Hitler also appointed him Reich Protector in Czechoslovakia. He immediately impressed in this job too, by doing what might have seemed contradictory – he offered Czech industrial and agricultural workers parity of pay with their counter parts in Germany. The effect was remarkable in that this was followed by a 70 per cent reduction in acts of sabotage by local vigilantes. The Czechs, it seemed to Heydrich and to the German authorities, had been pacified; but not all.

Heydrich became so confident that his pacification programme had succeeded that he flagrantly disregarded measures for his own security and travelled around Prague in an open top Mercedes. He would pay the price for his vanity. On 27 May 1942, as he did every day at precisely 10.30 am, *SS Obergruppenführer* and *General der Polize* Reinhard Heydrich left his home in his open-top, green Cabriolet Mercedes 320 B to be driven the nine miles to his headquarters at Prague Castle. Nearing the city, at a tight curve on the road, two trained assassins, sent by the Czechoslovak government-in-exile and trained by the British Special Operations Executive (SOE) to kill the Reich-Protector in Operation Anthropoid, awaited his arrival. Further up the road another Czech signalled the approach of Heydrich's car. As it slowed for the bend, Jozef Gabčík stepped off the pavement, pulled a British Sten sub-machine gun out from under his coat, pointed it at the car and pulled the trigger. It had jammed. He tried again, it still jammed. Heydrich then made the mistake of not accelerating away but ordering, probably in anger, his driver to stop. He stood up, drew his Luger pistol and began firing at Gabčík.

At that moment, the other attacker, Kubiš, threw an anti-tank grenade at the car, but he missed and it rolled under the car. It exploded, throwing fragments of metal and upholstery all around. Heydrich was hit, but he jumped out of the car and tried to give chase, the pain stopping him before he could reach Kubiš, who had also been injured in the explosion. Gabčík ran into a butcher's shop for help, but the shopkeeper was a Nazi sympathiser, and as Gabčík ran out he collided with Heydrich's driver

On 27 May 1942, *SS Obergruppenführer* and *General der Polizei* Reinhard Heydrich left his home in his open-top, Green Cabriolet Mercedes but two SOE operatives assassinated him by throwing a grenade under his car.

who he then shot twice in the leg. Gabčík jumped on a passing tram and escaped, as did Kubiš. They were both sure the attempt had failed; it had certainly been a fiasco.

Heydrich, now in considerable pain, was taken to the hospital in a passing van. He had immediate surgery to try to remove the many tiny pieces of shrapnel and over the next couple of days seemed to begin to recover. Himmler sent his top surgeon and he visited Heydrich a few days later.

Heydrich was a Roman Catholic and in a moment of great irony he said to Himmler '*the world is just a barrel-organ which the Lord turns Himself. We all have to dance to the tune that is already on the drum.*'

The next day Heydrich had deteriorated as the many fragments of wood and other material in his wounds turned septic. He may also have got botulism from the infected grenade shrapnel. He was not given penicillin, although it was available. He did not, by all accounts, ask for the last rights and a day later, aged 38, he died.

Heydrich's regime of murder, massacre and cold-blooded slaughter did not end with his demise. Nazi intelligence falsely linked the Czech/Slovak soldiers and resistance partisans to the villages of Lidice and Ležáky.

Both villages were razed; all men and boys over the age of 16 were shot, and all but a handful of the women and children were deported and killed in Nazi concentration camps.

At the funeral, Hitler said that Heydrich had been *'one of the best National Socialists and greatest opponent of all enemies of this Reich'*.

Heydrich had appeared at precisely the right moment for Hitler – when he needed the vilest and most evil of actions carried out that he was certainly not capable of doing himself.

Hitler could not have been more lucky than when Heydrich had walked into Himmler's office.

Wilhelm Keitel 1882–1946

Hitler's most loyal, dedicated, obedient and unquestioning *'Yes-man'*. Seldom was Hitler seen without General Keitel by his side, reassuring his Führer of his genius and his place as a man of destiny. In 1940, after the Blitzkrieg victory over a weak and unprepared Poland, Keitel named Hitler *'the greatest commander of all time'*.

Keitel was the most sycophantic of Hitler's disciples and was reviled among his military colleagues, who often referred to him by the nickname *Lakeitel,* a combination of Lackey and Keitel.

Göring said Keitel had *'a sergeant's mind inside a field marshal's body'*. General von Kleist described him as *'stupid'* and when another officer apologised to General Halder for failing to salute Keitel, he told him *'Don't worry, it's only Keitel.'* [24]

Aged 19, Keitel joined the Prussian army as an officer cadet. As a commoner, he could not join the cavalry, so he went to a field artillery regiment. He married the daughter of a wealthy landowner in 1909. He was eventually promoted to captain after being injured in the First World War, and was posted to the staff of an infantry division. Retained in the army after the war, he progressed steadily, working in the Ministry of War as a colonel. Once Hitler became chancellor in 1933, he was involved in the re-armament programme in the Soviet Union. Despite becoming very ill with pneumonia following a heart attack, he recovered and by 1934 had command of an infantry division. Hitler liked Keitel's unquestioning attitude, and when he took control of the Wehrmacht in 1938, he made Keitel a field marshal and Chief of the Armed Forces.

The Führer liked to have General Keitel by his side constantly reassuring him that he was 'the greatest commander of all time.'

Keitel was easily manipulated by Hitler because of his limited intellect and nervous disposition, but Hitler valued his hard work and blind obedience. Keitel was happy to agree and to sign all of the Führer's directives without ever considering the consequences.

At one major conference before the invasion of Russia, Hitler asked infantry General Georg Thomas to make a study of economic matters pertaining to Operation Barbarossa. When Keitel saw the first report, highlighting problems with fuelling and rubber supplies, he promptly told Thomas to take it away, as Hitler would not want to see that and to return with a new report giving a glowing recommendation to the Führer's plan.

After the failed 20 July assassination plot in 1944 (Ch.11) Keitel sat on the court martial board that condemned many of the officers who had been involved, and some who had not; 5,000 were executed.

Even after Hitler's suicide on 30 April, Keitel stayed on as a member of the three week Cabinet under Grand Admiral Karl Dönitz. Albert

Speer recalled later that Keitel grovelled to Dönitz in the same way as he had done to Hitler. Stalin considered the first signing of Germany's surrender by Field Marshal Jodl an insult but a day later seemed content when Keitel signed the German surrender to the Soviet Union.

After the war, Keitel was found guilty at Nuremberg on all counts of crimes against humanity, crimes against peace, criminal conspiracy, and war crimes. He was sentenced to death and he asked to be shot like a soldier, but the request was denied.

At his hanging in 1946, Keitel's last words were: *'I call on God Almighty to have mercy on the German people. More than 2 million German soldiers went to their death for the fatherland before me. I follow now my sons – all for Germany.'* The trap door was too small and Keitel banged his head on it as he dropped, resulting in a suffocating death struggle that lasted twenty-four minutes. [54]

Field Marshal Keitel had been the Führer's most trusted and obedient general throughout the war. Hitler had been very lucky to have a Chief of Staff who never disagreed or contested the major decisions that he made after he had appointed himself Commander in Chief of all German armed forces.

Martin Bormann 1900–45

None of Hitler's henchmen were closer to the Führer for longer that Martin Bormann. He was not a general, nor was he a philosopher, and he certainly was not a speech-maker. Bormann was a 'toady', a crawler, a creep, a disciple, a follower, a believer, a 'gofer' and a consummate sycophant. But once Hitler found him, he kept him two steps behind him everywhere he went. No matter what Hitler asked for, even when he did not ask for it but looked like he may want it, Bormann was one step ahead, often surprising his master with his wish before he had even ordered it. That was what made Bormann unique, invaluable and irreplaceable to a megalomaniac who trusted no-one.

Bormann was a Nazi, for sure. Soon after the end of the First World War, he joined a local *Freikorps* paramilitary group in Northern Germany. He was no soldier but he was a 'Party-man', which was just what most other paramilitaries were not; an administrator, an unqualified accountant and a natural business manager. He quickly found these skills brought power and influence in their own way, and he knew this was a route to advancement within the Nazi Party. In 1924, he got involved, along with a number of fellow *Freikorps* activists, in an assault on a man they claimed had betrayed them. The victim died and Bormann was imprisoned as an accomplice. He was released after a short sentence and immediately joined the burgeoning National Socialist German Workers Party, the NSDAP or Nazi Party under its celebrity and ex-prisoner leader, Adolf Hitler. His invaluable Party management skills took him gradually to the post of chief of staff to the then Deputy Führer, Rudolf Hess. Hess was no administrator either and he soon came to rely on the ever-present Bormann to get things done properly.

Bormann was the complete sycophant but Hitler trusted him. To a megalomaniac who trusted no-one, Bormann was unique, invaluable and irreplaceable.

Hitler told Hess to greatly improve his summer house, the *Berghof* at Berchtesgaden near the Austrian border, but this was well beyond Hess's abilities, and he immediately passed the task, which carried with it the full authority of the Führer, on to Bormann.

This was the opportunity Bormann had been looking for as it now gave him direct personal access to Hitler and it was not long before Hitler saw before him, by great good luck, the personal executor he had long wanted.

Bormann was a ruthless project manager, and had the Berghof built to fulfil all of Hitler's wishes including the removal, one way or another, of all the surrounding houses and farms, to give the Führer a perfect, uninterrupted view of his favourite scenery, the valleys and mountains of the Obersalzberg. Hitler was very impressed.

After Hess's enigmatic flight to Scotland in May, 1941, Hitler appointed Bormann as *Reichsleiter*, deputy to the Führer and head of the Nazi Party, which included control of all its finances. Bormann was now the Führer's right-hand man in every respect; no-one could get to see Hitler without first going through him. Bormann was also able to subtly manipulate Hitler as he observed his weaknesses, his needs and his eccentricities.

He became Hitler's personal secretary, drawing up the Führer's schedule and appointments and shielding him from those who Bormann did not like or trust. Not surprisngly, with this power came many enemies; in fact, everyone in a senior position, whether military or political, soon grew to hate the *'Brown Eminence'* as he was mockingly called in reference to the machiavellian Cardinal Richelieu.

As the war progressed, Hitler spent more time in the *Wolfsschanze* or Wolf's Lair, his bunker nearer the Eastern front, and so Bormann was given more power and authority over almost all domestic matters. Ideologically, Bormann was a rigid and unbending guardian of Nazi orthodoxy; he was a major advocate of the use of slave labour and the persecution and extermination of Jews and Slavs. He was signing decrees that said that the 'Final Solution could be solved only with the use of ruthless force in special camps' meaning, of course, extermination camps like Treblinka and Auschwitz.

In 1929, Bormann had married the 19-year-old Gerda Buch. She was the daughter of a senior Nazi party official and lawyer, who introduced Bormann to Hitler; Hitler served as a witness at their wedding. Martin and Gerda had ten children, in line with Party demands for many 'pure' Aryan children. Bormann, however, also had a series of mistresses, one of whom, an actress called Manja Behrens, he told Gerda she should accept as his second 'wife'. He also had a number of other children to other mistresses.

When the final moments of the war came, Bormann appeared lost and afraid when his beloved Führer took his own life on 30 April 1945 in the Berlin Bunker, deep under the Reich Chancellery. By all accounts, he then tried to flee the heavily shelled bunker with three others, scrambling over the debris of shattered buildings. He did not get far, only to Lehrter Station where he was last seen.

His body was never recovered, so he was found guilty of war crimes and sentenced to death in absentia by the International Military Tribunal at Nuremberg in October 1946. For many years thereafter, rumours circulated that he may have escaped and still be alive, perhaps in South America. In 1972, his skeletal remains were found at the place of his last sighting and showed that he had bitten into a cyanide pill at the last moment, taking his own life.

If Hitler was a 'lazy dictator', he was also a very lucky one. He had lots to say, and he wanted many things done, but he was not interested in doing them; that was for his henchmen. Every dictator or tyrant in history has longed for a right-hand man, a secretary who he could not only trust to the end but who could and would understand his every need – and, most of all, get it done. There have been very few: Henry VIII's Cromwell, Elizabeth I's Walsingham, Stalin's Beria. So Hitler was a very lucky dictator who just happened to get what few others did – and Martin Bormann was the best.

Rudolf Hess 1894–1987

Hess played an important and influential part in Hitler's life during the 1920s and 30s. He had seen active service during the First World War, being wounded several times and awarded the Iron Cross, second class. In 1918, having just learned to fly, the war ended, and he left with the rank of *Leutnant der Reserve* or Lieutenant of the Reserves. This gave him the right to go to university, which he did in Munich, and where he studied geopolitics. This was a big influence on him as his lecturer was a proponent of the concept of *lebenstraum*, the idea that the German people needed and were entitled to more 'living space', an ideology he took on board with great enthusiasm and was to pass on to Hitler when they ended up in prison together a couple of years later.

As soon as he left university in 1920, he joined the Nazi Party after hearing and falling under the spell of one of its speakers, Adolf Hitler. His commitment to the cause saw him march alongside Hitler, Göring and many other disillusioned former war veterans in November 1923 on the front line, at the failed Munich Beer Hall Putsch (Ch.2).

He was, however, very pleased to be put into Landsberg am Lech Prison alongside his beloved leader, Adolf Hitler.

Hess considered himself lucky, and yet the real luck was with Hitler, who, left on his own, spoke of giving up the struggle and forgetting about National Socialism completely. But Hess was full of ideas from his university lecturer, Karl Haushofer, and he soon was re-invigorating Hitler back to his old self. Hitler was always full of ideas and words but

Hess offered to write *Mein Kampf* as Hitler spoke – a perfect duet.

did not have the natural writing skills of Hess, so Hess offered to write while Hitler spoke – a perfect duet.

The outcome was the new 'bible' for all existing National Socialists and for the many yet to be converted – *Mein Kampf*. The more Hitler spoke, the more Hess was transfixed. He wrote home to his fiancée, Ilse Prohl,[1] telling her, '*I am devoted to him, I love him.*'

After Hitler became chancellor in January 1933 (Ch.3), Hess was almost overwhelmed with pride to be appointed Deputy Führer of the Party and then a cabinet minister in the Council of Ministers for Defence of the Reich, signing into law much of the new Nazi legislation, including the Nuremberg Laws that stripped away the rights of German Jews.

Hess was also private secretary to Hitler and as the absolute Party man, spoke at many rallies and meetings in ecstatic praise of the new '*Messiah*' – the saviour of Germany, the great leader. He had the crowd on its feet when he said, with great sincerity, '*My Führer, if you lead them, the people*

---

1. Ilse Prohl, later Mrs Hess, became a well-respected author after the war. She outlived her husband and died aged 95.

will follow; Hitler is Germany, Germany is Hitler!' But for all that, Hess did not have much else to offer at a time when Hitler needed men with other particular talents.

By 1939, Hess was beginning to feel as if he was no longer within the 'magic circle' of Hitler's henchmen, and he was shocked and deeply hurt when the Führer announced that his official successor was now Hermann Göring, and that Hess was then next in line. Hess's behaviour became noticeably odd as he seemed at times to become detached from reality and believe in unworldly powers such as astrology, the occult and telekinesis.

Hess now felt his position was being weakened by others, so he strived ever harder to impress his Führer. At one meeting of top military brass, held shortly after the Battle of Britain, an aide entered Hitler's room and announced that *'Britain refuses'*, to which Hitler ranted on in an angry mood, shouting out, *'Do they want me to go over there myself and go down on one knee?'*. [15]

There was no further explanation, but Hess seems to have taken this as proof of his own belief that Hitler had offered Britain some kind of terms. He knew that Hitler had met with the previous prime minister, Neville Chamberlain, who had done all he could to appease Hitler. Hess had also met the Duke of Windsor in 1937 and after a very brief conversation, had got the impression that some kind of deal could still be done with Britain. Hess had also been sure, in his own mind, that Hitler had allowed the British troops to escape from Dunkirk to leave open a window for negotiations.

But that was all before Churchill took control. Nevertheless, Hess had the idea he could do what others could not and decided to carry out a most outrageous plan that had been growing in his ever more paranoid mind. On 10 May 1941, Hess was driven in his Mercedes car to the Messerschmitt works in Augsburg, forty miles north of Munich.

There, he had arranged to have the use of a fully fuelled twin-engined Messerschmitt Bf110, a captain's flying suit and a parachute. He took off at 6pm and somehow, with almost no navigation experience and little experience of flying, flew one thousand miles over northern Germany and the North Sea, following the east coast of Britain, before heading west over the Scottish lowlands towards his unmarked target, the estate of the Duke of Hamilton, fifteen miles south of Glasgow. Three Spitfires and a Defiant were scrambled to attack the unidentified aircraft, but they could not catch it before Hess, somehow identifying his location in the darkness and with no training of parachute jumping, opened the aircraft cockpit, turned the aircraft upside down and dropped out.

Hurting his leg on the edge, and falling towards the ground, he managed to pull his parachute chord and drift down towards the fields below, leaving his plane to crash some distance ahead. He landed safely, but his injured leg made it difficult to stand and release his harness. A local farm worker called Donald Maclean from Floors Farm, near the village of Eaglesham, approached him, asking if he was German. Hess said that his name was Hauptman Alfred Horn, that he was unarmed and that he had an important message for the Duke of Hamilton.

It was, by any standards, a most remarkable feat; almost unbelievable that an inexperienced pilot had flown a light bomber 1,000 miles on his own, mostly in darkness, without navigation and with no parachute training but had landed almost exactly on the spot for which he had been aiming. His plane had crashed into a hillside some miles ahead.

Donald Maclean, William Craig and a local Home Guard stand by the wreckage of Hess's Messerschmitt Bf110.

Maclean and another local man, William Craig, helped Hess to his feet and took him back to Maclean's cottage where Mrs Maclean offered him a cup of tea. Craig went for help, and soon a member of the Home Guard, smelling of whisky, arrived and poked Hess with an old pistol. They then took him to a nearby Scout hut that was HQ for the local Home Guard. Hess, still claiming to be Captain Horn, was recognised by one man who then sent a message to the duke's house.

The duke, who was a wing commander in the RAF, got a message that a German pilot named Horn had landed nearby and wanted to see him, but the duke just went to his bed, saying that he would deal with it in the morning. The next day, realising that the prisoner was Rudolf Hess, the duke immediately flew south to Ditchley Park, an Oxfordshire country house weekend retreat used by the prime minister, there hoping to explain the situation directly to Winston Churchill.

Churchill and his guests were in the middle of dinner when the duke arrived. '*Come on, tell us your funny story*', demanded the prime minister. After a short explanation, Churchill decided that the full debriefing could wait because he'd already had enough bad news that day concerning the severe bombing London had suffered the previous night, and that he needed to have his mood lifted by the Marx Brother's film that had been arranged for him to watch that evening. Churchill, by then in his usual ebullient mood said, '*Hess or no Hess, I am going to watch the Marx Brothers!*' [15]

At the same time, Hitler was handed a letter telling him that Hess had written to explain his plan. Hitler was apoplectic; his face turned white, and he bellowed, '*Bormann immediately, where is Bormann?*' Then he lifted the telephone and called Göring in Nuremberg, shouting only, '*Göring, get here immediately, something dreadful has happened!*'

Hess had written that his aim was to bring about Hitler's long-standing deal with Britain through one of his own contacts, the Duke of Hamilton.

If Hitler did not think this was a good plan then he should declare Hess insane; which is exactly what Hitler did, as soon as he had gathered his thoughts. First he dismissed Hess and replaced him with Bormann as Head of the Party Chancellery. After Göring arrived he asked the former pilot if he thought Hess's journey could have succeeded. Göring thought he would probably have crashed into the sea as he was sure Hess did not have the expertise for such a technically difficult operation on his own.

Hitler was not convinced. He sent Ribbentrop to Rome to pre-empt any misunderstanding by Mussolini, who may well have thought that it was an attempt at a secret peace deal with Britain behind his back.

Hitler must have been panicked, because he did not immediately call in his propaganda minister, Joseph Goebbels. Desperate to put out his side of the story before the British broke the news on the BBC, he issued a hasty communiqué that evening. Working on the assumption, or blind hope, that Hess had crashed and was dead, Hitler mentioned the letter saying it showed that Hess had been mentally deranged and a victim of hallucinations. Goebbels arrived shortly afterwards and was horrified at the way the whole incident was being handled, particularly critical of the idea that the man seen as next in line to the Führer was an idiot, a madman, a head-case. What, asked Goebbels, did that say about the judgement of Hitler himself? The next day, 13 May, the BBC announced that Rudolf Hess, Deputy Führer, had been captured and was being held prisoner in the Tower of London.

Goebbels tried to salvage the situation by making up different, but more palatable lies that Hess had been tricked by the British Secret Service, and that he had lost his nerve and made a cowardly attempt to reach Britain. It didn't help much. The damage had been done. Party and public morale sunk and even the Führer's popularity was damaged.

Rumour-mongers had a field-day as stories and criticisms spread like wild-fire. Harsh jokes abounded inside the Reich, even about Hitler himself. In one, it was said that when Hess had been questioned by Churchill himself, Churchill had asked him, 'So you're the madman are you?' 'Oh, no', replied Hess, 'only his deputy'. [15]

Goebbels, as ever the sharpest mind in these circumstances, was resolute. 'The Party will have to chew on this for a long time', he foretold. Hitler was affected very deeply; possibly for the first time ever and certainly since he had become leader of the party, he felt real human emotion. Being deceived by someone who loves you most sincerely, but feeling that person has betrayed you and even created a situation that could ruin you, is one of the harshest emotional distresses anyone can suffer, and for Hitler this was his first time; always the hardest to bear.

At a meeting of his closest confidants shortly afterwards in the Berghof, those present record saying that Hitler, incredulous that such betrayal could have happened, had never been so affected by any other event. They had, *'never seen the Führer so deeply shocked'* and after he spoke he leaned on the table by the window and was *'in tears and looked ten years older'*. [15]

There was, it seems, a human soul deep down inside that cold murderer, after all.

The British held Hess in custody until the end of the war. When he returned to Germany to be put on trial at Nuremberg, he was shocked to see the ruined cities and his surviving fellow henchmen ragged and bent in defeat. During much of the trial, he claimed to be suffering from amnesia, but he later surprised the court by confessing his great pride and admiration for Hitler. He had, he believed, done his faithful duty to Germany and his Führer. The court convicted him of crimes against peace and of conspiracy to commit crimes, even though he had not been there since May 1941. He was sentenced to life in Spandau Prison. During the 1960s there were many attempts by family and friends, ultimately supported by the British, to have him released, but the Soviet Union blocked them all. For many years, he was the sole occupant in Spandau and in 1987, at the age of 93, Hess put an end to his lonely life by hanging himself with a light cord in the garden summer house. The prison was then demolished.

Hitler had been very lucky to have had the blind devotion of Hess throughout his rise to power. Hess had worshipped him since his first speech, been by his side at the Munich Putsch, encouraged and inspired him to write his book while in prison, carried out his every demand without question and spoke, with the greatest sincerity, about his charismatic leader at every opportunity.

But this time he had broken his Messiah's heart.

Albert Speer 1905–81

'One seldom recognizes the devil when he is putting his hand on your shoulder.'

Speer

If Hitler could have been anyone else in peacetime, it would surely have been Albert Speer. Hitler was, after all, a frustrated and failed artist, his first career choice when young but when Professor Christian Griepenkerl, the Principal of the Academy of Fine Arts rejected Hitler's second application for entry to train as an artist in 1908, it was suggested he should apply to the College of Architecture as his drawings were mainly of buildings. History would probably have been very different had he taken that advice. Twenty-five years later, however, when Speer entered his close entourage, Hitler belatedly realised that architecture was his passion. It soon became his only recreational interest.

There can be no doubt that Hitler was wholly committed to his ideology, the victory and dominance of the Germanic race over all others.

After he became the Führer, he must have spent almost all his waking hours either thinking about, or planning for, the next battle or campaign in the war; except when Albert Speer was around. Then he could talk about his favourite, non-political subject of architecture, to his favourite, non-military 'pal'. Hitler and Speer were strongly attracted to each other, though neither man was homosexual. They revelled in each other's company, admired each other, shared the same interest, and loved each other in the way that fathers and sons love one another.

Speer was the son of an architect and he followed in his father's footsteps by studying in Munich and then qualifying in Berlin in 1927. The year after, he married Margaret Weber, the daughter of a successful businessman, and together they had seven children.

Albert Speer had been born in 1905 and so was too young to have served in the First World War, but he joined the NSDAP in 1931 to, as he put it, '*save Germany from Communism*'. He was tall, handsome, young and athletic, so was soon recruited into the Aryan SS.

Speer was very ambitious and competitive, and his professional status soon had him appointed to the staff of Rudolf Hess, then Deputy Leader of the Party, where his architect's vision was quickly noticed by Hitler, who promptly gave him the task of organising the 1934 Nuremberg party rally. The result was a breathtaking blend of scale, space, Nazi propaganda and classical architecture. The bond between the two men was sealed.

Working together, they spent many hours planning the most ambitious future for the new Germany; first the Olympic stadium was modified and then Speer designed the German Pavilion for the 1937 Paris 'Expo'. Hitler had found the man through whom he could now fulfil all his youthful dreams, so he appointed Speer General Architectural Inspector of the Reich with orders to build a New Berlin that would reflect the new

Germany. Speer was extremely flattered and set about a major programme of designing state offices, such as the new Reich Chancellery, monuments and new cities. Hitler awarded him the party's Golden Badge of Honour.

The building ambitions of the two men knew almost no limit. The capital city would have a three mile long boulevard called the *Prachstrasse* or Street of Magnificence; at one end would be a domed hall, much larger than any other in the world, at the other end a great triumphal arch to dwarf the Arc de Triomphe in Paris, and two new state-of-the-art railway stations would bring people into the city to wonder at its magnificence. [55] Such were the hopes and plans of the Führer of the Third Reich: a legacy that was to last for a thousand years.

The new Reichstag was the first priority, but labour and materials presented problems, so Speer was given plenipotentiary powers with orders to finish this project by the end of 1938. This was when Speer's hands were first soiled in the 'dirty' side of the Nazi regime; he had inmates of an SS concentration camp work twelve-hour shifts quarrying stones and making bricks. When questioned about this he said *'The Yids [Jews] got used to making bricks while in Egypt'* – one of a number of statements that led to his long jail sentence at the Nuremberg Trials seven years later.

As the war progressed, industry struggled to keep up with the ceaseless demand for the huge range of materiel, machines, vehicles, planes, boats and especially weapons that were permanently in short supply. By good luck – and for Hitler, that was what it was – his Armaments Minister was killed in an aircraft accident, and Hitler immediately turned to his erstwhile trusty friend and gave him the task of reviewing and greatly improving the whole armaments industry. Speer had shown himself to be an excellent administrator and project manager for the many constructions completed up until then, but it was a risky appointment, nevertheless.

Speer was again flattered and put his whole being into making this mammoth aim succeed. Once again, Hitler had gambled and once again his good luck produced another henchman who was perfect for the job required.

As the new Minister for Armaments and then also the head of Todt, a massive state-controlled construction company, he saw little of his wife and family as the efficiency changes he was making throughout the whole arms industry took him all over Germany, inspecting, questioning, reforming and greatly improving productivity.

Above: Hitler and Speer revelled in each other's company, shared the same interests, and enjoyed mutual admiration.

Left: Tank production was constantly being delayed by the Führer himself who loved to inspect and then change detailed specifications of the new models.

Below: By April 1945, the two men could only walk around the half-ruined Reich Chancellery, looking aghast at the downfall of their joint dreams.

For the last four years of the war, Albert Speer was effectively the man in control of the German war economy, the relentless pressure to keep on improving inevitably involving greater use of slave labour, which was sourced mainly from concentration camps. Speer later claimed that he had argued loudly with Himmler, the *ReichsFührer-SS*, that camp factories were inefficient; that he had actually saved lives by using paid labour in the occupied countries. The preference, however, was probably more to do with productivity than with any moral scruples.

Now Speer had tasted real power, his ambitions raced, and he became more and more unrelenting and ruthless as he set his sights on gaining the control of all the armed forces, such was his level of self-belief. [55]

The production of tanks was always a priority, especially in Hitler's eyes, and Speer did all he could to increase the number being built, but new models were constantly being delayed by the Führer himself. Speer tried many times to persuade Hitler that a larger part of production should be for spare parts as the attrition rate on the battlefields, especially in Russia was colossal and hundreds of damaged tanks were being abandoned due to the lack of spares, but Hitler only wanted more and more new tanks built to replace those left lying useless on the battlefields. To make matters worse, Hitler loved minutiae and he had a terrific memory for detail. Consequently, he knew the size, calibre and measurement of every vehicle and weapon, past and present, and so was forever suggesting or ordering changes to this or that part with each change causing further delays in production. Hitler's meddling was to prove very costly in the great tank battles of the Russian Steppes.

One of Speer's greatest technological achievements was that he oversaw the building of the V-1 flying bombs and the ordering of the world's first ever ballistic missiles, the V-2 rockets. While it lasted, the effect that both super-weapons (Ch.18) had on their victims was devastating, but as far as Germany was concerned, it was a case of too little, too late.

Another of Speer's great successes was the change he made in the production of the weapon that Churchill believed was the only thing that truly frightened him, the German U-boat (Ch.15).

Britain came so very close to being blockaded in the first couple of years of the war, but Admiral Karl Dönitz, Commander in Chief of the *Kriegsmarine,* did not have enough U-boats to cover the vast Atlantic Ocean. This was entirely due to Hitler's own obsession with all types of Panzers and his general disdain for naval matters. Speer, however, in close association with Dönitz, understood this shortcoming and by the end of the war had increased production of U-boats from one a month in 1940 to forty-two a month by 1945. [56]

All of these, and more, were achieved while British and American heavy bombers reigned free over the skies above German cities and ports. Looked at dispassionately, the German productivity level of munitions, maintained right up to the surrender, was a most remarkable feat of planning and organisation, controlled personally by the Minister for Armaments.

However, in 1944, after three years of relentless pressure, Speer fell seriously ill with a lung embolism. Addicted as he was to his power and control, he simply could not pass authority on to a deputy. Weak and in hospital, he continued to work from his bed. As if this was not enough, there were massive Allied bombing attacks on many German factories, particularly those involved in aircraft construction, and the desperately needed planes were not being produced.

With great power come great enemies and his rival henchmen were using these set-backs to undermine Albert Speer. He even lost the unconditional support of his close friend, Hitler. [55]

Nevertheless, Speer and Hitler formed a new Fighter Staff Committee and production of fighter aircraft more than doubled, although these models needed updating and proved easy prey for the technically superior Allied aircraft. Productivity was increasing at a great human cost as more work was being done by slave labour supplied by the SS. The situation was becoming desperate, and Speer introduced a system of punishments for the workers; anyone who did not, or could not, maintain the pace was sent back to concentration camps to starve.

The human cost was appalling and on this indictment, Speer was seen during the Nuremberg trials as no longer just Hitler's architect but as a director of the abuse and death of tens of thousands of concentration camp prisoners, most of whom were Jews.

Loyal till the end, Speer refused to have anything to do with the assassination plot of July 1944 but in the aftermath, Speer lost favour with those who took revenge and his earlier power and authority was greatly diminished. He still remained close to Hitler, whose mental health was steadily worsening in the aftermath of his near-death experience at the

Wolfsschanze, and Speer was tasked with keeping the Führer informed of the ever-worsening news on the armaments front.

By the turn of 1945, most of the territory conquered previously by the Nazis had been recaptured. The Ardennes Offensive (Ch.19) Hitler's last big military attempt, had failed and the Allies were closing in on Berlin from the east and from the west. Hitler would not even consider the unconditional surrender demanded by the Allies. Instead, he took the nihilistic view that life was now pointless and human values were worthless, and he ordered the destruction of all property and constructions in the face of the advancing enemy. Hitler ignored Speer's personal plea to stop the destruction and instead gave out his written order that would become known as his 'Nero Decree', the destruction of his own Reich. [57] Speer appealed once more to his depressed leader and, at the end of March, the order was rescinded, although the army continued to blow up bridges and strategic buildings. Speer spoke to Hitler one last time on 22 April 1945. The two men walked around the half-ruined Reich Chancellery, looking aghast at the downfall of their joint dreams.

A few days later, on 30 April, Hitler and his new wife Eva Braun committed suicide together.

After the German surrender, all living or missing Nazi leaders were put on trial at Nuremberg. There, Speer expressed remorse for crimes committed by the Nazis but denied first-hand knowledge of the plan to exterminate Jews. His credible appearance, manner and claims of having no direct involvement in the extermination of Jews, probably helped him avoid the death penalty, but he was sentenced to twenty-five years imprisonment for war crimes and crimes against humanity. Thereafter, he continued to publicly assert that he knew nothing of the 'final solution' until, in 1971, he finally admitted to having been present at a meeting when Himmler declared that all Jews would be killed. Speer also claimed that he had planned to assassinate Hitler (Ch.11). This was one of a number of unsubstantiated events that later became known as the 'Speer myths'. [58]

After being released from Spandau Prison in 1966, Speer published two books of his memoirs, *Inside the Third Reich* (1970) and *Spandau: The Secret Diaries* (1976). He also was in considerable demand by documentary makers and historians. He appeared in a number of documentaries about Hitler and the Reich, as he was the only free survivor of Hitler's eight henchmen. He remained married to Margret but had lost all contact with his family and lived in London with a German woman. His daughter, Margret Nissen, wrote in her 2005 memoirs that after his release from Spandau he spent all of his time constructing the '*Speer Myths*'. [55]

But once again, Hitler had been very lucky in acquiring, by chance events and random opportunities, yet another dedicated and loyal henchman; one who was extremely skilled, very able and only too willing to carry out the ideological madness that Hitler could never have achieved without him.

Chapter 9

The Manstein Plan 1940

'In war, avoid what is strong, strike what is weak.'

Sun Tzu, 500 BC

By the spring of 1940, Hitler was feeling very pleased with himself. His conquering of Poland had been swift and at a relatively low cost in men and machines and he had established a supply of iron-ore from a now occupied Norway, although this would tie-up more than a quarter of a million troops for the rest of the war. Up to this point, he had planned military operations only in the broad sense of naming an objective and giving an order to attack, leaving the details and day to day command decisions to his experienced and able generals.

In the eyes of the German people of course, all credit was attributed to their now adored Führer. Hitler enjoyed the national adoration and the sycophancy of all those around him, military, political and public. It would be difficult for any human being not to be flattered by all the attention and Hitler certainly revelled in it.

His next target was to be France, which he knew was expecting him to invade in the foreseeable future. Having no formal training whatsoever in the theory of warfare, Hitler was nevertheless not short of his own ideas, and he liked nothing more than taking risks. He was, as evidenced so far in the Rhineland, Austria and Czechoslovakia, an incredibly lucky gambler.

There had been an invasion plan on the table for some months, named *Fall Gelb* or Case Yellow. It had been designed and approved by the OKW, the Army High Command. Case Yellow was based closely on the First World War Schlieffen Plan which saw the German army invade rapidly through Holland and Belgium, only to get bogged down for four years in the muddy fields of Flanders.

Hitler was not keen on repeating that mistake and had a feeling there should be some alternative, but the generals were adamant that there was no alternative as the French Maginot Line presented a sophisticated and solid defence on the border between the two countries.

The forest and mountains of Luxembourg were impenetrable for any large mechanised army to move safely or at speed, as it would expose them as sitting ducks to enemy air attack.

Hitler had an astonishing memory for minutiae, and he often took great pleasure, as a former soldier-corporal in criticising and deriding any general who had failed or whose ideas he did not agree with or who he could embarrass by citing detailed technical specifications to some weapon or vehicle.

He had already voiced his opinion on Plan Yellow by saying it was no better than 'the ideas of a military cadet'. [6] It was only by good luck that a totally different plan emerged.

It was bad luck, however, for Major Reinberger of 7 Airborne Division, killed when his light aircraft crash-landed in Belgium. Worse still, he had failed to destroy his copy of Case Yellow. But it turned out to be good luck for Hitler as this meant that the OKW (Oberkommando der Wehrmacht) which was nominally in overall command of German armed forces, then had to look to a different plan as they were sure the Allies would have now gained full knowledge of it.

Hitler heard from one of his adjutants of a more unconventional idea going around so he invited its creator Generalleutnant Erich von Manstein to explain his plan. Manstein was Chief of Staff at Army Group A but not part of the OKW.

Manstein began his outline plan and Hitler was instantly excited by the big gamble. Manstein had earlier developed his plan with fellow General Heinz Guderian who was a pioneer and advocate of the Blitzkrieg method – the rapid and mass deployment of tanks and armour – having already led an armoured corps in the invasion of Poland.

Crucially, Manstein also had the full support and backing of his immediate superior, the commander of Army Group A, Generaloberst Gerd von Rundstedt. So Manstein was well rehearsed, and he greatly impressed Hitler with his intelligence, knowledge, and expertise.

Manstein captured his Führer's full attention when he ably demonstrated on the table maps how modern, fast moving Panzers could cut through the Ardennes Forest of Luxembourg in the south, while the French and their Allies would be pre-occupied with the expected attack in the north.

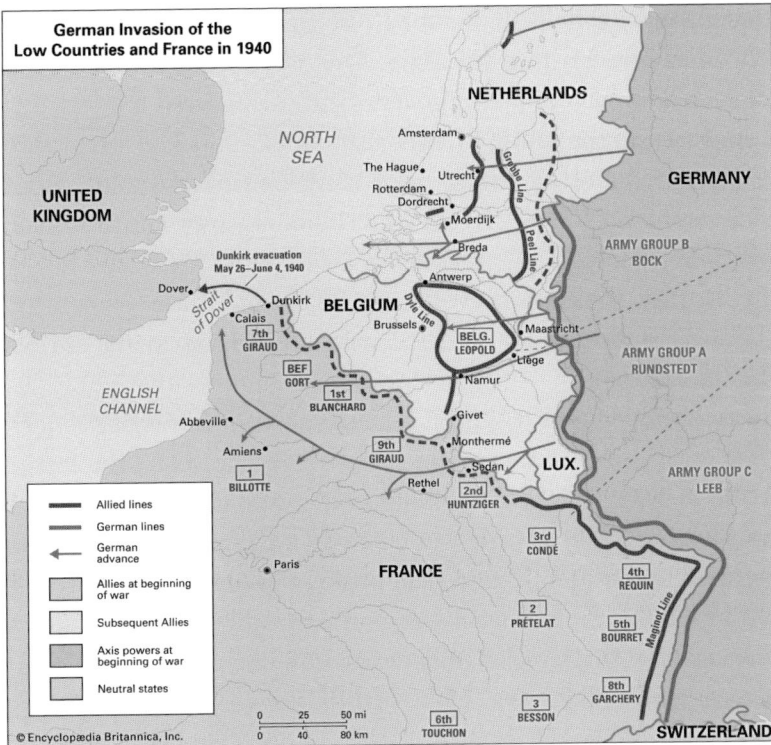

German Invasion of the Low Countries and France in 1940

NETHERLANDS

NORTH SEA

GERMANY

UNITED KINGDOM

Amsterdam

The Hague

Utrecht

Rotterdam

Dordrecht

Moerdijk

Breda

ARMY GROUP B BOCK

Dunkirk evacuation May 26–June 4, 1940

Antwerp

Dover

Dunkirk

BELGIUM

Brussels

Maastricht

Calais

7th GIRAUD

BELG. LEOPOLD

Liège

ARMY GROUP A RUNDSTEDT

BEF GORT

Namur

ENGLISH CHANNEL

Abbeville

1st BLANCHARD

Amiens

9th GIRAUD

Givet

Monthermé

LUX.

ARMY GROUP C LEEB

1 BILLOTTE

Rethel

Sedan

2nd HUNTZIGER

Paris

FRANCE

3rd CONDÉ

4th REQUIN

2 PRÉTELAT

5th BOURRET

8th GARCHERY

6 TOUCHON

3 BESSON

SWITZERLAND

Allied lines

German lines

German advance

Allies at beginning of war

Subsequent Allies

Axis powers at beginning of war

Neutral states

0   25   50 mi
0   40   80 km

© Encyclopædia Britannica, Inc.

Hitler invited its creator *Generalleutnant* Erich von Manstein to explain his plan and Hitler was instantly excited by the big gamble. Manstein captured his Führer's full attention when he ably demonstrated on the table maps how modern, fast moving Panzers could cut through the Ardennes Forest of Luxemburg. Then his Panzers would swing north in a 'sickle-cut' manoeuvre, cutting off the allies in one fell swoop. The whole operation was to be a masterpiece in Blitzkrieg, or lightning war, that was created first by air artillery, dive-bombers attacking behind enemy lines followed by fast moving mechanised armour, tanks and field artillery, then massed troops on vehicles such as trucks, motorbikes, and bicycles.

The Panzers would then swing north in a 'sickle-cut' manoeuvre, racing to the English Channel and cutting off the Allies in one fell swoop.

Hitler loved it; it was, he believed, exactly what he had been thinking about himself, and he immediately gave the order to OKW to prepare for this action as rapidly as possible. This plan was to be top-secret and the date of attack was set for the 10th May 1940.

The Belgians had in fact, retrieved the *Fall Gelb* details from the wrecked plane but, fearful of revoking their neutrality in case of German reprisal, only passed on a brief account of the plan to the British, who anyway suspected the whole set-up to be a German deception plan.

When the attack on Holland did start on 10 May, the Allies were not surprised that it did not look like any deception. An undefended Rotterdam was mercilessly bombed just as Warsaw had been and the Dutch surrendered within five days. One week later, the Belgian King Leopold fled into exile and his government surrendered too.

Meanwhile, in the south, German armoured units had swept through the Ardennes Forest, pushing aside any French resistance and then crossing the River Meuse. By 20 May 1940, advance Panzer squadrons had reached the coast.

The British Expeditionary Force (BEF) and their French Allies, numbering 340,000, were cornered with their backs to the sea on the beaches of Dunkirk.

The whole operation had been a masterpiece of Blitzkrieg – *lightning war*. Surprise and speed were the two primary elements, the former by air artillery – dive-bombers attacking strategic points behind enemy lines without warning. Then speed was created on the ground by fast moving mechanised armour, tanks and field artillery followed closely by massed troops on vehicles such as trucks, motorbikes, and bicycles.

Although the master plan was created by one of his most loyal and talented generals, Erich von Manstein, Hitler was happy to claim that this very bold and largely successful operation was all his.

Many were quick to believe him, and he was soon being hailed as a '*genius*' strategic military planner by his devoted soldiers; but it was, in reality, purely a result of his continuing good luck.

Chapter 10

Barbarossa – the End of the Beginning 1941

'Speed is the essence of war. Take advantage of the enemy's unpreparedness; travel by unexpected routes and strike him where he has taken no precautions.'

Sun Tzu, 500 BC

Although the invasion of Russia in June 1941, named by Hitler as Operation Barbarossa, was ultimately to cost Hitler his great plan for a German Empire, the Third Reich, it was to prove his greatest mistake of all. He interfered and personally changed his generals' original plans, wholly against their wishes, when he had, in fact, been presented with a chance series of events and the best conditions for victory right from the start, thanks entirely to his good luck.

But good luck cannot last forever

Hitler was under the very false impression that Britain had been effectively defeated, or at least was no longer a real threat in the West, as Hitler's single biggest dread had always been another war on two fronts. In many ways, he was right to be optimistic by the summer of 1941, given all the circumstances up to that moment. Hitler's successes included the defeat and capitulation of Britain's European Allies Belgium, Netherlands, Czechoslovakia, Poland, and France. He had been able to fool Stalin into a secret, non-aggression pact while his Blitzkrieg tactics had also pushed back the British army and forced it off the beaches at Dunkirk. German U-boats had, at this point, been able to effect a blockade of Britain by sinking many merchant ships in the Atlantic Ocean, Italy had allied with Germany by declaring war on Britain, and Japan had also joined the Axis, as had Romania and Hungary. Norway, Yugoslavia and Greece had surrendered, the *Afrika Korps* still seemed to be in control of

North Africa, and the cities and ports of Britain were being relentlessly bombed by the Luftwaffe.

Circumstances and events had therefore merged to give Hitler what he figured was the ideal opportunity to fulfil his greatest dream of all, the defeat and conquering of Russia. And he was almost right.

The British government, headed by Winston Churchill since May 1940, still regarded Russia or, strictly speaking, the Soviet Union, and its president Joseph Stalin, as an ally. So, Britain passed on to Stalin its clear warnings, obtained by its still very secret code breakers at Bletchley Park, that Hitler was planning to invade his country in midsummer 1941.

Stalin had also received similar warnings from other sources, including agents in Washington and Japan, but Stalin trusted no-one, except the one person who had lied, deceived, and tricked Britain, France, Poland and Czechoslovakia. Stalin had chosen to dismiss such information as deliberate misinformation aimed at keeping Russia on the Allies' side, describing Churchill as *'Angliyskaya provokatsiya!'* a *'double-crossing war-monger'*. [8] This was to be Stalin's big mistake as, unbelievably, he still trusted Hitler. But that was Hitler's great good luck as he was able to plan and organise the largest military invasion in history right under Stalin's unsuspecting nose.

Hitler had, of course, made his aim of conquering the *'land of the Slavs'* very clear two decades earlier in *Mein Kampf*, writing, *'We must stop the endless German movement to the south and west, and turn our gaze toward the land in the east – we can primarily have in mind only Russia and her vassal border states.'* [19]

Why Stalin preferred to trust a man who had shown his deceitful hand so clearly over the past years is difficult to understand but it was perfect for Hitler who had outlined his Plan Barbarossa to his senior generals in some detail in his Führer Directive No.21 of 16 December 1940.

Hitler envisaged another Blitzkrieg invasion using an overwhelming number of armoured thrusts supported by the Luftwaffe. Surprise and deception were again to be the key elements. Following the Ribbentrop-Molotov Pakt, where one year before the Russians had been given a free hand by Hitler to invade and occupy eastern Poland, the Russians had become complacent allowing the whole Red Army to be spread out over a vast area, deep into the western reaches, a long way from Moscow.

'Whoever wants victory should start attacking first.'

Mein Kampf

Hitler knew that a 'Stalin Defence Line' was being created but also that it was incomplete and that it had gaps.

On 22 June 1941, Hitler was able to give the order that was, in its way, the epitome of his personal aims, ambitions and achievements and can be considered both his finest moment and his biggest mistake. He was very lucky to have a range of individually brilliant *Generalfeldmarschalle* (Field Marshals) and *Generaloberts* (Colonel-Generals) to lead the 180 divisions that swept into and through the vastness of the eastern Russian empire. Field Marshal Walther von Brauchitsch was the commander-in-chief of this immense force consisting of three Army Groups. Army Group North was led through Lithuania, Latvia and Estonia towards Leningrad by Field Marshal von Leeb commanding, among many others, Sixteenth Army led by Busch, Eighteenth Army led by Küchler, Panzergruppe 4 led by Reinhard, and LVI(56) Motorised Infantry Corps led by Manstein, that included the SS Totenkopf Division (see Ch.8).

Army Group Centre was advancing directly through Belarus on the same route that Napoleon had taken 129 years before, via Smolensk to the capital, Moscow. It was commanded by Field Marshal von Bock, leading von Kluge's Fourth Army, Strauss's Ninth Army, Guderian's Panzergruppe 2 and rising star Model's Third Panzer Division, plus many, many others.

Army Group South, led by Field Marshal von Rundstedt, drove over the endless flat land of the Ukraine to Kiev, on towards the Black Sea and the primary target of the oil wells of Baku and the Caucasus. With him were von Reichenau's Sixth Army, von Kleist's Panzergruppe 1 and Kempf's XXXXVIII (48) Corps of Motorised Panzers, plus many other corps including Hungarians, Slovakians and Romanians. [59]

The numbers were unmatched in history. In excess of three million German troops, armed with over 3,000 tanks, more than 3,000 aircraft, 7,000 guns, and even three-quarters of a million horses combined to overwhelm the 10,000 outspread, and mostly radio-less, Russian tanks. One third of Russia's 6,000 planes were destroyed as they sat in neat lines on the well-known airfields scattered over western Russia. [8] Stalin's

One hundred and eighty German Divisions invaded in three Army Groups on 22 June 1941, all led by Hitler's finest Generals, including the redoubtable Heinz Guderian a pioneer and champion of Panzer battle tactics. The Soviets had, perhaps the greatest General of the whole war, Marshal Georgy Zhukov.

generals were slow to tell him the Motherland had been invaded by the Germans, too afraid of his psychopathic wrath. When they did, he went instantly silent, reportedly so stunned by the news he simply could not bring himself to believe that he had been utterly tricked by Hitler.

He just disappeared off to his country Dacha and withdrew, dazed and bewildered. It was almost a week before his most senior general, Marshal Zhukov, could get the Russian dictator's permission to counter-attack.

Events could not have played out any better for Hitler, and he may well have felt great self-satisfaction as his army raced ahead, sweeping aside all Russian defences, occupying all the Soviet states, taking thousands of Soviet prisoners, and most of west Russia up to within 100 miles of the capital, Moscow.

Stalin's long hesitation was Hitler's good luck and it was to cost Russia over two million casualties by the end of August.

The Soviet Union was always going to be the most difficult nut to crack, Hitler was well aware of that, but the speed and glory of the invasion added to his already inflated his ego.

The political deceptions, the massive build-up of more than three million troops and tens of thousands of mobile armour and weapons, the suddenness of the attack, the unreadiness of Soviet forces, and the stunned reaction by Stalin made up the perfect storm. Hitler, with a combination of these circumstances and his experienced General Staff, had been almost unbelievably lucky in that they all came together at precisely the same moment.

Once again, it seemed as if Blitzkrieg was about to win the greatest victory of all for Hitler. The speed of advance had bewildered Stalin and surprised Hitler himself, dazzling his followers at the same time.

Little wonder his Chief of Staff, General Keitel, gushed admiration for his Führer, describing Hitler as '*the greatest warlord of all time*'. [15] Perhaps he should have called him '*the luckiest warlord of all time*'.

But luck eventually runs out and that is when military skills, cool judgement and calculated decisions are needed.

These are the skills of a great commander; but none of them belonged to the Führer.

Chapter 11

Assassination – Luck of the Devil

'The only preventative measure one can take is to live irregularly.'

Adolf Hitler, *Mein Kampf*

When it comes to good luck, perhaps escaping an unexpected deadly event is probably the best luck you can have. While any contentious public figure always faces a risk of attack by either someone of another view or just a madman, it would surely have to be considered lucky beyond any laws of average, or chance, not to have your life shortened by twenty-two assassination attempts over twelve years.

In Chapter 1, between 1914 and 1918, Hitler avoided death from artillery explosions, stray bullets and gas attacks when hundreds of thousands of his comrades were killed around him. This invisible shield of protection that had surrounded him over these four years of war did not disappear after 1918.

In Chapter 2, Hitler avoided death again when he was on the front line of his 2,000 party supporters as they marched on the Marienplatz in Munich in 1923. On his left arm was one of the leaders, Max von Scheubner-Richter, and to his right was Hermann Göring. The group were met with a hail of bullets from the police cordon and sixteen Nazis were killed including Richter. Göring was shot in the thigh. Hitler was dragged over by Richter as he fell, but the bullets all went elsewhere.

1932

There were two attempts to kill Hitler in 1932. While dining at the Hotel Kaiserhof in Berlin several members of Hitler's company were poisoned, but Hitler avoided the attempt as he was a vegetarian and did not eat the poisoned meat. Shortly after that, Ludwig Assner, a member of the Bavarian state parliament, sent a letter containing poison to Hitler. There was a tip-off by a fellow politician, and the letter was intercepted just in time.

1934 and 1935

There were two further conspiracies in 1934 and another two in 1935, all in Berlin. The first two plots were uncovered by the Gestapo and despite the next two involving officers of the army along with Foreign Office officials, university professors and some businessmen, they too failed.

1936

A German Jew named Helmut Hirsch came close to success in 1936 when he planted two suitcases full of explosives in the Nazi Party headquarters in Nuremberg when Hitler was due to visit. A Gestapo double-agent revealed the plot, and Hirsch was caught and executed by decapitation.

1937

Two attempts to shoot Hitler dead occurred in 1937; the first was by Josef Thomas who travelled over 300 miles from Elberfeld, near Cologne, armed and with the intention of shooting both Hitler and Göring. Thomas was intercepted by the Gestapo.

A few weeks later, during the annual Nazi rally at the Berlin *Sportpalast*, an unidentified man, dressed in full SS uniform, managed to get close to Hitler but was arrested before he could fire his weapon.

1938

While Hitler toyed with British prime minister Chamberlain in so-called negotiations over the future of Czechoslovakia, many officers of the Wehrmacht feared the outcome would be war, so planned to storm the Reich Chancellery, execute Hitler and restore the exiled Kaiser Wilhelm to power. The plan collapsed when Hitler was appeased by the British and French and was allowed to annexe the Sudetenland. This group was not exposed and many of them formed part of future attempts, most notably the plot of July 1944.

A few weeks later, a Swiss theology student, Maurice Bovard, had his plan to shoot Hitler as he passed in a parade, spoiled when his view was blocked by the ecstatic crowd. Bovard followed Hitler to try again but could not get close enough. On his way home on the train his suspicious behaviour was noticed by the conductor, and he was turned over to the Gestapo. He was executed by guillotine.

1939

By the time Hitler ordered the invasion of Poland on 1 September 1939, all the attempts and plots for his assassination had been foiled, either by the inner workings of the Gestapo or just by chance. By the end of October, Hitler had avoided certain death only by the greatest of good luck on three different occasions. At the beginning of that month a Polish general and his men concealed half a tonne of TNT by the side of the road that Hitler was to pass on his victory parade through Warsaw. At the very last moment, the parade was diverted, by chance, and the targeted dictator was driven out of range.

Over the preceding few weeks, however, the most audacious attempt yet was being set up by a German carpenter called Georg Elser. He had read that Hitler was due to be making his annual speech at the *Bürgerbräukeller* on 8 November in commemoration of the Munich Beer Hall Putsch. Elser had been planning this for over a year, regularly stealing small amounts of explosives from his workplace in Heidenheim and hiding it in his bedroom. Esler realised the bomb case would have to be an exact size to fit inside the column he had identified the previous year. This was directly behind the podium from which Hitler would be giving his speech.

He travelled to Munich with his camera and took photographs inside the Beer Hall, and he changed his job to work in a quarry where he was able to gather an arsenal of blasting cartridges and detonators.

While living in a rented room he designed a timer system using some clock parts and a car indicator switch. He then moved to Munich in August and frequented the *Bürgerbräukeller* where he dined most evenings. From there he could secretly stay behind after it closed at

Anyone would surely be considered lucky beyond any laws of averagenot to have lost their life after 22 serious assassination attempts over 12 years.

One of the closest calls was in 1939 when a German man named George Esler carefully planted a bomb that went off in the *Bürgerbräukeller* directly behind where Hitler had been giving a long speech only thirteen minutes earlier.

night and then, over the next few weeks, he worked on creating a cavity in the pillar and installing his bomb and timer. This was a remarkable achievement and showed a surprising lack of security on the part of both the Bürgerbräukeller and Hitler's bobyguards, as Elser was able to work till the early hours of the morning using a torch. He was then able to sleep in a storeroom and leave by a back door in the morning.

On the night of 1 November, Elser installed the explosives; he returned three nights later to fit the twin-clock mechanism that would trigger the detonator. Hitler's speeches were famously long so Elser calculated his bomb should explode at 9.20pm, right in the middle of the speech.

With Hitler standing with his back to the pillar, inside which was a box full of TNT, there was no doubt the explosion would kill him. On the morning of 7 November, Elser departed Munich, travelling the 120 miles to Friedrichshafen by train and then taking the 6.30 pm ferry across to Konstanz.

Adolf Hitler and several high-ranking Nazis, including Goebbels, Heydrich, Hess, Rosenberg, and Himmler, arrived on the evening of 8 November for the celebrations at the Bürgerbräukeller as scheduled.

Hitler had in fact cancelled the visit the day before as he was pre-occupied with planning the forthcoming invasion of France but had changed his mind again at the last moment and arrived to start his speech at 8pm.

This was half an hour earlier than had been planned as Hitler had decided he would not fly back to Berlin the next day but instead return by train that evening.

As the train was due to leave at 9.30pm, Hitler cut short his speech, and he and his entourage left the building at 9.07pm. Thirteen minutes later the bomb exploded with great force. The walls, pillars and half of the ceiling blew out and collapsed, killing eight people and severely injuring sixty-two others. Had Hitler been at that podium, he would certainly have been killed, as would some of his closest henchmen sitting next to him.

When his train stopped en route at Nuremberg, Hitler was given the news. According to Goebbels, his response was *'A man has to be lucky'*. After a little further thought, he added *'My leaving earlier than usual is proof to me that Providence wants me to reach my goal.'* [62]

The luckiest and probably the most famous near-miss was the Valkyrie plot on 20 July 1944.

Colonel Claus von Stauffenberg placed TNT explosives under Hitler's table. By the greatest of luck Hitler was only slightly burned but greatly shocked.

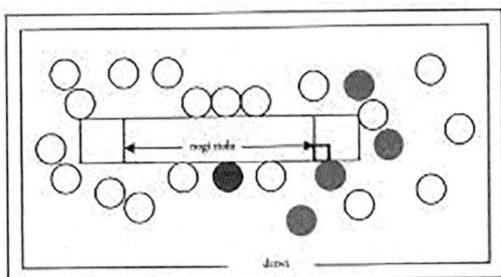

This was an understandable reaction that Hitler would repeat many more times over the next five years when he came just as close to being assassinated, only to escape death by sheer luck.

Earlier that same evening, before the explosion, Elser was only twenty yards from the Swiss border in Konstanz when he was, by chance, apprehended by two border guards and told to empty his pockets. Unwisely, he still had on him wire cutters, notes and sketches about explosive devices, firing pins and a colour postcard of the interior of the Bürgerbräukeller. The guards decided to detain him, as a matter of routine, for further questions. Shortly afterwards news of the bombing arrived by teleprinter.

The next day Elser was handed over to Gestapo headquarters in Berlin. At the crime scene, pieces of brass plates with the patent numbers of a German clock-maker were picked out of the debris, and Himmler offered a reward of half a million Marks for information. Names of many suspects were soon flooding into the Munich Gestapo offices. Elser was soon identified as a regular diner at the *Bürgerbräukeller* by a waitress who said he was the odd man who never ordered more than one drink. Another shopkeeper said Elser had bought material to deaden the sound of a clock ticking. One Gestapo chief made Elser show him his knees. They were both badly bruised from his night work in the Beer Cellar. All of Esler's relatives and associates were quickly rounded-up back in his home-town.

Elser was badly beaten for over a week before he finally confessed. He had to make full-size drawings of the bombs to show that he was the sole activist and that no-one else was involved.

But many people had to pay the terrible price. Those with whom Elser had associated were regarded as suspects and many spent some time in prison or were beaten.

Elser was not executed at the time, as the Nazi party wanted to stage a show trial. He spent the rest of the war in a concentration camp and was finally 'liquidated', as the order read, in secret in April 1945 in Dachau concentration camp.

1941

Some of the conspirators from the second 1935 plot, known as the Solf Circle, led by Beppo Römer, had not given up their aim. They had been keeping constant tabs on Hitler's movements through a contact in their Berlin command centre, awaiting their opportunity, but each time Hitler would change his plans, or his security would prevent it, or some other small matter would disrupt any possibility. The longer the plot went on, the greater the likelihood of detection and that is just what happened; once again, the deep penetration of Gestapo informants paid off, and Römer was arrested and executed in 1944.

1943

Two Werhmacht generals claimed later that they had plotted to arrest and then kill Hitler on a planned visit to their army detachment in the Ukraine. It was a big idea – General Hyazinth Strachwitz would surround Hitler with his tank squadron, and General Hubert Lanz would arrest the Führer. Once again Hitler changed his plans and only pure luck prevented them from carrying out the deed.

In the same year, however, one of the best organised, and most likely to succeed, plots happened when a small group of the most determined would-be assassins tried twice to kill Hitler and his deputy, Himmler. The first was an unsophisticated plan. Major von Boeselager and Colonel Tresckow would stand up as Hitler and Himmler approached and, at a given signal, fire their pistols point blank. Himmler failed to appear, and the plot was abandoned.

Undaunted by this unlucky event, Colonel Tresckow and General von Schlabrendorff then came up with another plan that had the best chance of success since Georg Elser's bomb plot in 1939. Hitler had flown to Colonel Tresckow's base at Smolensk so he put two bottles of Cognac in a box under which he placed a large block of explosives. He handed the box to a colleague who was flying back with Hitler in his Junkers Ju 52 – explaining it as a gift to von Schlabrendorff in Berlin. Set to explode during the flight, the result would unquestionably have been the death of Adolf Hitler.

The package was placed in the unpressurised hold and the freezing temperature at altitude prevented the detonator from setting off the explosives. When von Schlabrendorff heard Hitler had landed safely he had to go urgently to retrieve the box before the plot was uncovered.

He succeeded in that part, but Hitler's astonishing good luck seemed never ending.

The same conspirators became frustrated and more than a little desperate. Tresckow's close friend, Major General von Gersdorff, offered his own life in return for the elimination of Hitler to, in his words, 'save Germany'. Von Gersdorff, an expert in Russian weapons, was due to guide Hitler, Göring, Himmler, Keitel, and Dönitz on a tour of an exhibition of captured Soviet weapons in a museum in Berlin one week after the failed attempt on his flight from Smolensk. Hitler and his henchmen turned up on time, and Gersdorff immediately primed the timers of the explosives hidden in his coat pockets.

This time a full follow-up plan for a *coup d'etat* had been devised as the whole top brass of the Nazi government was likely to be taken out in one fell swoop.

Hitler, however, seemed disinterested in the exhibits, hurrying through the building, scarcely looking at any item and preventing Gersdorff any chance to get close enough. Not for the first time, Hitler cut the visit short without notice, leaving the building after only ten minutes.

Hitler was again very lucky, but so too was Gersdorff who had just enough time to reach the toilet to defuse the bomb. Soon afterwards, he was transferred to the Eastern Front, having evaded any suspicion.

Six months later another suicidal attempt was made on the Führer's life. It, too, would surely have succeeded but for Hitler's apparent innate good luck. A young major, Axel von dem Bussche, had been chosen to model the latest Nazi winter uniforms in a fashion show being held for the Führer in the *Wolfsschanze* bunker deep in the Masurian forest of East Prussia (now Poland). He was tall, blond, blue-eyed and everything Hitler wanted his future Aryan Empire to be, but Bussche was willing to give up his life to stop Hitler's destruction of Germany. It was a simple plan involving him wearing a back-pack full of high explosives.

Although the train carrying the new uniforms was destroyed during an Allied air attack, the plan remained in place when another date was set for the review a few weeks later. Again, the uniforms failed to arrive, so the whole show was eventually cancelled.

1944 – Berghof

Major von Bussche was given another opportunity a couple of months later when he was asked to attend a briefing by Hitler on 11 March in his Berghof near Obersalzberg in Austria. This time the plan was to shoot Hitler in the head at point-blank range with a Browning 7.65mm pistol concealed in his trouser pocket. But at the very last moment, the SS guards were told that staff officers only could join the Führer in the conference room, aides having to wait outside.

Without knowing anything about it, Hitler's life was once again spared by sheer luck.

1944 – 20 July – Valkyrie

By a long way, the best organised and most forward thinking plot to kill Hitler, replacing his regime with one that would immediately try to negotiate a peace deal with the Allies, was carefully and painstakingly planned in the summer of 1944.

What became known as the 20 July Plot was actually based on an already prepared Nazi plan, known as Operation Valkyrie by the perpetrators. It was to become immortalised by the 2008 film of that name, directed by Bryan Singer and starring Tom Cruise who depicted, with astonishing accuracy, the central character, Colonel Claus von Stauffenberg's very nearly successful attempt to kill Hitler. Perhaps even more significant in the film was how it showed that killing Hitler itself was only one part of a bigger plan for it was by no means certain that the Führer's death would be welcomed by all.

There were, after all, thousands of highly loyal SS soldiers and officers who would have to be prevented from taking control and replacing Hitler with an equally dangerous new leader, or even worse with a far more skilful military leader who would present the assassination as a martyrdom and rally the armed forces and the people of Germany into prolonging the war.

The conspiracy to kill Hitler was a long way from being a one-man show; it had in fact been growing and developing for some years. Most of the failed attempts mentioned previously involved some, or all, of a group of thirty-seven senior army officers that had formed back in 1942. [74] The three leading figures were General Olbricht, General-Major von Tresckow and Colonel-General Beck. The Finance Minister, Johannes Popitz, believed he could persuade Himmler to lead a coup against Hitler, and a meeting was arranged by Himmler's lawyer, Carl Langbehn, who was one of the few non-military members of the group. At this meeting, Popitz flattered Himmler's ever inflating ego and vanity by telling him that only he, Himmler, could restore the true National Socialist ideals and lead the Party away from the road to disaster to which it was heading under Hitler; he would be the new Führer of Germany.

Although Hitler had long believed Himmler was one of his few and most trusted henchmen, the fact was that Himmler was as corruptible as any of them when it came to self-aggrandisement. Popitz also pointed out that the British, in the shape of Winston Churchill, and the Americans, as stated clearly by President Roosevelt, would never negotiate a peace with Hitler, but he told Himmler that they both would be willing to do so with a leader who they were sure would stand up against the real enemy of the democratic west, the communist Soviet Union.

Himmler was easily flattered and, having the morals of a weasel, agreed to meet again for further discussions. However, the Gestapo reported to him that Popitz was being investigated, so Himmler had to act quickly to distance himself from Popitz and, at the same time, get the Gestapo off the scent. To be sure that he was never implicated, Himmler ordered the execution of Popitz immediately after the failed assassination attempt in July 1944.

Claus von Stauffenberg was born in Bavaria in 1907 into a distinguished aristocratic family. His father had been Privy Chamberlain to the King of Bavaria, and his mother was the granddaughter of a Prussian baron and army general.

Stauffenberg was a tall and strikingly handsome young man, and in 1930, aged 23, he was commissioned as a second lieutenant into the family's traditional regiment, 17 Cavalry.

In 1933 he married Nina von Lechernfeld with whom he had five children. Although Stauffenberg, like most army officers, had been impressed by Hitler at first, after *Kristallnacht* had developed over the years a distaste and eventual hostility towards his Führer. By 1940, his Panzer regiment had taken part in the invasion of Poland and he had become concerned at the way the Poles, and in particular the Jews were being treated. He had been approached by some conspirators at that time but had declined to join them then.

In combat, Stauffenberg had shown courage and was awarded the Iron Cross First Class. [76] He was sickened, however, by the mass shooting of civilians and Jews that he witnessed during Operation Barbarossa and, as a direct result, he resolved to do everything in his power to remove Hitler and overthrow the regime. [77]

In 1942, Stauffenberg was promoted to Lieutenant Colonel and appointed to the General Staff as the Operations Officer of 10 Panzer Division in North Africa. While travelling in a column to a forward group he was strafed by an Australian Kittyhawk P-40G and received wounds to his face, arms and legs.

He spent the next three months in a Munich hospital where his life was saved but he suffered the loss of one eye, the amputation of his right hand, and the removal of part of his leg and three fingers from his left hand. Not surprisingly, his recovery was slow and as he convalesced in his castle home in the Swabian Alps, he was introduced to General von Tresckow, one of the leaders of the conspirators' group.

As Stauffenberg could no longer serve on the front line, he was promoted to Colonel and appointed Chief of Staff at the Berlin headquarters of the *Ersatzheer*, the Reserve Army. This was the perfect place for Stauffenberg to develop and execute his primary aim, to assassinate Adolf Hitler.

There was already a plan made that would let the *Ersatzheer* take immediate control of all communications should there be any internal disruptions or an attempted coup by the SS; it was named *Unternehmen Walküre* or Operation Valkyrie. Stauffenberg's senior commander was General Olbricht, also a conspirator, and together they amended the original plan, Valkyrie, that had previously been authorised by Hitler. This new plan was to trick the Reserve Army into the seizure and removal of the civilian government of wartime Germany under the false pretence that the SS had attempted a *coup d'état* and that Hitler had been assassinated.

Their one big problem was their commanding officer, General Fromm. Only he had the authority to enable Operation Valkyrie, but he would not wholly commit to the conspiracy. He knew of it but did not report it to the Gestapo; like many other senior officers, he was a man more fearful for his own skin than for the future of the Fatherland. Olbricht and Stauffenberg knew this and decided they would falsify Fromm's authorisation and deal with him afterwards if it became necessary.

As Stauffenberg now had direct access to the Führer, he was able to get Hitler to authorise and sign-off the new plan without him actually reading the changes. This was typical of Hitler; on the one hand he would indulge for hours in the minutiae of weapons or tank specifications but was lazy when it came to paperwork, preferring to let his officers just '*get on with it*'.

This mistake very nearly cost him his life.

At this moment, General von Tresckow was deployed to the Russian front and so control of the plot was taken over by Stauffenberg. He brought a new impetus and dynamism to the group and offered himself to be the man to do the deed.

He also wanted to be sure that the aftermath of a coup should be fully organised and that the new government would not be a replacement of the old but would be a true and proper Republic. The conspirators agreed, and a new cabinet of senior ministers in waiting was named that included Beck as President, von Tresckow as Chief of Police, Popitz as Finance Minister and Olbricht as State Secretary for War.

Stauffenberg's plan was to take explosives with him to his next meeting in the company of Hitler, and there he would be able to set-off the bomb that would kill not only the Führer but, he hoped, Himmler and perhaps Göring too.

The first time Stauffenberg met Hitler was on 7 June 1944, the day after D-Day. He accompanied his commander General Fromm to a meeting at the Berghof and when Hitler solemnly clasped Stauffenberg's one, two-fingered hand between his two hands and gazed his blue eyes intensely into Stauffenberg's one eye, Stauffenberg did not feel any of the hypnotic charisma that so many others had spoken of when they had come close the Führer. This was a gathering of Hitler's henchmen: Himmler, Göring, Keitel and Speer. Stauffenberg wished he had taken his explosives as this was the moment he had been waiting for. He vowed he would not miss such an opportunity again as he felt physically sick in the company of what he described as *patent psychopaths*. [87]

The next chance came sooner than he could have hoped. On 11 July he was summoned to another meeting at the Berghof, and this time he would be fully prepared. He packed two 1Kg blocks of explosives and two acid-filled pencil tubes in the bottom of his briefcase and arranged for a plane to be on stand-by at Obersalzberg airfield to get him back to Berlin as soon after the assassination of Hitler as possible. There, he and Olbricht would put Operation Valkyrie into action immediately. That was his plan.

When Stauffenberg arrived at the Berghof there were a number of SS guards at the door. He knew that if they checked his briefcase, he would be a dead man; but they just saluted as he passed by.

When Stauffenberg entered the same large lounge area, he immediately noticed that Himmler was not present. It was the resolve of the conspirators that Himmler had to be killed at the same time, as he was the most likely to take over from Hitler and was even more sick in the mind than his Führer.

Very reluctantly, Stauffenberg decided he would wait for another opportunity, confident that there would be further such meetings.

On 15 July 1944, Stauffenberg was attending a meeting of senior officers for the third time in as many weeks. This meeting was at the *Wolfsschanze*, Hitler's Headquarters in East Prussia.

At previous meetings, Stauffenberg had the explosives in his case, but on this occasion he could not set the timers as he needed to use pliers to squeeze the detonator timer, and his one hand did not have the fingers to do the job. Again, he decided to defer to another time as neither Himmler nor Göring was present.

Urged on by General Beck, he decided that he would go ahead with the plan at the next meeting, whether or not Himmler or Göring were present; he may not be given many more chances to be so close to Hitler again.

Stauffenberg realised he could not do this alone, so for the next visit he took with him his adjutant and fellow conspirator, Lieutenant von Haeften.

So it was, on 20 July 1944, that von Stauffenberg and von Haeften flew the 400 miles from Berlin to the airstrip at Rastenburg. The open top Mercedes that awaited their arrival drove them the five miles to the *Wolfsschanze*. The main building was of thick concrete and had been built as the base for Operation Barbarossa, the invasion of Russia in June 1941.

Over the four years of its existence, Hitler spent a lot of his time, more than 800 days in fact, that's almost two and a half years, in the *Wolfsschanze*. He felt secure below ground and behind the bunker's bomb-proof walls, and it was also a long distance from Allied air attacks. Stauffenberg knew, however, that the very thickness of the concrete would multiply the explosive power of the bomb, as the pressure waves would be compressed and the shrapnel would slice through the human flesh of all those within range.

In Haeften's briefcase were two 1Kg blocks of British explosives wrapped in brown paper and two pencil-thin copper-tube detonators containing acid. When squeezed, the acid would take approximately ten minutes to eat through the wire, thereby releasing the firing-pin onto the percussion cap. That was the plan.

The first obstacle was the weather. It was mid-summer and the heat was stifling, so Hitler had decided to hold this day's meeting in a ground-level, wood-framed building where the windows could be left wide open. Stauffenberg was unfazed; the plan was going ahead, whatever.

During the late morning he had to attend two briefings, the first in General Jodl's quarters and the second in Keitel's bunker. [79] At 12.30pm, Keitel announced that it was time to go to the Führer's meeting, so Stauffenberg asked if he could have a private place to change his shirt. He insisted that Haeften came with him as, due to his injuries, he needed his help. An orderly nodded and took them to a private room while Keitel waited in the hallway. But this was to be one of the moments of simple luck that probably saved Hitler's life.

The meeting was about to begin so there was some urgency as the two of them quickly, but nervously, unwrapped the first explosive block and were about to unwrap the second, when Keitel shouted from the hallway, '*Stauffenberg, please hurry up!*' [82] At the same time, the orderly tried to enter the room to urge them to hurry as the meeting had already begun. The two men had to push the primed bomb into Stauffenberg's case before they could even get the other one out of Haeften's case. This was a crucial moment, as there can be no doubt that if both bombs had exploded – everyone in the room would have been killed, including Hitler. But that is what luck is – '*the arbitrary distribution of events or outcomes*'.

It would be unacceptable for them to be late to Hitler's meeting so the two men walked briskly from one security zone to a higher one and although the place was busy with SS *Begleit* commandos (FBK) and SS guards of the *Sicherheitsdienst* (SD), no-one attempted to check them, or their bags. When Stauffenberg entered the meeting room, he bowed his head towards Hitler and apologised. Hitler acknowledged him and Stauffenberg took his place less than ten feet to the Führer's right. He had been allocated the position close to Hitler as he had made it known that he was suffering deafness due to his injuries.

He then placed the briefcase, containing the primed bomb, by his feet just under the large wooden table and as near to Hitler as he could reach. A few minutes later, he excused himself from the room. This did not raise any suspicion, as there was a great deal of sympathy for the discomfort it was assumed that he felt as a consequence of the dreadful injuries sustained on active service.

Minutes later, another officer, Colonel Heinz Brandt, [78] stepped into the space and kicked the briefcase by mistake. He then bent down and moved it a little further away and, crucially, behind the thick wooden support beneath the centre of the solid oak table.

Meanwhile, Stauffenberg walked as nonchalantly as he could over to Haeften, and they both walked on to the black Mercedes with the driver that had taken them there earlier that morning. At 12.41 – a huge explosion ripped through the air – Stauffenberg saw the wood-framed building blow apart and felt no doubt that his mission had been a success. An officer standing nearby had only heard the deafening crack and exclaimed it was probably a mine in the woods being set off by a wild animal. Stauffenberg and Haeften boarded the car instantly and instructed the driver to make haste as they had been ordered to return to Berlin immediately. What mattered now was to get back to Berlin as soon as possible to make sure Valkyrie was put into operation as quickly as possible.

The car passed out of the gate without being stopped but further on, at the perimeter of the compound, guards halted the Mercedes. This guard was more vigilant, and he refused to allow Oberst Stauffenberg to pass at first. Stauffenberg stepped aggressively out of the car feigning offence at the insubordination; the check-point barrier lifted, his staff car passed through and they drove quickly to the airfield and his waiting plane.

Over the previous thirty years Hitler had survived, or avoided, many instances when he could have been killed. Whether it was by his wartime enemy or by his would-be assassins, he had on each occasion usually by sheer luck, either not been at the place of likely death, or had been late, or had been early, or had changed his plans, or by some other wholly unplanned event had not even been injured.

On 20 July 1944, however, Hitler came closer to death than ever before.

There had been twenty-four people in the conference room. The explosion killed three officers standing near the briefcase, but the thick wooden support under the oak table had taken the first impact of the blast, while the wood-lined hut, with its windows wide open, had dispersed the shock waves outwards and away from Hitler. He had been blown off his feet and his trousers were ripped to tatters, but he emerged from the shambles with no more than a few bruises.

Communications between Berlin and Rastenburg had been severed as part of the plan, but this led to much doubt in Berlin for some hours, and Valkyrie was not put into operation immediately. When the order was eventually given by Olbricht, the plan began to work. Then, another moment of good luck for Hitler but bad luck, or careless planning, for the conspirators.

Goebbels, hearing that Hitler was dead, telephoned the *Wolfsschanze* on his direct line – no-one had thought of cutting this line of communication. He was able to speak to the Führer in person, so when the guards came to arrest Goebbels, as part of plan Valkyrie, he was able to turn the whole operation around and announce that the Führer was alive as he had just spoken to him personally on the telephone. Goebbels immediately arranged for Hitler to make a radio broadcast to the nation and it was from this point that Valkyrie could no longer succeed.

As soon as General Fromm, the official commander of Valkyrie who had never fully committed to Stauffenberg's plan, heard this, he immediately acted in his own personal interests and arrested Olbricht, Stauffenberg, Beck, Haefte, and a number of the other known conspirators.

Fearful of the passive part he had played, Fromm had them summarily shot in the garden outside his office, backlit by the headlights of nearby army trucks.

General Fromm did not escape. Two days later he was arrested – Goebbels said, '*You were in a damn hurry to get your witnesses below ground.*' [80] He was put on trial, and although no evidence was brought that proved his direct involvement, there was still enough to have him shot by firing squad.

In the immediate aftermath, the Gestapo had a field-day – 7,000 people were arrested on the slightest of connections and 4,980 were executed or took their own lives. These included three field marshals, the most notable of whom was Erwin Rommel, nineteen generals, twenty-six colonels, two ambassadors, seven diplomats, four ministers, and the head of Berlin police. Those closest to Hitler were hung up by the neck with piano wire, and their suffering was filmed for his evening entertainment.

General-Major Henning von Tresckow, the instigator of the conspiracy group, had been seeking a way to assassinate Hitler since the start of the war. In 1939, he told a colleague, '*Both duty and honour demand from us that we should do our best to bring about the downfall of Hitler and National Socialism to save Germany and Europe from barbarism.*' [81] However, as soon as von Tresckow received the news, far out on the Eastern Front, he

The room was destroyed as was the Führer's trousers. Three senior officers were killed and twenty others injured.

drove into the forest and took his own life by pulling the pin on a hand grenade held under his chin.

His last recorded words were, *'A man's moral worth is established only at the point where he is ready to give his life in defence of his convictions.'* [82]

July 1944 – Foxley

Britain and her allies knew nothing of Operation Valkyrie during its planning stage, but at exactly the same time the British Special Operations Executive (SOE) was hatching its own plan to eliminate Hitler. He was to be assassinated during one of his visits to his Austrian home, the Berghof, some time in the summer of 1944. The plan was named Operation Foxley. [84]

SOE had been created in 1940 at the behest of the newly appointed prime minister, Winston Churchill. The mission, he told them, was to, '*set Europe ablaze*'. [85] Their full remit was to conduct espionage, sabotage and reconnaissance in occupied Europe, as well as to aid resistance movements. SOE had not been looking at possible assassination opportunities for some time, but an agent in France sent a coded message saying that Hitler was at that moment, 27 June 1944, staying in a named chateau for a couple of days. The agent suggested the chateau could be accurately bombed by the RAF. The idea was presented to the SOE directors, but they were split on going ahead with this mission as some felt there was not enough certainty of success. However, they agreed to look at other options.

One director, code named LBX, considered that, given Hitler's constant and unpredictable movements every day and his security protection by large numbers of SS and SD men, the best and possibly only opportunity could arise when he was in, or around, the Berghof, his home near Obersalzberg in the southern Alps.

Among several of the somewhat bizarre ideas put forward was one to attack the special train Hitler often travelled in – oddly named '*Amerika*' – later renamed '*Brandenburg*'.

One option was to have SOE commandos hide in the forest near a small, remote station that Hitler was known to stop at on his way from Berlin to Obersalzberg. He could be killed either as he stepped off the train or as he returned to it. On this occasion, they considered using a PIAT, a Projector, Infantry, Anti-Tank weapon.

The thinking, it seems, was that a powerful explosion was more likely to kill Hitler than a sniper's bullet. However, effective though the PIAT was at hitting tanks, it was not considered accurate enough at over 100 yards, and no sniper would be likely to get that close.

Another plan considered was to derail his train with an explosive in a tunnel, as SOE had a lot of experience with this technique. But perhaps the most unlikely plan was to put some tasteless but lethal poison in the drinking water supply on Hitler's train. However, this plan was considered too complicated because of the need for an inside man and in any case it was thought that Hitler probably drank bottled water with his meals.

It was already known from sources such as former guards who had been taken prisoners of war that Hitler was at his most relaxed and exposed at the Berghof, his alpine home. There he would rise mid-morning, and every day, between 10 and 11am, he would stroll for twenty minutes, down the private 2 kilometre road to the *Teehaus* – in the village below – for his favourite tea and cakes.

Often, he would walk with a minister or a general but at times he would be alone, apart from a couple of SD men who would keep well behind him so as not to spoil the pleasure he clearly felt in the peace and quiet of the fresh alpine air.

SOE Director LBX felt that there, at the Berghof, lay the best chance of assassination. The idea was to be explored in depth and would be named Operation Foxley. The plan was to drop trained, German-speaking snipers, wearing the exact uniform of the Mountain Regiment, into the forest near the Berghof. There they could hide in the thick woodlands that overlooked Hitler's house, the ideal scenario for a sniper to assassinate him. What is more, it was known that a Nazi flag was flown only when Hitler was at the Berghof and that it was visible from a nearby café.

The selection and training of a team of two marksmen would take some time. The perfect candidates were identified – the leader was Captain Edmund Bennett, an experienced intelligence officer who specialised in small arms – a crack-shot who spoke fluent German. The other was a German-speaking Pole.

Time had moved on and it was 22 March 1945 before the SOE finalised the plan.

The two snipers, wearing the correct kit, would be parachuted into the area. They would contact a local SOE agent, who was an anti-Nazi shopkeeper living near Salzburg, and he would hide and protect them. The snipers, disguised as German troopers, could then approach the Berchtesgaden area and find the best vantage point to hide overnight for the attack the next morning when Hitler took his walk down to the *Teehaus* for his daily tea and cakes.

The two men would have practised by firing at moving dummy targets with a German Karabiner 98K rifle fitted with a Mauser telescopic sight. They would also be armed with a Luger pistol and silencer to deal with any threats during their approach to the target and hand grenades that may be needed in their escape. The difficulty of landing by parachute near the target was always a potential hazard, as were the accuracy of local maps and the number of patrol dogs the guards would be using; but these were problems for every SOE agent in foreign territory.

Although Churchill approved the plan, there was division among the top brass, with some feeling that there was no real benefit to eliminating Hitler at this late point of the war. Hitler was seen by the British as such a poor military strategist that it was better the devil you know than the risk of a much more able replacement leader. It was also argued that as Germany was almost defeated, an assassinated Hitler would become a martyr figure to some Germans and give support to the myth that Germany might have been victorious if he hadn't been killed by underhand means. This in turn could re-invigorate the whole National Socialist movement and prolong the war rather than end it promptly. So, the operation never happened, and Hitler once again avoided likely elimination because of events way out of his control.

Hitler left the Berghof for the last time on 14 July 1944, never to return.

1945 – Poison Gas

The last known attempt to kill Hitler was in the mind of Albert Speer – he claimed it was a serious consideration – but it never actually happened.

Albert Speer had a special relationship with Adolf Hitler. It could be described as a father and son relationship, or perhaps like two pals who shared the same interests.

In Chapter 8 of this book, Speer's relationship with his Führer is looked at from the point of view of Speer as one of Hitler's henchmen, as indeed he was. The relationship did not start as such though. Speer first saw and heard Hitler at a political rally in the university at which he had recently graduated and where he was to become a lecturer in architecture

– the Technical University of Berlin. There was a huge audience in the main hall, as the National Socialists were very popular in the university during the 1930s. Speer said he was immediately captivated by the great orator's voice. [86]

Shortly after this, Speer joined the party and in 1932 he was given the task of redesigning the new party offices by Joseph Goebbels. Goebbels was pleased with the work and gave Speers the huge job of designing the whole backdrop for the forthcoming Nazi mass rally. Speer said he wanted to make the Führer look very impressive and he succeeded. Hitler was also impressed, and Goebbels elevated Speer to the position of designer of sets for all Nazi rallies. At this point, Hitler had his own architect, Professor Troost. Troost was very able, but he treated Hitler more like an enthusiastic pupil when Hitler believed his ideas deserved more respect. At the beginning of 1934 Troost died; Hitler wasted no time in appointing Speer as his successor.

He was immediately told to redesign the massive arena at the *Zeppelinfeld* in Nuremberg. The building had to be able to hold a third of a million people. Speer's completed project was used many times for the great Nazi rallies, often held by flaming torchlight or with upturned searchlights, all to glorify the Führer and his Reich.

After that Hitler wanted to spend as much time as he could in the company of the man who had realised his boyhood dreams and with whom he could share his most ambitious ideas for a future Germany and a new Berlin. Hitler helped him to design a stadium so large it would accommodate nearly half a million people, all under a massive roof. The two men spent many hours together discussing, planning and admiring the perfectly made models of the city of the Führer's wildest imagination.

Speer was a very busy architect for the next eight years, designing and overseeing many more massive projects such as the 1936 Olympic Stadium and the 1937 German Pavilion for the International Exposition in Paris. Hitler was never far from his side, revelling in the active participation of his greatest passion. Speer later rightly described himself as the only person who Hitler treated as a friend. Speer treated his Führer as an architectural equal and nothing made Hitler happier.

By 1942, Germany was struggling to maintain production of weapons, tanks and vehicles at a rate fast enough to match the attrition rates being suffered, the consequence of losses on the eastern front in battles against ever strengthening Soviet forces, and damage being done to German factories from ever increasing air raids by British and American bombers.

In February of that year, the mega-industrialist and armaments minister, Fritz Todt, died in a plane crash, and Hitler immediately appointed Speer as his replacement. This demonstrated the absolute trust and faith Adolf Hitler had in his friend. That trust was well rewarded as Speer showed a remarkable natural ability, many said '*genius*', to take control of this massive responsibility that included the running of the Todt industrial empire.

There is little doubt that Speer was the most intelligent of Hitler's henchmen, and for the rest of the war he was able to use his wits and guile to exploit his very close personal relationship with the Führer (Ch.8).

As Minister for Armaments, Speer now had to take on a role that was totally committed to Nazi causes. He had enjoyed years of playing games with his Führer, but now he had to become a full-blown Nazi. His early results were seen as miraculous, as his reorganisation of all production, including prioritising the manufacture of tanks and the development of concentration camps, were all unrelentingly successful. However, it did not last; the Allies were controlling the sky and the sustained heavy bombing of strategic targets took its toll. He was no longer content to be just an architect of fine buildings – he had become ambitious for more success and, now that he had tasted it, for more personal power. The consequence of so much work and responsibility, however, was that in January 1944 he was committed to a sanatorium suffering from exhaustion and nervous collapse. [87] He had been under tremendous pressure and was now distrusted by his fellow henchmen (Ch.8). As he recovered, he saw the writing was on the wall for the war effort, and as he had been detached from developing events he now felt sure that his period of illness was to cost him dear. He could see that he was well out of favour with his former friend, the Führer. Speer said that at that moment '*the veil was lifted... I could see omens of the war's end ... [Allied] bombers... not a German fighter plane anywhere... [we were] totally defenceless*'. [87]

By March 1945, Hitler was confined to his Berlin bunker, deep under the Reich Chancellery. Soviet forces were shelling the centre of the city and by mid-April their tanks were at the Brandenburg Gates.

The British and her Allies had crossed the River Elbe and were closing in on the capital from the north. Speer continued to use his wits, and he visited Hitler on a number of occasions. He was particularly sickened by what became known as the *'Nero Decree'* in which the Führer had ordered the destruction of all buildings, factories and bridges ahead of the enemy advances.

This was *'scorched earth'* taken to the extreme, as it was not aimed at preventing the enemy from enjoying supplies and resources but was the annihilation of everything that Speer, often along with Hitler, had planned and built. The destruction order was being carried out with astonishing enthusiasm by some German troops, and Speer was appalled. He pleaded time and again to Hitler, appealing to him by saying that Germany would soon fight back and that these places would be needed again. Hitler relented a little, in response to Speer's sound arguments, and for a few weeks in February and March 1945, Speer was able to issue orders that saved from demolition Paris, the old city in Hamburg, the mines in Belgium, France and Finland, the canals in Holland, and the oil fields in Hungary. [87]

But the Führer was, by this time, wholly unhinged and such appeals were either lost on him or more often seen as some kind of betrayal. Speer was perhaps fortunate not to have been shot for countermanding Hitler's express wishes. Many others, including Göring and Himmler, were either executed or condemned to be shot for treason during those final months in the Berlin bunker (Epilogue).

At this point in the winter of early 1945, Speer was reminded of Hitler's own words that he had written two decades earlier in *Mein Kampf* and that were the antithesis of what the madman was doing now. At this revelation, claims Speer, he vowed to *'eliminate Hitler'*. He also hoped he could kill Bormann and Goebbels at the same time despite thinking that that had *'a touch of the ridiculous about it'*. [88] That was true, as Speer was the least likely assassin ever.

Speer had never been involved in any war action and had never directly killed anyone, so he couldn't even think of how to carry out his vow to himself. He still had personal access to Hitler but to shoot him, face to face, would be well beyond him. In any case, since the 20 July plot, no-one could get in to the Berlin bunker with any weapons whatsoever; without exception, all had to accept a full body search. He needed to find a more remote or detached method, and while walking in the Reich gardens he had noticed the inlet ventilation shaft to the Bunker was only hidden behind a small bush. As there were no guards, he felt it would surely be simple enough to introduce some poison gas down through the vent. After all, by this time millions of people, mostly Jews, had already been exterminated with ease using that very method. He discussed his plan with a colleague named Dieter Stahl, his head of munitions production whom he knew was of the same mind.

They knew that Hitler had a massive stockpile of the colourless and tasteless nerve agent *tabun*, and Stahl said that he could acquire some. Shortly after, Speer revisited the garden only to find all had changed. There were now SS patrols, and worse, the inlet ventilation chimney had been extended to a height of over 3 metres, well beyond reach. When he returned the next day to see Stahl, he told him that *tabun*, though deadly, could not be used anyway as it did not evaporate or form smoke, and could only be activated by the explosion of the shell that carried it to its target.

Speer was no natural killer, and when he later overheard some workers expressing their undying faith in their Führer, he abandoned his plot to kill Hitler. In his last visit to the bunker on 22 April, the two men walked through the badly damaged Chancellery, no doubt deeply shocked at the destruction of their joint plans. Speer then left his Führer and Berlin and returned to Hamburg for the last few weeks of the war.

This claim by Speer may well have been some clever ruse by him at his trial in Nuremberg shortly after the war – to make himself appear distant and blameless of the terrible crimes that had been committed by the Nazis. However, if it had been just made up, then surely he could have made it all sound so much more convincing?

If such ideas and actions had taken place, and if a suitable poison gas had been available and if the vent pipe had remained easily accessed, then maybe Hitler would have been assassinated after all. If so, it would have been an added irony that he would have been killed by the one man in his life with whom he shared a genuinely close friendship, bordering perhaps on a kind of love.

Whether true, partly true, or all false, the story played a large part in saving the impressively eloquent and apparently honest demeanour of Albert Speer from the gallows of Nuremberg. [88]

Regardless of all these factors, Hitler had, by sheer luck, once again avoided death by an assassin. Hitler's good luck had guided him from one astonishing success to the next. It had prevented him from falling foul of others' errors, had allowed him to benefit from others' misfortunes, it had presented him with fait accompli successes, and it had enabled him to side-step countless bullets and bombs without him even noticing.

Hitler's run of good luck had gone on for twenty-five years and in all that time he was sure that it was he who was responsible for all the fortunate events that had befallen him and that it was he who controlled events; not his good luck but his imperious, infallible omnipotence – and that was his first big mistake!

Part Two

Hitler's Big Mistakes

'Hitler has sown the seeds of havoc, now he must reap the harvest of the chaos he created.'

Air Marshal Arthur T. Harris

Chapter 12

Ideological Obsessions

'The ultimate end of any ideology is totalitarianism.'

Tom Robbins

The big mistake that Hitler made, perhaps the one mistake that over-arches all his mistakes, was the priority he gave to the ideological option when seeking to solve any problem, whether political, social or military. His ideology had been clear since 1924, when he wrote his first volume of *Mein Kampf*. The second volume followed shortly after his release from Landsberg am Lech prison and the complete set was reprinted in English in 1933. By 1939 it had sold over five million copies and had been translated into eleven languages. No contemporaneous individual could justly claim that he had no idea what Hitler's aims were in the decade before the Second World War.

Although his book could never compete for a literary prize in terms of writing expertise as it is very much a drudge to work through, it nevertheless revealed, without a shadow of doubt, the key to Hitler's ideological thinking. Three extracts that demonstrate all of these points are:

'Only the Jew knew that by an able and persistent use of propaganda heaven itself can be presented to the people as if it were hell and, vice versa, the most miserable kind of life can be presented as if it were paradise. The Jew knew this and acted accordingly. But the German, or rather his Government, did not have the slightest suspicion of it. During the War the heaviest of penalties had to be paid for that ignorance.

'As opposed to this, we National Socialists must hold unflinchingly to our aim in foreign policy, namely, to secure for the German people the land and soil to which they are entitled on this earth. And this action is the only one which, before God and our German posterity, would make any sacrifice of blood seem justified.'

'I know that fewer people are won over by the written word than by the spoken word and that every great movement on this earth owes its growth to great speakers and not to great writers.'

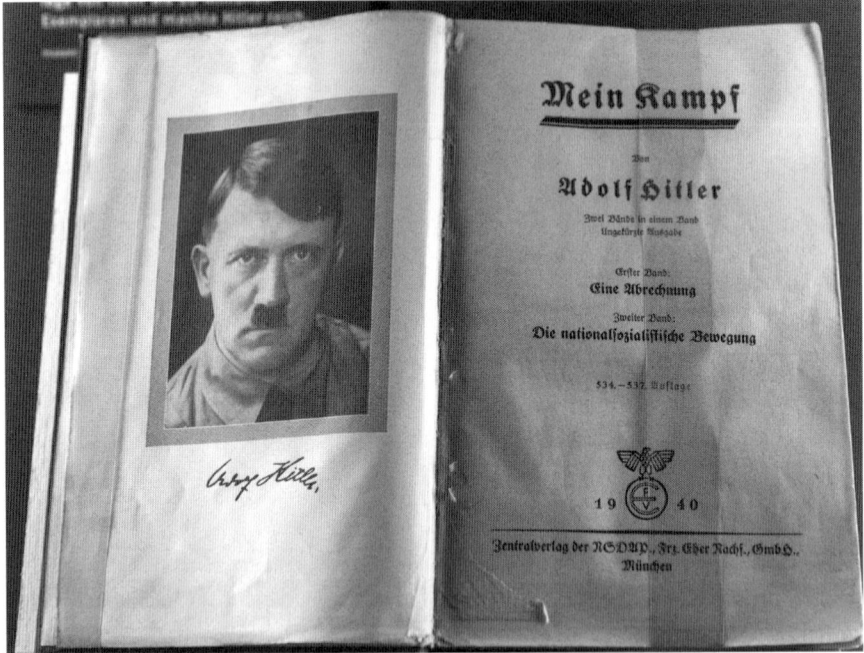

After the abortive Munich Beer Hall Putsch of 1923, Hitler was imprisoned at Landsberg am Lech in Bavaria. There, in relative comfort, Hitler, aided by Hess, wrote his first volume of *Mein Kampf*. His basic philosophy was that for Germany to be great again, he would need to rid society of the causes of its problems: Jews and Bolsheviks. (*Shutterstock*)

Hitler made it clear to his readers that it was all, in his mind, at least, a clear and unequivocal statement of his ideology and aims when he concluded,

'I know exactly where I am going and nothing is going to prevent me getting there.' [10]

Hitler's beliefs and ideology were evidently well entrenched long before he got anywhere near the reins of power. His First World War experience and sheer dismay at Germany's surrender and defeat was explained simply: Germany had been *'betrayed by Jews and Communists'*. The German soldier had never wanted to give up as he was Aryan, part of the genius race. Communists were the political enemy and they were spreading their *'Bolshevik lies'* westwards following the Russian Revolution of 1917.

Hitler called for *'revenge'* against France and stated plainly he would make Poland a vassal state and that he would humiliate Russia by conquering it. Although these can be seen as just the geographical objectives of *lebensraum*, they were, in Hitler's mind, countries occupied by *untermensch* (sub-humans), thereby justifying rule by the master race.

German society, he stated, was *'infested'* by the *'parasite'* that was the Jew. The elimination of Jews *'must necessarily be a bloody process'*, he wrote.

Hitler's aim was to create a Third German Reich that would last a thousand years. This new German Empire would be *Volksgemeinschaft*, based on the *'traditional values of the ancient German people'*. It was to be a new ideal German society which rejected old religions, ideologies, and class divisions, and instead formed a united German identity based around ideas of race, struggle and state leadership.

This traditional society included the subjugation of women's interests, restricting them to being house-wives and mothers, as it was *'the sacred mission of the German people… to assemble and preserve their most valuable racial elements… as all who are not of a good race are chaff'*. [11] This narrow definition of a woman's role resulted in the costly mistake that would prevent women working during the war in the production of vitally important war equipment, food, material, machinery and weapons. [9]

Nazi ideology and Hitler's beliefs were also unequivocally racist. The enforced emigration of German and Austrian Jews between 1933 and 1939 was an appalling way to treat citizens who were integral and equally loyal members of their society, but Hitler's ideological obsession with ridding Europe of all Jews had no rational or pragmatic element to it. This was a mistake that can be measured as having cost him victory in the war as well as the lives of six million Jews.

After the *'Night of the Long Knives'* (Ch.5) cleared out the SA leadership and cut back their high profile attacks on the Jewish community, Hitler could have found a way to use the Jewish people to the benefit of the imminent war preparations; not to abuse and eliminate them. [10]

Hitler did show that he could conveniently sideline his racist beliefs when he sent Joachim von Ribbentrop to make a deal with the Slav and Bolshevik Vyacheslav Molotov to share the spoils of a conquered Poland. Hitler had also previously set aside his religious prejudices by making the *concordat* with the Head of the Roman Catholic Church. [10]

Hitler's constant desire to always be ahead of enemy technology in weapons, equipment and intelligence and later his programmes of 'super-weapons' (Ch.21) would have developed much more quickly and successfully if the best Jewish scientific brains had been involved. This was to be evidenced later by the five Jewish intellectuals who had already each won a Nobel Prize before transferring to the USA in 1937, and there became part of the team that developed the Manhattan Project to build the first atomic bomb by creating a plutonium 239 implosion. This big mistake was another unavoidable consequence of Hitler's ideology that very possibly also cost him his dream of a new Empire.

Hitler did not examine or even consider how those Empires like the British Empire and the Roman Empire that he admired so greatly, had been so successful. He failed to understand how they had lasted so long, not through subjugation, slavery, poverty, punishment and racist ideology but by *'allowing the common man some measure of hope'* [10] through sharing economic benefits, retaining their customs and religions, and by not specifically excluding them from opportunities for personal gain.

Instead, Hitler believed all conquered peoples were *Untermensch* and therefore needed to be controlled by force, subjugation, enslavement or annihilation.

In 1922 Hitler said *'Once I really am in power, my first and foremost task will be the annihilation of the Jews. As soon as I have the power to do so, I will have gallows built in rows…then the Jews will be hanged indiscriminately…. until the last Jew in Munich has been exterminated. Other cities will follow suit, precisely in this fashion, until all Germany has been completely cleansed of Jews.'* [107]

Hitler's ideology also damaged what had been an established legal system by creating a police state that would ultimately turn his planned

The *Enabling Act* effectively swept away Democracy and put all powers of law-making into the hands of a Führer who then described himself as 'Germany's Supreme Judge'.

Hitler made it clear that the Judges he wanted 'must not speak of State power but of Führer power'.

empire into a slave state. The breakdown began in 1933 with the Reichstag passing the *Enabling Act,* effectively sweeping away democracy and putting all powers of law-making into the hands of a Führer who then described himself as *'Germany's Supreme Judge'.* Hitler made it clear that the judges he wanted were *'men who were deeply convinced that the law should NOT safeguard the individual but… first and foremost see to it that Germany will not perish'.* [10]

The rot spread very quickly through the whole legal system when Hitler immediately replaced all state governors with Nazi Party nominees. Known as *Gauleiters,* every one of them was corrupt, ruling each state like gangsters and racketeers and compelling magistrates to swear an oath to Hitler personally. Hitler was *de facto,* omnipotent. As the German constitutional lawyer Ernst R Huber said *'We must not speak of State power but of Führer power.'*

In 1941, Himmler, the new Minister of Justice, was ordered by Hitler to *'pay no attention to any existing law that might interfere with the establishment of the Nationalist Socialist administration of Justice.'* This meant that Himmler could condemn all *untermensch* to death without trial or sentence by a court. [10]

Hitler had more or less abrogated his law making authority to others in the pyramid of power below him. He was shielded from awkward questions by his right-hand man, the rapacious, ruthless and ideological fanatic, Martin Bormann. By 1941, Bormann (Ch.8) was the sole channel to Hitler's ear and one of the very few that Hitler actually trusted. [10]

Hitler's ideology had its biggest negative impact on his military decision making. The Germans were on the point of victory a number of times between 1938 and 1945, but each time they managed to *'snatch defeat from the jaws of victory'* and each time that was as a result of Hitler's interference based on his ideology.

Hitler's first and arguably his greatest mistake therefore, was to allow his fascist, racist, irrational beliefs to over-ride his political, legal, social and military decisions. Although these prejudices served him well in the beginning of his climb to fame and public acclaim, they gradually but inevitably came to be the cause of, or at least have a bearing upon, all of his mistakes; mistakes that would lead, one after the other, to his ultimate failure and demise.

Chapter 13

Failure to Invade Britain after Dunkirk 1940

'On the Plains of Hesitation, bleach the bones of countless millions, who, at the Dawn of Victory, sat down to wait, and there, waiting – died.'

George W Cecil 1923

If Adolf Hitler had been that *greatest commander of all time*, if he had shown the sharp opportunist decision making of Caesar or Napoleon at that moment when only the remains of a defeated British Army and all its equipment, weapons and vehicles were trapped on Dunkirk beach, he would not have hesitated to implement his invasion plan, and, most likely, would have conquered Britain.

Hitler's big mistake was that he did not have such a plan.

When the *Führer* agreed upon General Erich von Manstein's plan to conquer France, Manstein was Chief of Staff at General Rundstedt's Army Group A and was already well recognised as an innovative and meticulous planner. Hitler, however, failed to look to what the next step would be if the plan succeeded. In *Mein Kampf*, Hitler did not propose invading Britain, and as he often told one of his closest ministers, Albert Speer, the English were *'our brothers, why fight our brothers?'*. [23] Hitler was convinced, ideologically, that as the British were Anglo-Saxons they were therefore racially Aryans, the same as all true Germans.

Even without a detailed plan a *great commander* would have gone forward, crossed the narrow fifty miles of the English Channel with whatever forces he could muster in those few days, establish a foothold on the Kent coast around the port of Folkestone, and then flood in as much support as possible, as quickly as possible. From there it is only seventy miles up the A2 to London, the very threat of which would surely have forced the surrender of the British government.

There is no doubt there were risks attached to such action, but speed and aggression, with overwhelming armour and air support, had already proved to be the ace cards of the Blitzkrieg victories in Poland and France.

That enigmatic maverick Scotsman, Colonel David Stirling who created the first elite commando force, the SAS, summed up its number one attitude with the clearest of military philosophies – '*He who dares, wins.*' Surely the truly great conquering commanders of the past, like Alexander, Caesar or Genghis Khan, would undoubtedly have dared to cross the English Channel as soon as they saw their enemy being pushed back into the sea at Dunkirk.

But Hitler hesitated and the opportunity was lost forever.

In the weeks up to the Dunkirk situation, German tanks, supported by mechanised transport, dive bombers and mobile infantry, had swept through Holland and Belgium in the north. However, Manstein's plan had critically taken seven tank divisions from the north Army Group B and relocated them to his own Army Group A in the centre. Army Group A then swept through the Ardennes Forest of Luxembourg, making the first break through the Maginot line at Houx by 7th Panzer Division led by their brilliant major-general Edwin Rommel. They then swung north in a right hook called Operation *Sichelschnitt* or 'Sickle-Cut'.

The Allies had fallen for the deception by moving their main strength in the north into Belgium to counter the Army Group B attack. Although General List's Twelfth Army in Army Group A encountered a strong challenge from 1 Tank Brigade supported by the British 50th Division, and from an earlier attempted counter-attack by Charles de Gaulle's French Tank Brigade, these were nullified by Rommel's tanks.

General Guderian's advance from the other breakthrough at Sedan meant that by 15 May the whole of Army Group A could press on north with great speed, leaving a large French army of tanks so far behind them as to be of no threat. In any case by 21 May the French army was effectively leaderless due to a series of near farcical events. [12]

The whole of the BEF under General Gort, and the remains of the French army, were now backed up against the English Channel on the beaches of Dunkirk. One more German attack would surely wipe out all the Allied forces trapped in the Dunkirk zone.

Guderian's forces were within twelve miles of the beach by 24 May 1940, so all the pieces were in place at that point for the defeat of the Allies when, on that day, Hitler made the big mistake of giving the still

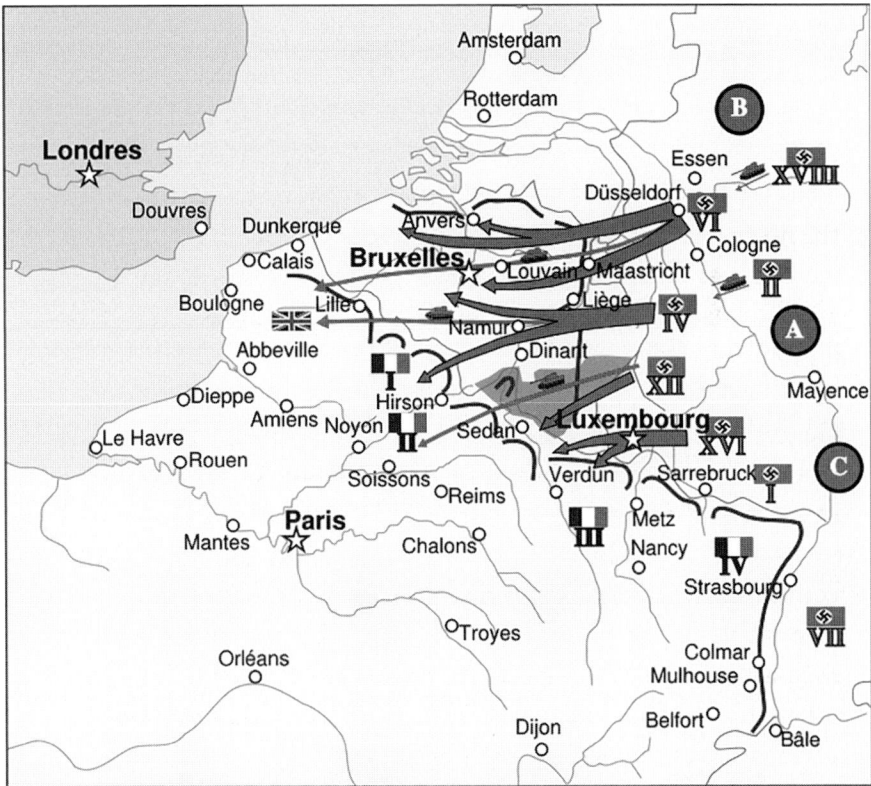

The Manstein Plan was so successful that the Germans had forced the British on to the beaches of Dunkirk. Had Adolf Hitler been that 'greatest commander of all time', he would not have hesitated to invade and conquer Britain.

unfathomable order to halt, to not advance into Dunkirk but to pull back to the designated canal line.

This single order gave Britain's new prime minister the briefest of opportunities.

Winston Churchill had been in the top job for only two weeks when he had to face what looked so very like the final defeat of the British Army and the grim likelihood of having to surrender to Hitler. A few days before, on 13 May, Churchill, in perhaps his finest ever speech, had told the House of Commons:

We have before us an ordeal of the most grievous kind. We have before us many, many long months of struggle and of suffering.

You ask, what is our policy? I will say: It is to wage war, by sea, land, and air, with all our might and with all the strength that God can give us; to wage war against a monstrous tyranny never surpassed in the dark, lamentable catalogue of human crime. That is our policy.

You ask, what is our aim? I can answer in one word: It is victory, victory at all costs, victory in spite of all terror, victory, however long and hard the road may be…We shall go on to the end.

We shall fight in France, we shall fight on the seas and oceans, we shall fight with growing confidence and growing strength in the air, we shall defend our island, whatever the cost may be.

We shall fight on the beaches, we shall fight on the landing grounds, we shall fight in the fields and in the streets, we shall fight in the hills…we shall never surrender.

Winston S Churchill, Prime Minister.

Churchill immediately summoned Vice Admiral Bertram Ramsay out of recent retirement and appointed him to lead Operation Dynamo. His task, to organise and execute the most remarkable of wartime escapes ever known, a near-miracle that almost certainly prevented the Germans from gaining, at the very least, an armistice with the British government and at most, total victory.

The evacuation began on 26 May and all troops were off the beach by 4 June. Operation Dynamo had been the most remarkable of military withdrawals in which 350,000 troops were safely transported by ships and boats of all sizes and returned to Britain, one third of whom were French. The BEF had been saved, but almost all of its heavy equipment, tanks, artillery, and motorized transport had been left behind.

In addition, more than 50,000 British troops were unable to escape as they heroically held back the German infantry for just long enough. Of these, 11,000 were killed and the bulk of the remainder were made prisoners of war. Only a handful were able to evade capture and eventually make their way back to Allied or neutral territory. Especially notable among the losses was the 51st Highland Division that gallantly held a stiff rear-guard under French command. When they were finally over-run on 12 June, 10,000 troops were captured. Britain was helpless in the face of a seemingly all-conquering foe that stood just a few miles away, across the open water of the English Channel. [12]

To this day, the reasons why Hitler gave the order for his Panzers to halt ten miles out from Dunkirk remain unclear and certainly debatable. He may have remembered the marshes from the First World War and may have been fearful of his tanks becoming bogged down if they drove any further north. [12] Hitler is not recorded as giving a clear reason, but he did say to Kleist a few days after the halt that '*I did not want to send the tanks into the Flanders marshes, and the British won't come back in this war*'. [8]

His order came as a shock, and a disappointment, to his commanders and indeed to his officers and soldiers, who must have been in a state of euphoria having moved so swiftly and cleared away all resistance with seeming ease and then reached their goals in such a short time.

The big question remains, however, what was the real reason Hitler gave the order to halt?

Various theories have been speculated by historians, such as:

- Hitler wanted to show good will to the British and to give them a chance to negotiate as Britain would be more willing to make peace if its pride was not wounded or humiliated by seeing its army surrender
- General von Rundstedt impressed on Hitler the need to conserve the armoured divisions for the next stage of the offensive.
- It had been a masterful plan, executed to near perfection, and with so much speed that Hitler was not only dazzled by its achievements but also bewildered by the situation in which he now found himself.

- Hitler wanted to move on and he had been assured by Göring on 23 May that he could easily leave the mopping up to the Air Reich Marshal and his Luftwaffe. Hitler, it seems, took him at his word.
- Hitler was so ecstatically happy about his defeat of the French, through his personal feeling of revenge for the First World War, that his thoughts were diverted to arranging a humiliating signing of a French surrender; and even a tour of the sights of Paris!

But Hitler's most likely reasons for calling a halt were, as ever, determined by his ideological mind-block. To the creator of *Mein Kampf*, it was because:

i.   Hitler's understanding of the British was that they were descended directly from the Anglo-Saxon invasions 900 years previously. This made him reluctant to attack fellow Aryans, feeling sure of their co-operation, convinced that history made British and German people 'brothers'.

ii. And he believed above all, that the British were admired as an 'Aryan' people – with typical *'ruthlessness'* they had *'subjected millions of brown- and black skinned people to their rule... a model for how the Germans would rule Russia'*. [17]

iii But the most likely of all perhaps, was that Hitler's priorities and attention were now elsewhere as he anticipated the opportunity that this apparent defeat of Britain and France meant for his real, over-riding ideological ambition, the invasion of Russia.

Although Hitler was surprised at the speed of his success; he did have a plan 'on paper', to invade Britain. It was called *Unternehmen Seelöwe* or Operation Sealion, but his one army at Dunkirk was a long way short of being able to execute such a massive sea invasion.

Whatever the real reason, the fact remains that this was one of Hitler's biggest mistakes. Even two of his generals who were *in situ* at the critical moment were in no doubt. General Wilhelm von Thomas, looking down on Dunkirk from his tank sent a message to OKH (Army High Command) urging permission to attack. He later said *'Hitler spoilt the chance of victory'* and General Kleist, commander of the Twelfth Army, said that as a result of Hitler's order, the British had *'managed to escape that trap in Dunkirk that I had so carefully laid'*. [8]

Hitler stamps his foot in celebration of his defeat of the French. (*Shutterstock*)

Revenge for the First World War as the French sign a humiliating surrender in the same railway carriage.

Hitler made a big mistake taking the time out to make a tour of the sights of Paris!

Failure to follow-up the massive evacuation of British and French troops from Dunkirk was not the only mistake Hitler made at this most critical point.

His next mistake was two-fold – his personal priority for revenge against the French, and his lazy decision to listen to Air Reichsmarshal Göring's blasé claim that his Luftwaffe would open the door to an easy invasion of Britain.

Hitler had taken his eye off Britain, even while the troops were on the beach at Dunkirk, and turned it towards Paris. After the humiliation of the German surrender in 1918, in which the French made the Germans board a train carriage in the Forest of Compiègne to sign an unconditional surrender, Hitler wanted, more than anything else at that moment, to bask in the surrender of the French. He got it on 22 June and he had the same railway carriage dragged out and used to repeat the surrender, but this time it was the French whose humiliation he now enjoyed.

Hitler then rubbed salt in the French wounds by having himself driven around Paris in his open-top Mercedes, stopping to be photographed at the famous sights, including the Eiffel Tower.

Instead of developing an action plan to invade Britain while the opportunity was wide open, Hitler preferred to put on a display of the vengeful conqueror by having his troops goose-step through the Arc de Triomphe and down the Avenue des Champs-Élysées.

The French surrender was a sideshow that distracted Hitler, and caused him to miss the opportunity to put Britain out of the war for certain, before moving onto his next objective. Göring had at his fingertips a massive, well equipped and, following the Spanish Civil War and the invasion of Poland, a well-trained and battle-experienced airforce. Perhaps it is no surprise that he exuded extreme over-confidence and that his Führer was easily convinced of his invulnerability. That is a mistake often made in history, when a successful commander starts taking victory for granted and underestimates his enemy. History was about to be repeated, but not straight away.

Göring's first attacks on Britain began on 10 July 1940 using his 'Stuka' or Junkers Ju 87 dive-bombers, and Messerschmitt Bf 109E3s fighter aircraft to target ports and coastal-shipping, but with RAF fighters soon intercepting them, he switched his targets to airfields, infrastructure, factories producing aircraft and communication sites in the south of England.

This was a sound enough strategy to start with. Although the Royal Navy was the biggest obstacle to an invasion, control of the skies was the first priority, as no German vessels could ever cross the English Channel exposed to attack from above. Göring was sure that the RAF was inferior to the Luftwaffe in all aspects – numbers of fighter aircraft, light and heavy bombers, trained and experienced air crew, advanced designs and technical superiority. He was right only on the numbers and the battle experience of his pilots.

What he did not know was that British scientists had already developed RDF or 'radar', had sited many masts along the south coast, and had created CH or 'Chain Home'. This was essentially the first ever early warning radar system in the world, and it took a relatively long time before the Germans realised what they were up against. Of course, the bravery and skills of the RAF's pilots, the quality of the established Hawker Hurricane fighter, and the new, hot-off-the-design-board, Supermarine Spitfire fighters were the visible reasons the Germans did not succeed, but the fact is that without the CH Britain would have been overwhelmed in a short time. The information from the radar stations and the eyes and ears of the Royal Observer Corps, was initially taking too long to get to RAF headquarters so British fighters were not able to take-off and reach the enemy before they had already attacked their targets.

A faster method was developed very quickly, using dedicated telephone landlines that became known as the Dowding System, named after the commander in chief of the RAF, Air Chief Marshal Sir Hugh Dowding, nicknamed 'Stuffy' by all who worked with him.

The vital information about approaching enemy aircraft, their distance, speed and direction was quickly transposed onto a huge table map, providing the overseeing commanders with a clear visualisation of the situation at that moment.

The Spitfire was a worthy rival to the Messerschmitt Bf 109 (Me109) during the Battle of Britain in 1940, albeit one with different flying qualities. The Spitfire was superior to the Me109 in a dogfight, since it had considerably better turning ability while the Me109 had better climbing and diving qualities. [165]

But two of the RAF's greatest fighter pilots agreed that -

'The Me 109F has a slightly superior performance to the Spitfire'

Air Vice-Marshal Trafford Leigh-Mallory, September 1941.

'I also thought the Bf 109F was slightly superior to the Spitfire V'

Squadron Leader Douglas Bader, circa 1941.

The Dowding System resulted in the most efficient use of the limited resources and meant that fighters could be sent up from the nearest airfield at the last moment to intercept and try to shoot down the enemy planes. The German aircraft had flown much further so they had only limited fuel and were therefore forced to turn about within a very short time-frame.

Even so, the strain and stress on commanders, pilots and ground-crew was immense, and the Luftwaffe's inevitable successes were causing so much damage to airfields and aircraft production that after only a few weeks the situation was looking very marginal.

The Germans were bewildered – *'How were the British able to intercept so accurately?'* asked every German pilot – and so did Air Reichsmarshal Göring. The Germans had some idea about the new technology and suspected the many small masts dotted along the coast had something to do with it so dive-bombers were told to target them and knock them down – not easy as they were fairly small and made of steel framing. Some were hit but were replaced or repaired within hours without any significant effect on CH.

Despite the relative success of the Dowding System, British airfields had been seriously affected and repairs to airstrips and aircraft, as well as the losses of fighter planes and their pilots, was pushing the situation towards make or break.

After his exciting distractions in France, Hitler finally set in motion his plan to invade Britain, Operation Sealion. Vast numbers of German troops were trained and specialised landing craft and weapons were gathered along the north coast of France, awaiting the order to cross the few miles of sea to the south coast of England. However, Hitler had decreed that no such invasion could take place until Germany had control of the English Channel, on the sea and in the air; the Luftwaffe's failures thus far put the plan on hold.

If Hitler or Göring had only known it, following almost endless mass bombing attacks on RAF airfields the Germans called *Adlerangriff* (eagle attacks) by hordes of Heinkel He 111 light-bombers, the situation in Britain had reached its most critical state by the end of August.

Instead, German pilots were returning with often exaggerated reports of the huge squadrons of fighters that the RAF seemed to have, and so Göring decided to change his main tactic from attacking airfields to the bombing of ports and industrial sites.

Hitler's mistake this time was his blind faith in the hugely self-confident Göring who had assured his Führer that he was next going to bomb the British into submission.

This was the beginning of what became known as the Blitz and throughout the winter of 1940–41 many British cities felt the wrath of endless waves of heavy night bombers carpet-bombing with tons of explosives and incendiary devices, killing many thousands of civilians and making millions homeless.

But the Battle of Britain was over, Göring's Luftwaffe had failed.

More significantly, Hitler had made that second big mistake. Had he kept up the pace of tactical bombing of airfields for just a few weeks longer, the RAF would not have had the resources to defend against a German invasion that autumn.

Chapter 14

Gibraltar, North Africa and the Mediterranean 1940

'He who hesitates is lost.'

Marcus Porcius Cato,
Roman Senator 160 BC

Instead of his disastrous invasion of Russia in July 1941 (Ch.11), Hitler could have used his enormous resources of men, equipment and weapons that had been stockpiled by 1940 to win control of the Mediterranean Sea. This would have been a far superior use of his power than wasting it on an attack on the Soviet Union, who were offering no threat whatsoever and who were in fact partners in crime in the invasion and occupation of Poland.

Strategically, taking Gibraltar, followed by Libya, Egypt and then Iraq, would have had two major, long-term benefits – it would cut off Britain's oil supply and it would give control of that most vital resource to Hitler for his planned invasion of Russia. Not doing so was a big mistake and one that a more intelligent, less arrogant commander-in-chief would never have made. His senior generals could see it, but Hitler already believed he had the magic touch so remained hell-bent on forcing Britain to make a deal that would let him move swiftly on to his ideological obsession, the conquering of Russia.

There was, of course a third likely benefit – control of the Suez Canal and the sea-lanes through the Mediterranean Sea, as all ports and German airbases were secured along the North African coast.

Just before the surrender of France in June 1940, General Guderian, commander of Second Panzer Army, had suggested to Hitler that he could quickly move his Panzers down through France and Spain to capture Gibraltar and cross into North Africa. Hitler's Chief of Staff, General Alfred Jodl suggested a similar plan as being a better strategic use of resources than the half-cocked Operation Sealion.

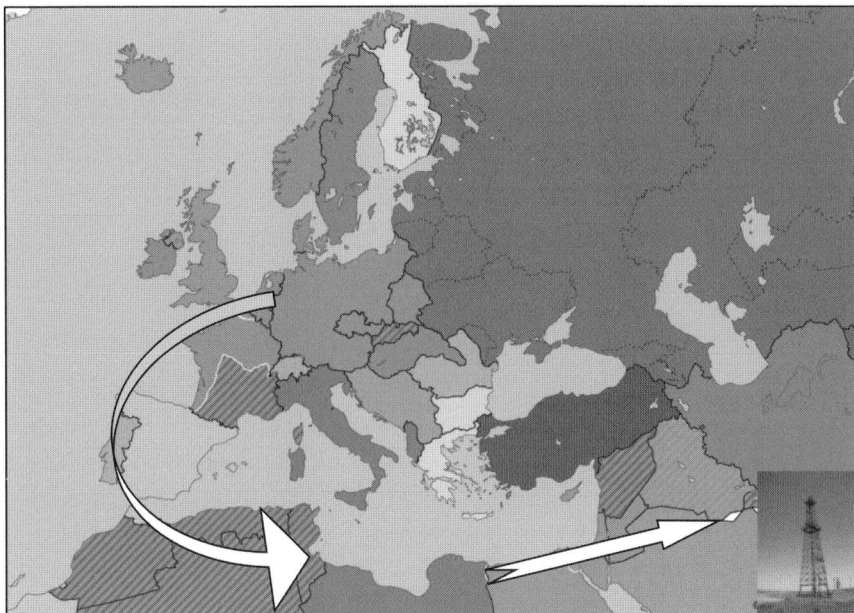

Operation Felix would have been a better strategic use of resources than the half-cocked Operation Sealion. Hitler described his meeting with Franco as being worse than 'a visit to the dentist'. (*Map by author*)

Hitler was also being urged by Admiral Raeder to take Gibraltar, and at this point Hitler seriously considered the idea. He had his head of the *Abwehr*, Admiral Canaris, carry out intelligence work in Spain and by November a plan had been acknowledged, but not quite agreed upon, by Hitler.

General von Reichenau had been put in charge of the plan, known as Operation Felix and a large force of artillery and dive bombers were put on alert for the occupation first of Portugal.

Time passed, due mainly to Hitler's usual dithering and persistent interference in the minutiae of planning. Instead of ordering those who knew best to get on with the plan, he could not resist being the '*great commander*' – an epithet only he and a few of his lackeys genuinely believed. Even the Vichy French air force and their navy minister were very keen to go to war with Britain and they were very much in favour of taking control of Gibraltar.

Hitler left it till the last minute before consulting his erstwhile 'friend', General Franco, in a meeting that Hitler described as being worse than '*a visit to the dentist*'.

As soon as Franco refused to co-operate, Hitler hastily made the big mistake of cancelling Felix immediately. Considering the enormous military support Hitler had sent to Franco during the Spanish Civil War and the far superior military might of the German forces in mid-1940, not to mention what should have been the natural reaction of a truly *great leader*, Hitler could have gone ahead regardless.

The suddenness of another Blitzkrieg would have ensured him the incalculable benefit of shutting off the mouth of the Mediterranean to the British, enabling him to conquer all the land and to take all the invaluable resources that it contained.

So, once again Hitler's big mistake was his now habitual swithering, changing plans and getting involved in detail beyond his experience, but just as significant was his decision, based on his mythical ideology, to look eastwards in preference to his generals' sound military advice to concentrate first on the Mediterranean and North Africa.

Chapter 15

U-Boats 1939–1943

'The only thing that ever really frightened me during the war was the U-boat peril.'

Winston Churchill

At the dawn of the Second World War, the island nation of Britain faced the grim possibility that it might be starved into defeat by a German naval blockade. Churchill knew it and confessed, after the war, that this was what he had feared most. Indeed, the German blockade in the Atlantic tends to be seen as something of a sideshow to other land battles during the Second World War but Churchill was not exaggerating his concerns. Great Britain, the British Isles, the United Kingdom – on account of it being an island, detached from the mainland of the European continent – required more than a million tons of imported material each week simply to survive, let alone fight a war against the Germans. Churchill later wrote: *'The Battle of the Atlantic was the dominating factor all through the war. Never for one moment could we forget that everything happening elsewhere – on land, at sea or in the air – depended ultimately on its outcome.'* [32]

Hitler's great mistake, or at least his greatest lack of foresight, was his failure to have recognised, long before he fired the first shots of war, that the Atlantic was the one place where he could have quickly brought Britain to its knees with the minimum cost to Germany. A massive U-boat blockade of the necessary raw materials from the Americas that Britain needed to fight a modern war would have left the Chamberlain government little option but to surrender, or at the very least, to negotiate withdrawal from hostilities.

Hitler, however, knew warfare only from the narrow view of the entrenched infantry soldier that he had been in the First World War. Despite his great vision of creating a new German Empire by conquering large areas of land using tanks and fast-moving armies, he did not have the mind of a true strategist, someone who could see the really big picture, its potential and its pitfalls.

Having fought through the First World War, it may be reasonable to think that Hitler would have looked at the real reasons why, and how, Germany had been defeated.

Instead of burying his head in his ideological obsessions and blaming traitors he named as Bolsheviks and Jews he should have observed that it was Germany's use of U-boats in 1914 and 1915 that had had a profound effect on the British people and, even more pertinently, that it was the British fleet's blockade of German ports over the 1916–18 period that was the cause of German civilian riots, protest marches, starvation and demoralisation which ultimately led to the German government suing for peace in November 1918.

That this same, powerful tactic could be used again in 1939, as soon as Britain had declared war on Germany, was completely ignored, or simply missed by the former foot-soldier, messenger, and corporal, Adolf Hitler.

The German Navy, the *Kriegsmarine*, never got the respect or support from Hitler it deserved, either before or during the war; at least, not until it was all too late. Led by the fanatical Nazi Admiral Karl Dönitz, the *Kriegsmarine* played second-fiddle to the *Heer* and the *Luftwaffe* throughout the war. By 1941, Hitler was only interested in his attack on Russia, believing the British threat had largely been removed and that Britain would not be able to fight on once he had defeated their ally in the east, Stalin's Russia.

This was, of course, a catastrophic mistake by Hitler as he had taken his eye off the much deeper, historic, and cultural relationship between Churchill's Britain and Roosevelt's America.

The USA was to be, as President Roosevelt put it in his radio address delivered from Washington DC on 29 December 1940, '*the arsenal of democracy*'. [31] To an American public that was broadly against any level of intervention in any European war, having paid the cost in American lives in 1918, he put the reality of the situation this way:

'*This is not a fireside chat on war. It is a talk on national security. The Nazi masters of Germany have made it clear that they intend not only to dominate all life and thought in their own country, but also to enslave the whole of Europe, and then to use the resources of Europe to dominate the rest of the world… For us this is an emergency as serious as war itself. We have furnished the British [with] great material support and we will furnish far more in the future. There will be no bottlenecks in our determination to aid Great Britain.'*

Franklin D. Roosevelt [31]

Hitler either did not hear this broadcast or, more likely, dismissed it at a time when his good luck was rolling along like an unstoppable Panzer tank. Although Hitler supported the use of U-boats and the wolf pack tactics, he was a man obsessed with land battles. He never understood the importance of a full-blown blockade of British ports. After the war, Dönitz attributed this shortcoming to the loss of the war.

In a recording of his conversation with his Minister for Armaments and chief architect, Albert Speer, when setting the budget for what was supposed to become the world's largest stadium in a 'new Berlin', Hitler not only showed his lack of interest in naval matters but also that his romantic, architectural dreams mattered far more to him.

Hitler told Speer: *'That [stadium costs] less than two Bismarck class battleships. Look how quickly an armoured ship gets destroyed, and if it survives it becomes scrap metal in ten years anyway. But this building will still be standing centuries from now.'*

Hitler was, after all, an artist by nature, and undoubtedly a frustrated architect. He was not, however, *'the greatest commander of all time'* as he had demonstrated once again.

If Hitler had been the visionary or master of warfare he came to believe he was, or even if he had simply referred back to the First World War, then he would have foreseen Britain's 'Achilles heel' and have prioritised the building of U-boats during the 1930s over the building of archaic, expensive and massive battleships (or capital ships as they were known). These floating leviathans may have looked magnificent, but they were destined to spend whatever life they had (usually very short) stuck in some port or fjord, hiding from air attack by British bombers and fearful of going to sea lest they be sunk by a Royal Navy task force or a submarine.

By 1945 Germany had lost forty-seven surface warships including the 'state of the art', massively armed pride of Hitler's surface fleet, the

Bismarck. Each one had been hunted down and destroyed before they could inflict any serious damage to the Royal Navy.

This was in sharp contrast to the relatively few U-boats that Dönitz had under his command in 1939. This was Hitler's big mistake.

There were only twenty-four U-boats active at the start of the conflict and they were immediately very effective. It is not an over-simplification to calculate that if Dönitz had had his 1,156 U-boats in 1939 – that were eventually built by 1945 – then not enough supplies would have reached British ports and Britain would have had to sue for peace as its citizens starved and its factories closed for lack of raw materials.

The British admirals, it seemed, had also forgotten their First World War experience when the Navy had come under attack from those early U-boats. They paid a high price for the delay in organising the convoys that would later give much greater protection to the large number of hapless merchant ships, full of vital supplies and oil, crossing the North Atlantic on their own and unprotected. For the few U-boats in 1939 and 1940 this was their first '*happy time*' as the submariner crews named it. They sent around 270 ships and thousands of seamen to the bottom of the Atlantic. The U-boats were so effective that Dönitz tried hard – in vain – to gain Hitler's approval to move ship-building resources from capital ships to U-boats.

Of course, every commander wanted more for his forces and Hitler was under constant pressure from all of them but it is surely the mark of a competent commander to identify where the best use of the inevitably scarce resources must be employed. Hitler did not do so.

Not foreseeing this great opportunity before the war, Hitler was offered a second chance in June 1940 to remedy the deficiency in U-boat construction. The geography of the war had changed since the surrender of France and the Germans now had the entire stretch of the French Atlantic coast from which they could operate.

There were several suitable ports from which U-boats could be built, safely harboured, and then launched against Allied shipping. At this time, Dönitz also revealed his new plan known as *Rudeltaktik* or wolf pack tactic, to his Führer. U-boats would spread out in a long line across the projected course of a convoy and as soon as a target was identified, they would come together to attack en masse and overwhelm any escorting warships. While escorts chased individual submarines,

Of all the threats facing Britain during World War II, it was the U-boat peril that frightened Winston Churchill the most. The USS destroyer *Reuben James* was torpedoed and sunk by *U-562*, killing 100 American crewmen. This was crucial in changing American public opinion to join Britain's war against the Nazis.

the rest of the 'pack' would be able to attack the merchant ships with impunity.

This was a radical move away from the 'loner' ambushing tactic used, up to this point, by submarines of all navies, where a submarine was stationed near an enemy port waiting to attack ships leaving or arriving. Hitler began to see his earlier mistake, though he never admitted it, of course. U-boat building was given a new level of priority and numbers began to swell.

But it was already too late as the Allies had been making rapid changes to their tactics and, more importantly, to their detection equipment and anti-submarine weapons.

Up to this point, defence against submarines consisted of inshore patrol craft – armed with a small gun and depth charges, patrolling close to ports. In the interwar years the Royal Navy had not considered anti-submarine warfare as a tactical subject since unrestricted submarine warfare had actually been outlawed by the London Naval Treaty of 1930. To the traditionalist, conservative-minded admirals, anti-submarine warfare was 'defensive' rather than attacking. Class snobbery also played a part as many naval officers looked down on anti-submarine work. It was also believed that, anyway, ASDIC or SONAR – using radio waves to detect submerged submarines – had rendered submarines impotent.

Royal Navy destroyers also carried depth charges and they too placed much faith in ASDIC to detect submerged U-boats – but from the summer of 1940 the U-boat menace grew. The conquest by Germany of Norway and France gave the Germans strategically advantageous sea ports that increased the range of the U-boats and also allowed Focke-Wulf FW200 'Kondor' long-range aircraft to patrol the Atlantic, carrying out reconnaissance and pin-pointing convoys for the U-boat wolf packs.

The Royal Navy was critically short of escort vessels, although this problem was eased somewhat by the arrival of fifty old American destroyers that President Roosevelt gave in return for bases in British territory in the West Indies.

From May 1941, the US Navy became a British ally in the struggle in the Atlantic and on Halloween 1941, the inevitable happened.

While escorting a British convoy, an American warship, the destroyer *Reuben James*, was torpedoed and sunk by *U-562*.

Two particular factors were to prove crucial to the outcome of the Battle of the Atlantic. The first was the new longer-range reconnaissance aircraft, the Liberator, which could, at last, cover a much larger area of the vast ocean, including the unprotected zone known as the 'mid-Atlantic gap'.

The second was Intelligence (Intel). Britain's ability to break the Enigma codes, and the resulting 'Ultra' intelligence was a priceless advantage, particularly after the Royal Navy (not, as a recent Hollywood movie would have one believe, the Americans!) seized an Enigma machine from a captured U-boat in May 1941.

The Enigma was a cipher machine invented by the Germans at the end of the First World War that scrambled typed messages into a code they were sure no-one would be able to break. When the codes were broken by Alan Turing and his team at MI5 headquarters, Bletchley Park, it became Britain's most valuable asset on the road to the final victory.

The British and their allies, now armed with top-secret information about where U-boats were patrolling, were soon able to move convoys into safe areas away from the U-boat wolf packs.

Nevertheless, a handful of U-boats operating off the North American and Caribbean coastal areas, where the residents and local shipping were culpably complacent about night-time black-out accounted for the loss of nearly 500 Allied ships in the first half of 1942. For German submariners, this phase, formally named Operation *Paukenschlag* or Operation Drumbeat, was soon to be called the second '*happy time*' and, even more disparagingly, the '*American Shooting Season*', by the crews of the marauding U-boats.

The crisis of the Battle of the Atlantic came in early 1943. Admiral Dönitz now had 200 operational U-boats. British supplies, especially of oil, were running out and it became a question of whether Allied shipyards could build merchant ships fast enough to replace the tonnage that was being sunk.

Mass production of Liberty Ships in US shipyards, however, helped to ensure that the Allies would win this race.

The Allies gradually gained the upper hand, defeating the U-boats by mid-1943, using convoys, code breaking, ASDIC, aerial reconnaissance Liberators, depth charges, 'hedgehogs', torpedoes, and bombs. Losses due to U-boats did continue until the war's end, but in much smaller numbers.

By April 1943 the U-boats were struggling to make an impact. Worse, from Hitler's point of view, was the fact that Allied sinking of German U-boats began to escalate, with forty-five being destroyed in April and May. At that same time, Dönitz's son, a U-boat captain, was killed in action and the *Grosadmiral* recognised that the U-boat's moment had passed. The *Battle of the Atlantic* was called-off on 23 May 1943.

In the final analysis, it was Allied sea power and British technology that prevented disaster. It is impossible, of course, to know for certain what greater success Germany might have had in the Atlantic, and elsewhere, if Hitler had been a true commander with the vision to have given priority to developing and building many more U-boats in the mid 1930s, thereby out-manoeuvring the British, long before they could have found new ways to save themselves from defeat.

This misuse of labour, materials, and time was a grave mistake. It was not until the end of the war that the Germans were able to produce a few of the new types of 'super-submarines' – perhaps the outcome might have been different had they been introduced earlier (Ch.21).

The *Battle of the Atlantic* was one of the longest campaigns of the war, and possibly the costliest. 3,500 merchant ships and 175 warships were sunk in the Atlantic for the loss of 783 U-boats (most of them Type VIIs), and 47 German surface warships.

Of the U-boats, 519 were sunk by British, Canadian, or other allied forces, while 175 were destroyed by American forces. The Soviets destroyed 15 and 73 were scuttled for various reasons by their crews before the end of the war. [53]

The human cost was appalling. Around 80,000 Allied seamen and 28,000 U-boat crew were killed during the Battle of the Atlantic. The stakes, however, could not have been higher. If the U-boats had prevailed, the Allies could not have won the war.

Hitler's big mistake was that he failed to appreciate the devastating effect a blockade of Atlantic merchant shipping by a large fleet of U-boats would have had. It would very probably have given him victory in the West at an early stage in the war by effectively starving Britain into submission. This mistake arose from a combination of his lack of command expertise, his inability to see the superior potential of U-boats over his pre-occupation with huge First World War type capital ships, his relative disregard for naval matters and as always, his over-inflated self-belief.

Chapter 16

Barbarossa to Bagration – War on Two Fronts 1943

'Only an idiot tries to fight a war on two fronts, and only a madman tries to fight one on three.'

David Eddings, 1985 [37]

O ne strategic lesson that 'Corporal Hitler' [41] certainly did learn from the First World War was that Germany's chances of winning were unrealistic because they were, up until the beginning of 1918, fighting a war on two fronts. It is not only one of the fundamental doctrines of military strategy but it is obvious, even to the layman, that having to divide your forces to attack or defend against two different enemies at either end of your country, is a situation a commander would never deliberately put himself and his armies into. And yet, this was exactly the mistake that this acclaimed *'greatest commander of all time'* actually made.

Seeking to fulfil Germany's ideological destiny in the East, Adolf Hitler was hell-bent on claiming the vast Russian territories for himself, while purging it of *untermensch*, namely Jews, Slavs and all other 'undesirable' elements that included Bolshevism, the arch-enemy of National Socialism. Convinced it would be a walk in the park, he brushed aside the warnings of military intelligence, telling his generals, *'We have only to kick in the front door and the whole rotten Russian edifice will come tumbling down.'*

At the beginning of 1941, Hitler and his generals were confident of a final victory. Britain had not been occupied like France, but Hitler was sure it had been well battered and was impotent following the debacle and narrow escape of the remnants of his army at Dunkirk. The Luftwaffe was relentlessly bombing cities and ports over Britain, causing immense collateral and industrial damage to British war production. His U-boats were taking a heavy toll on the convoys of supplies crossing the Atlantic

Ocean from America. Germany's fascist ally, the Italian Dictator Benito Mussolini, had been sent the support of Hitler's finest tank commander, Erwin Rommel. Together they had pushed the British army back to the east of the Sahara desert, almost to Cairo. The oilfields beyond were the targets and securing them would give the Reich untold wealth and supplies of that most vital of resources, oil. Control of the Suez Canal would choke Britain of her links to the jewel of her empire, India. On the continent of Europe, all countries were now either allies of, or under occupation by, the Nazis. His back was safe, deduced Hitler. It would only be, he was sure, a short time before Britain would have to sue for peace.

Little wonder, then, that Hitler saw the situation in the spring of 1941 as the perfect springboard for the invasion of the Soviet Union. This was, after all, his ultimate dream and the primary aim of his great plan for *lebensraum*, as laid out so clearly in his book *Mein Kampf*, written eighteen years before.

The Führer, drunk on these recent successes and further motivated by Russia's embarrassing defeat at the hands of Finland, decided to make the fateful move. The ensuing attack, on the morning of 22 June 1941, was the largest military confrontation in human history, involving a front line that extended 2,000 miles from north to south. At the outset, the operation involved nearly three million Axis soldiers in 166 divisions that included over 3,000 tanks, incalculable amounts of artillery, 5,000 aircraft, 600,000 vehicles and at least 750,000 horses. The Soviet's front-line strength amounted to around 3 million personnel in 220 divisions, including 34 armoured divisions, 10,000 tanks and around 6,000 aircraft. As always, it was all about advancing at pace. Blitzkrieg action swept the Germans across Belarus and the Ukraine, past Smolensk, to the gates of Moscow, then south into the Crimea where they took Sebastopol. Twenty-eight Soviet Divisions were wiped out and seventy others lost more than half their men and equipment.

The SS remained the foremost agency of security, surveillance, and terror within Germany and German-occupied Europe until the regime's collapse in 1945 and was a remarkable, if horrendous achievement by one of Hitler's most dedicated henchmen. (Ch.8)

Hitler allowed thousands of *untermensch* Slav, Jewish and Bolshevik prisoners and civilians to be executed, including farmers and skilled workers. Properties were destroyed and farms burned, depriving his own troops of food, materiel and labour. This deliberate act of terrorism in

Schutzstaffel
SS

Waffen-SS badge with SS motto
'Meine Ehre heist Treue!'
(My Honour is my Loyalty)

Skull & Eagle
SS Hat

The SS eventually consisted of four main sections; the *Allgemeine SS* (General SS) was responsible for enforcing the racial policy of Nazi Germany and for general policing, the *Waffen-SS* consisted of elite, initially all Aryan, combat units under separate control from the *Wehrmacht*. Although by 1944 the *Waffen-SS* made up less than 5 per cent of the *Wehrmacht,* it accounted for around a quarter of all Germany's panzer divisions and panzer grenadier (mechanized infantry) divisions.

A third component of the *SS-Totenkopfverbände* (SS-TV) or Death's Head Squadron, ran the concentration camps and extermination camps. Additional subdivisions of the SS included the Gestapo and the *Sicherheitsdienst* (SD) organizations.

They were tasked with the detection of actual or potential enemies of the Nazi state, the neutralization of any opposition, policing the German people for their commitment to Nazi ideology, and providing domestic and foreign intelligence.

The SS was the organization most responsible for the killing of an estimated six million Jews and millions of other *untermensch* during the 'holocaust'. Members of all of its branches committed war crimes and crimes against humanity during the war. The SS was also involved in commercial enterprises and exploited concentration camp inmates as slave labour.

After Nazi Germany's defeat, the SS and the NSDAP were judged by the International Military Tribunal at Nuremberg to be criminal organizations. Ernst Kaltenbrunner, the highest-ranking surviving SS main department chief, was found guilty of crimes against humanity at the Nuremberg trials and hanged in 1946. [11]

Among the Nazi troops used in the invasion of Russia were the *3rd SS-Totenkopfverbände* or Death's Head Division of the Waffen SS. Under Heinrich Himmler, from its creation in 1929, the SS or *Schutzstaffel* grew from a small paramilitary formation during the Weimar Republic to be one of the most powerful and feared organizations in Nazi Germany.

the Ukraine was only the first of several big mistakes made right at the start of the campaign that would have disastrous repercussions for the thousands of German troops stranded a long way from the Fatherland, over the next two and more years.

The peasant workers of Belarus, Ukraine, Lithuania, Latvia and Russia initially welcomed the German troops, seeing them as freeing the people from the collectivization madness of Communism, imposed by Stalin's NKVD over the previous decade, on perfectly productive farms, causing famine and death.

Here, Hitler made a costly mistake. Instead of *'exploiting nationalism as a tool'* [8] that could have rallied this proud Ukrainian labour force and so provided food for his troops and also prevented partisan groups from causing havoc with supplies and services, Hitler missed the opportunity to have at his command an enormous and potentially complicit workforce for agriculture and industry – a crucial factor that could have changed the outcome of Barbarossa from disaster to success. Of course, Hitler's ideology that he had spelled out clearly in *Mein Kampf* could not conceive of any respect or even fairness for Slavs, who were to his mind, all Bolsheviks and *untermensch*.

After the surrender and subjugation of France in 1940, Hitler had held a conference of senior commanders to assess the Führer's final plans for the invasion of Russia. No-one made any major objections, but Hitler asked General Georg Thomas to report on a study on economic matters. The first study had pointed out that there were most likely to be problems with fuel and general supplies, but Hitler's closest trustee and 'yes-man', Field Marshal Keitel, bluntly dismissed the problems, telling Thomas that Hitler would *'not want to see it'*. Thomas's rewritten second study gave Hitler's plan a glowing recommendation based on fabricated economic benefits that simply compounded his mistake. [25]

Barbarossa

'What a soldier most needed in war is a full belly and a good pair of shoes.'

Napoleon Bonaparte

The invasion of Russia, Operation Barbarossa, which would have been visible from space, began on 22 June 1941. The German armies swept over the massive open flat-lands at breakneck speed.

Thousands of Soviet tanks were punched aside, and many of their aircraft destroyed while still on the ground. Army Groups North, Centre and South each scooped up 300,000 shocked and ill-prepared Soviet prisoners. As Army Group Centre (AGC) charged through Smolensk, Army Group North (AGN) sped on towards Leningrad and Army Group South (AGS) towards Kiev.

By mid-July, German forces had captured Smolensk, a key city on the road to Moscow. Six months earlier, Hitler, in his Führer Directive No.21 of 18 December 1940, had identified Moscow's strategic importance, saying that *'The capture of this city means a decisive success politically and economically and … the elimination of this most important railway centre.'*

By February 1941, Hitler had completely changed his mind. His new priority was to take Leningrad and the Baltic coast, declaring *'Moscow is completely immaterial'*. [15] Despite the fact that German Army High Command (OKH) had always favoured making Moscow the key objective, not one voice was raised against their Führer's order to the contrary. He ignored the feeble words of caution from his generals, telling them *'I am convinced that our attack (on Russia) will sweep over them like a hailstorm.'* Of course, he was right, for a time, at least while surprise and good luck was on his side (Ch.10).

Even Hitler was astounded at the rate of progress, and his generals were, at this moment, truly impressed with their Führer and most likely now in full agreement with Keitel's adoring declaration that Hitler was *'the greatest commander of all time'*. [15]

This marked the high point of Hitler's arrogant self-belief in his infallibility and in his judgement in issuing strategic and tactical orders without any consultation whatsoever with his senior commanders. But his lack of command experience caused him to react with 'knee-jerk' ideas and with notions based on his ideological, not military, expertise.

Hitler also constantly changed his mind, sometimes from day to day. His generals wanted to keep to the plan, to focus on Moscow, which was, at this point, vulnerable and not prepared for defence. In mid-July 1941, with AGC only 100 miles from Moscow, Hitler changed his plan once again. He issued Directive No 33 stating Moscow was no longer the primary objective and ordering AGC to split its Panzer Corps off north to support the AGN attack on Leningrad and south to support AGS's thrust towards Kiev, south to Kharkov and into the Caucasus. [15]

(*Shutterstock*)

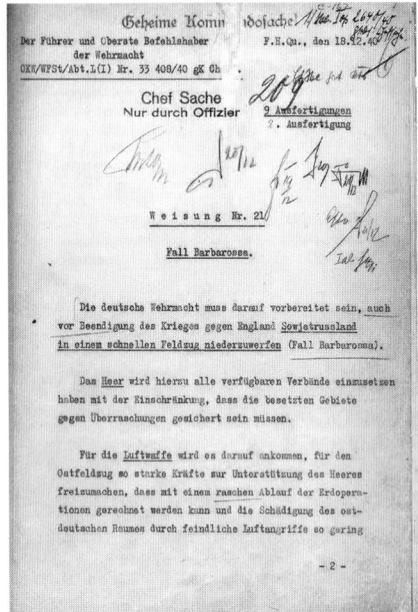

Adolf Hitler issued the Führer Directive No.21 on 18 December 1940 but Operation Barbarossa was not ordered to begin until 22 June 1941.

At the end of July, Hitler cancelled his previous *Supplement to Directive No 33* and issued Directive No.34, but his generals were to be disappointed for a while yet as it still did not name Moscow as the target. Hitler's closest military adviser, OKW Chief of Staff, Field Marshal Jodl, worked on his master and in the *Supplement to Directive No. 34*, there was a suggestion of a gathering of focus on Moscow.

But Hitler vacillated again and returned to his intransigent view, telling his generals that they '*knew nothing about the economic aspects of war*' – that Leningrad must be secured for '*the iron-ore route to Sweden*' – and that the fertile Ukraine was needed for '*agricultural products for a long war*'; Moscow, he added, could be taken at leisure. [97] His commanders were unable to counter these valid economic arguments, but they could have, and should have, insisted that the strategic and military value of taking Moscow outweighed both points.

General Bock, commander of Army Group Centre, was against the change, but he could not get Hitler to think again. Even one of Hitler's favourites, the straight-talking General Heinz Guderian, flew back to Hitler's HQ to protest but ended up being persuaded, or ordered, to comply with the Führer's directive.

Hitler's vacillations, hesitancy and incompetence gave Stalin and his generals of the Stavka, the crucial space they needed to reinforce the defences around Moscow.

The Battle for Moscow – Operation Typhoon – September 1941–January 1942

When the advance on Moscow was finally ordered on 26 September 1941, Marshal Georgy Zhukov, Stalin's greatest general, had reinforced the defences of the city.

The defence of Moscow was the first of three military masterpieces by Zhukov. On 5 December 1941, German Field Marshal Guderian wrote in his diary: '*the offensive on Moscow has failed… we under-estimated enemy strength and winter weather*'. [34]

The siege of Stalingrad is often seen today as the 'turning point' of Germany's war against the Soviets, but it was in fact, to use Churchill's analogy following the British victory at the Battle of El Alamein in November 1942, only the '*beginning of the end*'. The previous line of his wonderfully descriptive prose, '*the end of the beginning*' had, in fact, happened ten months earlier when the Germans failed to take Moscow in Operation Typhoon. The attack was doomed before it began, as Hitler had insisted that a large part of AGC be diverted to the Ukraine, thereby delaying and reducing his central forces that were en route to the capital and, worse, wasted the late months of summer that then allowed the inevitable power of the Russian winter to make its dreadful mark on the massive invading German army – just when it had started Operation Typhoon.

In a two-pronged pincer attack on Moscow by AGC commanders von Brauchitsch and von Bock, one thousand tanks of the 2nd, 3rd and 4th Panzer Groups of AGC were unable to defeat Zhukov's forces and had to abandon the attempt to take control of the Soviet capital city. Had they succeeded it is quite feasible to argue that this would have led to the submission of western Russia to Nazi control (see Ch.16). The success of the Red Army in preventing the loss of Moscow was the first major victory for the Russians in defence of their homeland and gave Stalin's Stavka the confidence and foundation for the massive rebuilding of their forces during the summer of 1943. From this point on, the Germans made no further incursions eastwards so the Battle of Moscow had, indeed been, '*the end of the beginning*'.

Incapable of rational multi-tasking when under pressure, Hitler's mental and physical health came under the scrutiny of those around him. Hitler was a hypochondriac but at this time was suffering debilitating attacks of dysentery. His mind was also distracted by the Italian invasion of Greece that had gone badly wrong some months before and was now requiring German support. Goebbels records that he was '*most concerned*' about his Führer's well-being as he seemed '*very irritable*' and was clearly unwell – he had even heard him talk of considering '*peace terms*' with Stalin and with Churchill. *Generalleutnant* Adolf Heusinger told Jodl that Hitler struggled psychologically with a '*An instinctive aversion to treading the same path as Napoleon… Moscow gives him a sinister feeling*'. [15] This fear may well have been the reason for his repeated rejection of OKH's plan to attack Moscow immediately. But Hitler's Chief of Staff, General Franz Halder, showed no sympathy for his leader, writing in his diary '*The Führer's interference is unendurable… [he] is to blame for the zigzag course caused by his successive orders.*' [15]

Hitler's ever-changing strategy had been a mishmash; a confused mess that, in the long run, can be argued was his biggest military mistake of the war. In early 1942, only weeks after he had taken command of all German forces (Ch.18), the *Felder* – the Supreme Commander – had personally allowed the best opportunity to take Moscow slip through his hands, never to be possible again.

Hitler insisted the oil in the Caucasus and the iron-ore through Leningrad must remain the priority and so ordered AGS to take Kiev as soon as possible to open the road to the Crimea. He did not fear the approaching winter as, he boasted '*it would all be over in a few weeks – first Kiev, then Leningrad, then Moscow.*' The Bolsheviks would be cut-off from their main industrial areas and the war would be as good as won. Hitler's brash predictions soon appeared to be proving correct as Guderian's Panzers swept through the Ukraine and by September had taken the city of Kiev, capturing an astonishing 665,000 Soviet prisoners and destroying 884 Soviet tanks.

Then the spectacular speed of advance and astonishing success of Barbarossa suddenly hit the buffers of reality – *panzers* are no use without petrol, guns no use without bullets, and soldiers cannot fight without food.

The German supply line was already under massive strain. It needed twenty-five goods-trains every day just to supply AGC with fuel, food, and kit. One thing that should have been obvious, even to Hitler before Barbarossa, was that the German and Russian railway tracks had different gauges – German trains could not use Russian rails. A massive and costly programme of replacing the tracks was a long way behind schedule. By the summer, less than half the required train loads were reaching their destinations.

In early November 1941, Hitler's health suddenly improved but his apparent 'God-like' ability to foretell the near future had not. He failed to see the ominous approach of the enemy that had defeated Napoleon – the Russian weather.

Torrential rain had already begun to turn roads, many of which were just un-tarred tracks, into thick mud that German soldiers called '*schwarze erde*' (black earth), and Russians called '*rasputitsa*'. Even tracked vehicles struggled to make progress, and transport by rail was not an option.

German forces were much weakened and then forced to fight without winter clothing or appropriate equipment in one of the worst Russian

Incessant heavy rain preceded the Russian weather causing what Germans called '*schwarze erde*' (black earth), and Russians called '*rasputitsa*'.

winters ever recorded. By mid-December temperatures dropped to between −20C and −30C requiring frozen grease to be scraped off each shell before being loaded and for engines to be heated up by lighting fires under them. Soldiers even had to watch special troops, nicknamed '*saw commandos*', thaw out and then strip frozen corpses to re-use kit and clothing.

Far from Hitler acknowledging his catastrophic mistake, however, he decided that failure was the result of inept generals and so sacked his commander in chief, Field Marshal von Brauchitsch and, in the most incredible piece of self-delusion so far in the war, appointed himself *Feldher, Oberkommando der Wehrmacht* – Supreme Commander of the Army, (Ch.18) thereby taking absolute control of all military decisions.

Hitler explained his decision to take on this ultimate responsibility (and thereby the blame) for every military action from then on that – *'Anyone can do the little job of directing operations in war, the task of the commander-in-chief is to educate the army to be National Socialists. I do not know any army general who can do this in the way I want it done!'* [15] Thereafter, to ensure minimal debate on his plans and orders, he made sure he was surrounded by staff officers with little or no recent combat experience. As before, and from then on, he compounded his unprofessional judgements with his ideological preferences.

In this deluded euphoria of self-belief, perhaps even of his own immortality, that was fed constantly by a few of his closest worshippers, the '*Messiah*' took the unmitigated decision on 11 December to declare war on the United States of America (Ch.6).

But his first instructions were to direct events towards his next huge military error: the decisive turning point of the war in the east, the siege of Stalingrad.

Stalingrad 1942

Stalingrad was a ten-mile-long industrialised, modern conurbation lying along the west bank of the River Volga. Strategically, it was not a military prerequisite to the conquering of Russia but the fact that the city was re-named in 1925 to honour the new Russian leader, Stalin, gave the place a certain prestige. It became of fantasised importance in the minds of both Hitler and Stalin, primarily because of this. To Hitler, the notion of capturing Stalingrad started as a passing bit of kudos, but day by day it became more entrenched in his mind, and in the end was to cost him everything he had dreamt of for the past twenty years.

Hitler's armies were actually heading for the highly strategic oil reserves of Baku and the Caucasus and the city of Stalingrad could have, should have, been by-passed and left to another day, but for the new *Feldher* pride was more important that petrol.

In July 1942, Manstein's Eleventh Army was poised to cross into the Caucasus when Hitler made another change to his plan and split Army Group B, ordering them to take Stalingrad first. This decision was made despite Hitler himself having previously said (prophetically but never repeated) *'If we do not capture the oil supplies of the Caucasus by the autumn… we cannot win this war.'* [8]

Hitler had taken full personal control of the operation, but he had, of course, never been to Staff College and had no experience of field command. He diverted the Fourth Panzer Army from Group A to Group B and then in his typically hesitant and indecisive way he transferred them back a few days later; only to change his order again to attack Stalingrad from the south.

General von Kleist whose First Panzer Army was leading the drive in the Caucasus later wrote, *'The Fourth Pz. Army could have taken Stalingrad without a fight [two weeks ago] but was diverted south to help me… I did not need its help [now] the Russians have gathered just enough forces to check it.'*

After the failure to take Moscow over the long cold winter of 1941/42, Hitler's forces began their offensive in the Crimea, besieging and taking Sebastopol over the spring months.

As the Germans pushed further into Stalingrad, they used so much heavy artillery and tank fire that much of the area became huge zones of rubble and half destroyed buildings.

At just this same time, between 12 and 14 August 1942, Stalin was hosting a visit by Winston Churchill in Moscow. This was the first time the two great leaders had met face to face, but for two and half days it was not a pleasant encounter. Stalin persistently accused Britain and America of failing to commit to a second front in Europe, Churchill contemplated going home early as he felt he was not making any progress. However, on the last evening, Stalin invited Churchill to dine with him in a private room; there they began to relax and laugh together, enjoying good food and quantities of wine, vodka and other imbibes. Churchill felt they had at last established a *'friendship'* with what he now called *'the great man'* and they parted on good terms but without any firm programme set for a future D-Day.

Days later, the Luftwaffe laid a massive bombing raid on Stalingrad. The whole city then became almost unconquerable, as troops could not move about without the highly likely chance of being picked off by a Russian sniper. As almost every building had been pulverised into

On a visit to Moscow on 14 August 1942, Churchill felt he had at last established a 'friendship' with Stalin, who he now called 'the great man'.

ruin, German heavy weapons were of little use thereafter and the siege of Stalingrad soon became a huge 'game' of hide and seek. Germans had to keep such a low profile that movement was through tunnels, passageways and sewers in what was soon known by the beleaguered soldiers as *rattenkreig*, 'rat-war'. Some Russian snipers, including female sharp-shooters such as Tanya Chernova, with a claim of 80 kills in three months, became folk-heroes.

Best known today is Vasily Zaitsev, following his depiction in the 2001 film *'Enemy at the Gates'*. There were, of course, snipers on both sides but it was the Germans whose morale was damaged most by this unseen enemy.

The deprivations suffered by both sides during the siege of Stalingrad took its biggest toll during the freezing cold winter months. Stalin's order from July 1941 that there should be *'not one step back'* was enforced by the ruthless NKVD, the Peoples' Commissariat for Internal Affairs (later to become the KGB) who did not hesitate to shoot any Russian who retreated or deserted.

Over the five months of the siege they killed 13,500 of their own people. However, under such dreadful conditions any lesser punishment would probably have meant widespread mutinies and mass desertion. [11]

Hitler's complete lack of expertise in field command caused him to overlook the most crucial of factors in any campaign conducted over a vast distance and that was his extended supply lines. Napoleon Bonaparte, who a little over a century earlier had tried the same military feat, famously said that an '*army marches on its stomach*' and he would no doubt have added after his Russian campaign that it also needs the right clothing for the extremes of climate. Hitler ignored or dismissed this, his calculations solidly based, as ever, on his ideological prejudices. He was convinced that the Russian soldier,

Female sharp-shooters such as Tanya Chernova became folk-heroes with a claim of 80 kills in three months.

being of an inferior Slav race, had no fortitude and could never match the pure Aryan blood and fighting skills of his Germanic troops.

At the end of November 1942, it was Russia's gifted General Zhukov who masterminded the simultaneous attacks from the north, against the Rumanian and Italians, and from the south of Stalingrad against another Rumanian army. At this point, while there was still a chance, the commander of the trapped Sixth Army, General Paulus, should have attempted a break-out, but Hitler forbade it (Ch.19). The whole Sixth Army therefore became surrounded and trapped. Hitler had already ordered General Manstein to lead an army of relief towards Stalingrad. He had believed Göring when he made the ludicrous assurance to his Führer that his Luftwaffe could fly in 550 tons of supplies every day to the Sixth Army; Paulus said he needed 750 tons a day. This offer reflected Göring's arrogance and lack of understanding of the logistics needed for such an airlift and Hitler's blindness towards the same man who had previously promised him that his Luftwaffe would take control of the skies over the English Channel in 1940 and force Britain to surrender.

These mistakes by Hitler meant that an average of only 100 tons a day was actually delivered and so the exhausted Sixth Army starved, froze and died from injury and disease. One German soldier of the 94th Infantry Division wrote in his diary, '*The horses have already been eaten, I would eat a cat, they say its meat is tasty… the soldiers look like corpses or lunatics, they haven't the strength to walk or hide.*' [11] Soldiers' hands were too frostbitten to operate weapons and frozen corpses lay all around. The Russians offered them surrender, food and warmth so long as weapons were not damaged, but it was refused on the instructions of Hitler.

Hitler claimed to have read a great deal about Napoleon's attempt to bring the massive land-space under his control so it is almost beyond belief that he should have made what was almost a perfect copy of the same fundamental mistake as one of the truly greatest field commanders of all time had made.

Hitler, unlike Napoleon, showed a completely detached disregard for the wellbeing of his soldiers. He made this quite clear to his generals at an earlier meeting in his warm comfortable home in Berchtesgaden, when

Hitler claimed he did not feel the cold when wearing lederhosen, even with temperatures below –10°C.

he was describing his own, apparently super-human ability to resist the cold. He boasted *'long trousers were a misery to me. Even with temperatures well below –10°C I used to go about in lederhosen… I never even noticed [the cold].'* He then displayed his moronic logic by declaring that he was going to create *'an SS Mountain Brigade dressed in lederhosen'*. [35]

At the same meeting, in direct contradiction to his ideological derision and contempt for people he would surely have otherwise considered *untermensch*, he said, *'one can't trust meteorological forecasts… we need men gifted with a sixth sense who live with nature… one of them will have a humped back, another bandy legs, another paralytic.'*

Hitler's callousness towards his troops was perfectly exemplified on 20 December 1942 when he responded to the request for a tactical withdrawal telling all the half a million men in Army Group Centre that they must *'stand or die'*. [8]

The Russians, meanwhile, were beginning to receive supplies in trucks driven across the now frozen River Volga, and on 10 January they launched a massive offensive to regain the city.

Paulus repeated his request for permission to try to break out to meet up with Manstein's advancing army, but Hitler sent him this message: *'Surrender is forbidden, Sixth Army will hold their positions to the last man and the last round.'* Hitler, in his *Wolfsschanze* that same day, referring more to the vast amount of equipment rather than the men, said to his officers, *'Under no circumstances can we give this up; we won't get it back once it's lost.'*

That same week, far away in Casablanca, Churchill and President Roosevelt, along with the Free French leader General Charles de Gaulle, were holding a summit meeting that Stalin was unable to attend due to the ongoing Stalingrad situation. Roosevelt publicly announced, without consulting either Churchill or Stalin, that the Allies would accept nothing less than *'unconditional surrender'* of all German forces. Now Hitler knew it could only be all or nothing from here on.

Erich von Manstein was one of Hitler's finest generals and following his brilliant taking of Sebastopol and the whole Crimea, he was now leading Army Group Don to relieve Paulus's Sixth Army, stranded in Stalingrad. Manstein, now less than fifty miles from Stalingrad, radioed ahead his order as a Field Marshal to General Paulus to break-out, but it was too late. Paulus no longer had the petrol to move his vehicles and most of his men would have been too weak anyway. At the same time, Manstein's right flank came under attack and progress was halted by the ferocious winter weather as icy wind blew in off the Steppe and temperatures dropped to –20C and below.

Soon after Paulus was captured, wrapped in a blanket, and then surrendered his whole army including twenty-two other Generals.

(*Shutterstock*)

One week later, Hitler cynically promoted Paulus to Field Marshal, thinking it would prevent him from surrendering as no German field marshal had ever surrendered before or, as Hitler would have more likely expected, his new field marshal would shoot himself in disgrace. But the next day, 2 February 1943, Paulus was captured, wrapped in a blanket, and surrendered the 91,000 soldiers that remained of all his armies that included twenty-two other generals.

Hitler was disgusted and furious and said that they all should have shot themselves with their last bullet, declaring *'I have no respect for a soldier who shrinks back from it and prefers to go into captivity.'* [102]

The invasion of the Soviet Union was a colossal mistake entirely of Hitler's own making. Creating a major war on two fronts was to prove one of his greatest follies. It not only resulted in a terrible cost in lives and immense suffering for both sides, but in the surrender of the Sixth Army, including its commander, Paulus. Defeat on the eastern front was to become recognised as the biggest turning point of the Second World War. The near six-month siege had cost Germany and her allies the surrender of their ten Armies and the loss of almost one million troops – killed, injured or taken prisoner.

For Germany, it was the beginning of the end – they did not have the numbers to fill the boots of their dead and their factories producing tanks and weapons were under constant air attack. Germany was never going

Almost one million Axis troops had been killed in Hitler's failed *Festung* called Stalingrad. Creating a major war on two fronts was to prove one of Hitler's greatest mistakes.

to match the now colossal output of the Russians, aided by their allies Britain and the USA.

Russian casualties, including the citizens of Stalingrad, were over a million, but the Russians had the reserves and the resources to take the huge cost in men and materiel.

Hitler had made four big mistakes in Operation Barbarossa:

I. His failure to see the obstacles clearly – obstacles obvious to his experienced, but blindly obedient, or fearful, generals.
II. His failure to appreciate the effect that the massive distances would have on his supply lines.
III. His failure to take Moscow and his obsession with Stalingrad.
IV. His underestimation of the enemy caused by his ideological blindness towards the resilience of the Russian soldier, the masterful tactics of Soviet generals, the resourcefulness of Russian industry, the Soviet leader's absolute and resolute determination to '*not take one step backwards*' and, inevitably, the Russian winter.

At the Nuremberg trials two years later, Hitler's then Chief of Staff, General Halder, stated, without reservation – '*Our final disagreement was the decision of an offensive on the Caucasus and Stalingrad – a mistake, and Hitler didn't want to see it… Hitler told me that I was an idiot… [he] flew into a rage of fury and threatened me with his fists.*' [106]

Hitler's nemesis in the west had survived the Nazi air and U-boat attacks and in November 1942 the Allied armies expelled the Germans and Italians from North Africa to expose what Churchill described as the '*soft underbelly*' of the Third Reich. The Allies now included soldiers from the many countries of the British Empire fighting alongside the massive forces of the United States of America. Together they were poised to launch the greatest ever sea-borne invasion in history onto the beaches of Normandy.

Hitler would now have to face the greatest fear that he had many times declared he must avoid – war on two fronts.

Hitler's generals knew Barbarossa had been a colossal mistake, but there were many more big mistakes to follow.

Chapter 17

Declared War on the USA – December 1941

'It's only hubris if I fail.'

Julius Caesar

Winston Churchill was enjoying a glass of his favourite brandy sitting by the log fire in the drawing room at Chequers, the official country retreat of the prime minister of Great Britain. It was just before 9pm that Sunday evening of 7 December 1941. Sitting next to him were two important American men, both special envoys from the US Embassy, who had been sent by the president of the United States of America, Franklin D. Roosevelt. Churchill reached over and switched on his radio to hear the latest news from the BBC. The reception was intermittent but all three men thought there had been something said about Japan when the butler, named Sawyer, came hurriedly into the room saying, *'It's true, the Japanese have attacked the Americans, we just heard it on our radio!'* [67] Churchill stood up instantly and declared that he was going *'straight away'* to declare war on Japan, just as he had promised the president. In his memoirs Churchill wrote, *'At this very moment I knew the United States was in the war up to its neck and into the death,'* and he said to himself, *'So now we shall win, after all!'* [68] The prime minister then telephoned President Roosevelt directly and in a short conversation heard it confirmed that it was indeed so – the US naval base at Pearl Harbor in Hawaii had been attacked without warning.

No more details were known of that moment but shortly afterwards, Churchill recalls in his own history of the Second World War of feeling *'saturated and satiated with emotion and sensation'* and of going to bed and sleeping *'the sleep of the saved and thankful'*.

At exactly the same moment, one thousand miles away, in his Wolf's Lair headquarters, the Führer's reaction to the same news was equally ecstatic, and what he said, remarkably similar: *'delighted!… now we cannot*

On 7 December 1941, in the drawing room at Chequers the butler told Churchill, 'the Japanese have attacked the Americans...'

The Prime Minister later wrote in his memoirs that it was at that moment he said to himself 'so now we shall win, after all!'

lose the war... now we have an ally [Japan] which has never been beaten in 3,000 years!' [15].

Hitler flew back to Berlin from the *Wolfsschanze* on 9 December. He had also been receiving less welcome news from his commanders, deep inside Russian territory, of major problems and of increasing resistance from Soviet forces. Following the successes of Operation Barbarossa during the first few months after 22 June, when Blitzkrieg troops had swept aside all Soviet resistance, the situation had become bogged down since October as Operation Typhoon had hit the buffers and German losses were beginning to look ominous.

Hitler had been expecting Japan to attack the USA at some point and had already made up his mind how he was going to react. Germany, Italy and Japan had signed an agreement called the Tripartite Pact in September 1940, but it did not oblige Germany to declare war on America as Japan had not, as was a condition of the pact, been invaded by another country; on the contrary, Japan had invaded the USA. Hitler therefore had the perfect reason not to feel any need to make such a monumental declaration, but he did have other reasons that convinced him that he should declare war on the USA. He felt flattered by the way the Japanese had completely surprised the Americans by attacking in force, without warning or declaring war beforehand – this masterpiece of deception was exactly what he had advised the Japanese to do; it was just as he had done to Poland and to Russia. [72] Hitler probably assumed the USA would have to switch its support from Britain and Russia to concentrating on the war in the Pacific against the massive navy and army of the Japanese Empire.

Hitler's opinion of America was narrow and naive in the extreme. It was based on his ignorance of facts that would have been easy to obtain about the huge financial and productive power of the USA, about its great wealth of people, and about its abundance of natural resources. Mostly, however, it was Hitler's ideologically racist views that obscured attempts by several of his advisers to enlighten him of the unpalatable reality but Hitler never wanted to hear anything that contradicted his own unequivocal knowledge. The USA was, he said, '*rotten from… Jews and Blacks*'. [8] He had convinced most of the Nazi hierarchy that despite America being originally an Anglo-Saxon country, it was now corrupt, decadent, filled with people of mixed races, and under the influence of Jews and '*Negroes*' – all living a life of dancing, drinking, and listening to '*negrofied*' music. [69]

Hitler, it seems, had conveniently forgotten about the one million soldiers that the USA had sent over to support the great Allied offensive in the spring of 1918 which was, in effect, the decisive action of the First World War that led to Germany's surrender later that year. He told his followers that he had little or no respect for the US military, that the American army was no more than 100,000 strong, that they were dominated by Jews, and that their armed forces were weakened by large numbers of African-American immigrants. It was one mistake dismissing America's military qualities, but an even bigger one ignoring the productive potential of a country so wealthy and resourceful that it would replace all the aircraft lost at Pearl Harbor in just two days of production and in the following year would produce 98,000 warplanes while Germany struggled to build 40,000.

Hitler could not have understood either, that Germany, Japan and Britain were geographical, as well as economic, minnows compared to the physical enormity and almost unlimited resources of the United States of America. By the end of the war the USA would have supplied her Allies

How big is the USA

Hitler would not accept that that Germany, Japan and Britain were geographical, as well as economic minnows compared to the enormity and resources of the United States of America. His adjutant later recorded Hitler's 'cluelessness and ignorance… of foreign countries'.

with 37,000 tanks and 800,000 trucks and there would be 14.9 million Americans in one or other of their military forces. [8]

Hitler's views were absorbed freely by the most sycophantic generals such as Jodl, and Keitel, but the wiser ones were well aware of the dangers. One of his adjutants from the Luftwaffe later recorded how he was astounded by Hitler's *'cluelessness and that such ignorance was a display of Hitler's dilettante methods and his limited knowledge of foreign countries'*. [70] Another comment made after the war by General Warlimont made it clear that the decision was made by Hitler alone and concluded, *'If they had been asked, the military leadership would have advised against expanding the war, given the extent of the crisis on the Eastern Front.'* When his Head of the Luftwaffe, Ernst Udet, heard of his Führer's plan to go to war against America he shot himself.

Both Churchill and Hitler were now convinced that the war would end in their favour. Churchill believed that Britain would have the unambiguous commitment and huge resources of a nation with three times the population of the UK and many times its wealth. Hitler was sure that Japan would take the attention of the USA away from supporting the Russians and from protecting the Atlantic convoys from his U-boats. The British would also suffer when Japan invaded its colonies and possessions in the Far East.

Both men could not be right.

This news would allow Hitler to distract attention from the current difficulties on the eastern front and enable him instead, to give a much-needed, morale-boosting speech to the Reichstag and therefore to the German people, a few days later.

Hitler had been concerned for some weeks how he was going to present the setbacks in Operation Typhoon in a more positive light. This new turn of events at Pearl Harbor gave him a positive angle. In fact, he talked of this exclusively, utterly ignoring any mention of the mounting losses on the Russian front. [Ch.16]

Hitler and Goebbels chose 3 pm on 11 December 1941 as the ideal time to deliver the speech to the Reichstag as it would be heard simultaneously in Tokyo at 10 pm and in Washington at 8 am. Hitler had also instructed Foreign Minister Ribbentrop to call Mussolini to make sure Italy declared war on the USA at exactly the same time. The main concern Hitler had was that Japan had, by then, also signed the agreement that prevented either member of the tripartite agreement from making a separate 'peace deal' with any of the Allies. [71]

It is without doubt that this speech was Hitler's next big mistake. He began by accusing the USA of violating the international rules of neutrality and maintaining that America had been provoking Germany with open military acts of aggression such as its destroyers opening fire on German submarines and seizing German merchant ships on the high seas. The USA had thereby created a state of war between the two countries. He concluded his speech by claiming that the German government had adhered to the rules of international law in her relations with America but as a result of these circumstances, all brought about by President Roosevelt, '*Germany now considers herself to be in a state of war with the United States of America.*'

Churchill's address to the House of Commons was equally positive, but he came to the opposite conclusion. He said, '*Hitler's fate was sealed. Mussolini's fate was sealed. As for the Japanese, they would be ground to powder... Many disasters, immeasurable costs and tribulations lay ahead, but there was no more doubt about the end.*' Churchill always felt a strong affiliation to America as he was the son of an American mother. He had previously made plain his faith in his half-homeland when he told a colleague '*The United States is like a gigantic boiler. Once the fire is lit under it, there is no limit to the power it can generate.*' [67]

This massive mistake by Hitler, to declare war on the United States of America on 11 December 1941, was not a knee-jerk decision. It had been made by Hitler alone, without consultation. It seems so obviously disastrous today, but it was made a full four days after Pearl Harbor, so it was not a hasty one, as far as he was concerned. According to the Tripartite Pact, Germany was under no obligation to do so as it only promised to help Japan if it were attacked. The Japanese Ambassador Oshima had demanded that Germany declare war on America, but Foreign Office Minister Ribbentrop recognised the untenable position Germany would find itself in by doing so. He advised against such action.

Hitler disagreed. He had been expecting such an event and had made up his mind sometime in the past how he would react. Why he did so was a matter of politics, pride, flattery and ideology. It was certainly not a decision based on sound military reasoning, as it was now a war that would have to be fought on three fronts.

Hitler's decision to declare war on the United States of America was one of the biggest mistakes he would ever make.

Chapter 18

Taking over as Commander in Chief – December 1941

'Anyone can do the little job of directing operations in war.'

Adolf Hitler 1941

The most astonishing run of good luck had carried Adolf Hitler a long way from the rejected, failed artist and foot-soldier he had been at the beginning of the First World War to a seemingly preordained route of destiny in which a ceaseless wave of good luck had delivered him to the crest of that wave by the summer of 1941.

Hitler had given the order to start the war by invading Poland, with the co-operation of Stalin's Russia, on 1 September 1939. His input to his High Command was simple – take Poland; he left the strategies and tactics to his skilful generals and their officers. They did a brilliant job, obtaining the surrender of Poland within one month. For the next two years this was how Hitler's forces conquered the entire European mainland and very nearly brought Britain to its knees.

Hitler was euphoric – he could not wait to turn his attention eastwards and on 22 June 1941, he ordered the German invasion of the Soviet Union. His best generals were not in favour. They understood their shortcomings in logistics, materiel and manpower, and the limitations of their armies, but it had been victory after victory so Hitler overruled them and insisted Operation Barbarossa (Ch.10) went ahead without delay.

Hitler already believed himself without equal, a man destined to rule Europe, to create a Third Reich and to rid the world of all *untermensch* such as Jews, Slavs, and Bolsheviks.

He knew he had been incredibly lucky but that was not how he would have explained events so far. He would have agreed with his Chief of Staff, General Keitel that he, Adolf Hitler, Führer of the new German Empire was now *'the greatest commander of all time'*. [8]

1941 had been another good year for Adolf Hitler. France had surrendered, and Britain, he was sure, was all but finished. The start of the invasion of the Soviet Union had been only slightly delayed, and by mid-July Smolensk had been taken. By the end of August German forces had begun the siege of Leningrad and by September they had taken Kiev. (Ch.10).

The military successes achieved by his armed forces since he became a dictator looked impressive. Impressive that is until it's clear that at no point had Hitler to face a serious challenge on the ground. The real test comes when faced with adversity; only then can a commander be judged to be great or otherwise.

The first serious challenge to his decade-long run of luck happened when AGC, slowed down by six days of heavy rain in Belarus, had given the Soviets time to build-up a six-army defensive line south of Smolensk. On 6 July 1941, the Germans were pounded by the Red Army in a massive counter-attack and were saved from annihilation only because the Luftwaffe were present, more by chance than by design, with their only squadron of new tank-busters, the Stuka Ju 87G.

Four weeks into the campaign, the Germans had used up most of their initial supplies and were beginning to realize that they had underestimated Soviet strength.

Hitler was interfering more and more in the day-to-day movements and tactics of his three massive army groups. Although he had given senior commanders their overall orders to take Leningrad, Moscow, and Kiev, Hitler continually made detailed changes during the advances and these led to confusion, disruption and, naturally, discontent.

Marshal Zhukov, Stalin's greatest general, had used the lull caused entirely by Hitler's change of plans, to reinforce the defences around Moscow and just as the Germans reached a position around twenty miles from the centre, the infamous Russian winter started early.

At first, heavy constant rain turned all the unmetalled roads to a sea of thick black mud that sucked in men, horses, vehicles and even the tracked but very heavy tanks. Predictably, but not accounted for, was the fact that Russian railway tracks had a different gauge so could not be used.

Within weeks, the real winter weather started to blow in off the wide-open steppes. Temperatures were well below zero and the ice and snow soon played havoc on men and machines. The Germans had already sustained around 150,000 casualties, many dying of the cold and lost hundreds of tanks and guns.

Hitler was incapable of any sympathy or understanding – he had withstood the privations of First World War trench life, so the least he could expect of his Aryan troops was to put up with a few setbacks and some cold weather; retreat in any shape or form was unacceptable, he reasoned.

But Army Group Centre, led by Field Marshal Fedor von Bock, had passed Smolensk and the Russians were pulling their scattered forces together when Hitler, contrary to his own declared priority, halted the advance on Moscow at the most crucial moment. Hitler had changed his own plan and divided Army Group Centre, sending one part of it to Leningrad and another south towards Kiev.

So, at the gates of Moscow, Hitler suddenly decided that the oil fields of Baku and the Caucasus were the new priority, and he changed his plan, in an instant, thereby saving Moscow and abandoning what could have been his most significant, possibly decisive, battle of Operation Barbarossa. (Ch.16)

Changing his plans was a fatal miscalculation. Before Barbarossa had begun, he had actually made it clear in his Führer Directive No.21 that taking and holding the Russian capital was the strategic key to the conquering and controlling of all of the Soviet Union. But he divided Army Group Centre to the north, towards Leningrad, and to the south, towards Kiev and Stalingrad because of his new aim of securing Ukraine's food and the Caucasus oil wells. During the planning of Barbarossa, Hitler had ignored all attempts to warn him of the likelihood of severe fuel shortages and none of his generals had the courage to argue with him.

Von Bock had been sure he was about to have the glory of taking Moscow, so when he received Hitler's order, he protested and tried very hard to persuade Hitler to take Moscow first and not to divide his forces. OKH Chief of Staff, Franz Halder also had no doubt this was the moment to press the attack on the capital city, as did every other German general involved, but Hitler had made up his mind and declared the new priority would be to defeat the Soviets by 'economic means'. [142] The Führer's new plan was to first seize the industrial centre of Kharkov, take control of the oilfields in the Caucasus and then to capture the military centre of Leningrad. The generals argued vehemently that now was the best opportunity to take Moscow, which would not only have the greatest psychological effect on the Soviets, on Germany's Allies and on the German people, but that the capital was also a major centre of arms production, the centre of Soviet communications and a crucial transport hub.

Bock and Halder then sent Guderian, one of the few commanders well respected by Hitler. Surely this master of tank tactics would be the one man able to convince Hitler not to change the plan; but it was hopeless. Bock had wanted to be the general who captured Moscow, but he was frustrated to see the chance was being missed. He wrote in his diary, '*It is not my fault.*' Bock was sacked and was immediately replaced by General von Kluge, as commander of AGC.

Halder had noted in his diary that '*He [Hitler] decides on his objectives and sticks to them, without considering what the enemy may do.*' He later added, '*In my view, the situation resulting from the Führer's interference is intolerable… counter-order and disorder and no one can be held responsible but he himself personally.*' [10]

19 December 1941 – good luck ends, mistakes begin.

> '*Luck always seems to be against the man who depends upon it.*'
>
> Ukrainian proverb

As Führer, Hitler always had the last word on all operations of war but much of the day-to-day decisions, strategies and tactics had been made by his highly able commanders on the ground. Victories had been granted to the Führer and credit assigned to him personally as the overlord of the successes so far.

As the situation around Moscow worsened, commander-in-chief of the army, von Brauchitsch asked permission to withdraw his forces. The next day Hitler sacked him. On 19 December 1941, Hitler gathered his senior commanders together and told them that they '*knew nothing about the economic aspects of war*'. He announced that he was now the new commander-in-chief, assuring them that '*anyone can do the little job of directing operations in war… I do not know of any Army General who can do this in the way that I want it done… I have therefore decided to take over command of the Army.*' [143]

Commander-in-Chief of the Army, Walther von Brauchitsch had asked permission to withdraw his forces but Hitler's reply was, as ever, to stand and die.

From this moment on it would be he, Adolf Hitler, the former Corporal and motorcycle messenger, who would be Supreme Commander, or *Feldherr*, of all German Forces – he would personally intervene and approve or reject every military decision. He did not say it, but his all-powerful rank now meant that he would be fully responsible and solely to blame for all the forthcoming disasters, defeats, retreats and losses of ground, men, machinery and, of course, the final national disgrace.

Commanders of vast armies on campaign must have the gift of scope of mind – a wide intellectual capacity, an ability to see situations on a broad scale and to have an appreciation of all options. Hitler had none of those attributes but he did possess absolute self-belief and unswervable certainty in his own opinions, ideals, philosophies, and military prowess.

Only in adversity can a commander's military skills be measured, when cool judgement and calculated decisions are needed. These are the skills of a great commander; but none of them belonged to the Führer.

This was the moment that Hitler began the journey to his final defeat and demise.

This was when his long run of good luck turned into a long run of big mistakes!

Feldherr

One of his first acts as *Feldherr* was to allow his U-boats to attack shipping along the east coast of the USA, convincing any doubting American citizen that they really were now at war. He authorised the first of the Luftwaffe's large bombing air raids on British cities but that only prompted the RAF to launch ever greater bombing raids on German cities like Cologne and Hamburg, followed in the summer by American Flying Fortresses' massive daytime air raids on the industrial heart of Germany. In July, Hitler planned and launched what is often seen as his biggest military blunder, and the decisive turning point of the war in the East, the siege of Stalingrad (Ch.16). In November he was humiliated by the defeat of his favourite – Field Marshal Rommel, at the Battle of El Alamein.

Hitler must have felt, possibly for the first time, real anxiety – the unequivocal defeat of his Afrika Korps and public hero-figure Rommel, the failure to take Moscow and the pending disaster at Stalingrad – none of these brought out the *'great commander'* in Hitler, because, of course, it was never in there.

Instead, they brought the true evil out of the Führer. First he issued Führer Directive 46 declaiming all partisan fighters in the eastern front as 'bandits' and ordering the destruction and depopulation of those territories – turning them into 'dead zones' *(Tote Zonen).* [171] This alone did not satisfy his frustration or his lust for vengeance and he followed it up a few weeks later with the infamous 'Commando Order' *(Kommandobefehl)* on 18 October 1942 in which he directed that all Allied commandos encountered by German forces would be killed immediately without trial, even if they were in uniform or attempting to surrender. German commanders were given no discretion in this and had to ensure Hitler's order was carried out forthwith, on pain of their own life.[2]

---

2. At the Nuremberg Trials, the Commando Order was found to be in direct breach of the laws of war (Third Geneva Convention 1929), [172] and German officers who carried out illegal executions under the Commando Order were found guilty of war crimes and sentenced to death.

At the Berghof, Hitler would rise mid-morning and every day, between 10am and 11am, he would stroll for 20 minutes, down the private 2km road to the *Teehaus*, in the village below, for his favourite tea and cakes. (*Shutterstock*)

Hitler's morality had sunk to a new low and if there had been any Führer magic in the past, there was no sign of it now. If good luck had lifted him out of difficulties up until now, there was no sign of that either.

1943 was to be one defeat, retreat or setback after another for Hitler – Axis forces are driven out of North Africa and chased through Sicily and up the spine of Italy – the Battle of the Atlantic is lost as Admiral Dönitz withdraws his last U-boats from operations – Mussolini is arrested and imprisoned – Soviet armies take Stalingrad, Kharkov, Kursk and then decimate a thousand German tanks at Kiev – the German offensive in Operation Zitadelle is a disaster – Italy changes sides and Berlin is pounded by the RAF. Every battle lost, every set-back and every retreat was a direct result of mistakes made by one person – Adolf Hitler.

1943 had been a very bad year for the *Feldherr, Oberkommando der Wehrmacht*.

1944 did not get any better. The Soviets pushed through the Ukraine and Belarus, and Leningrad was finally relieved after 900 days under siege. The Allies were in north Italy as German troops retreat from one defensive line to the next. In the summer, the final Soviet offensive,

Operation Bagration, begins (Ch.16); the Allies invade Normandy on D-Day; Hitler's Atlantic Wall crumbles; and his wonder weapons, (Ch.21) the V-1 and the V-2 are soon found and destroyed; Paris and Athens are liberated and the Soviet armies reach Hungary and Poland. The Third Reich is reduced to the old German borders, their enemies poised to the west and to the east.

Since he had made himself the supreme commander in December 1941, Hitler had made mistake after mistake; his good luck had totally deserted him. He was physically and mentally drained. He no longer gave great speeches, or any speeches, and he no longer held triumphal marches through the streets of Berlin or held mega-rallies in the massive arena at Nuremberg. After the attempted assassination on 20 July 1944 (Ch.11) he spent most of his time in the *Kehlsteinhaus* or Eagle's Nest chalet at the very top of the escarpment that overlooked the *Berghof,* his house at the foot of the Alpine mountain near Berchtesgaden, Obersalzberg.

Every day without fail, he would stroll the half mile to the local cafeteria for afternoon tea and cakes. This was where he dreamt up his one, last, mad plan. It was going to be huge but, he was sure, it was going to turn the tide of the war and make Germany great once again.

Battle of the Bulge, December 1944 – Cannae forgotten

Hitler's final big mistake as *Feldherr* happened at the end of 1944. Despite the dire situation in the east, where the Soviet forces, already in Estonia and Hungary, were looking to the new year and establishing their plans for taking Warsaw and marching through Poland to the Fatherland, Hitler was thinking big, unrealistically big.

His idea was simple enough – amass a huge army in the west, make a surprise attack against the Allies, thereby dividing their forces and forcing them to negotiate peace. That would allow him then to transfer all the Wehrmacht to the Eastern Front, where he would bring the Soviet advance to a standstill and defeat it. It was, of course, fantasy. All of his generals knew it, and some, like von Rundstedt, sent him several written protests cautioning against the unworkable timetable and suggesting alternative strategies. But all to no avail.

Rundstedt later testified '*All, absolutely all conditions for the possible success of such an offensive were lacking.*' [131]

Even if the first element of Hitler's plan had succeeded in halting and defeating the Allied advance from the west, the second part was doomed because, as Jodl, Chief of Operations Staff at OKW, said *'The Russians had so many troops that even if we had succeeded in destroying thirty divisions it would have made no difference. On the other hand, if we destroyed thirty divisions in the West, it would amount to more than a third of the whole invasion Army.'* [133]

After much arguing and debate between Rundstedt and Model, both trying different ways to amend or scrap Hitler's big plan, the final version of the order for the counteroffensive, named by Hitler as *Wacht am Rhein* (Watch on the Rhine), was approved on 9 December 1944.

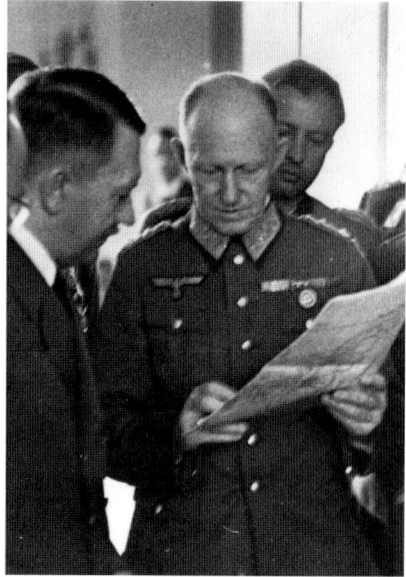

Generaloberst Alfred Jodl, Chief of Operations Staff at OKW said, 'the plan…[Ardennes or Hitler Offensive, 1944]… hasn't got a damned leg to stand on' …[and it] would have made no difference…'

The scope and objective were exactly as they had been conceived by Hitler in Obersalzberg and presented to his chiefs of staff on 22 October. Hitler had written on the orders, in his own hand, *'Not to be altered'*. This was to be entirely Hitler's offensive, although he later called it Rundstedt's offensive. It is best known today as the Ardennes Offensive and the main battle is named by the Allies as The Battle of the Bulge.

Hitler had taken over as Supreme Commander in Chief of all Wehrmacht forces three years previously, in the heat of the Soviet counter-offensives, and since that moment he had presided over one defeat after another. By the end of 1944, Italy had been invaded, Rome taken and the Italians surrendered.

It was never even a passing thought in the psychotic, fanatical mind of the Führer that all the defeats, all the withdrawals, the colossal loss of tanks and weapons, and all the millions of dead or captured German soldiers were entirely his fault. On the contrary, he remained certain that he was right, reminding himself that he was, after all, the *'greatest commander of all time'*. [15]

Earlier that year, on 20 July 1944 he had come to within a hair's-breadth of death when a number of his closest officers carried out an assassination attempt. (Ch.11). Hitler had been shocked alright, but never did he doubt himself – the very fact his assassins had failed was further proof that he had been saved by providence to fulfil his mission and win the ultimate victory for Germany.

On 20 November, 1944 Hitler left his eastern bunker for the last time and returned to Berlin.

The near-death explosion at the *Wolfsschanze* had made a big impact on Hitler's physical and mental health. After a minor operation to remove a polyp from his vocal chords, he then more or less withdrew from public events, spending a great deal of time in bed suffering from any one of his many symptoms and imagined illnesses. Every day he took a range of pills and stimulants including cocaine eye drops. Hitler was a hypochondriac and had several phobias, in particular his dread of dental treatment that his former dentist, SS officer Johannes Blaschke was keen

The near-death explosion at the *Wolfsschanze* had a big impact on Hitler's mental health and physical appearance.

Hitler's personal Doctor, Theodor Morell.

to tell his Russian captors at the end of the war, Hitler had '*terribly bad breath, abscesses and gum disease*'. He also had a fear of blades, a disgust of raw meat (he was a staunch vegetarian), smoking (he stopped smoking after the First World War), disease and germs (he often referred to Jews as parasites), prostitutes (it was rumoured that he had got syphilis from a Jewish woman in Vienna) and, allegedly, cats. Hitler also displayed bouts of hysteria for which he was given regular injections by his personal physician, Doctor Theodor Morell. Hitler no longer appeared in public, or made radio speeches and his physical appearance deteriorated so rapidly that rumours abounded that he was either seriously ill or even dead. [15]

Despite all this, Hitler in late 1944 was still convinced that he could win the war. He understood that to defeat the Russians, first he had to defeat the British and her Allies in the west. So he needed to think of something very special, very big, and something unexpected to halt the military reality that confronted him at that moment.

Confined to the *Führerbunker*, his mind had gone back to what he claimed was one of his greatest personal successes – the invasion of France in 1940. That plan, known today as the Manstein Plan (Ch.9) was devised by Field Marshal Erich von Manstein but adopted and claimed by Hitler as his own. The key to its success was the complete surprise of the attack westwards through what had previously been assumed to be the impassable forest and mountains of Luxembourg. It had worked in 1940, reasoned Hitler, so let it work again now.

The idea gave Hitler a great boost of spirit and he was again the 'old-style' Hitler, making sweeping hand movements over his maps in the planning room of his newly constructed headquarters – in the *Adlerhorst* – hidden below Kransberg Castle, just north of Frankfurt. He seemed rejuvenated, demonstrating to his generals how he was going to repeat his glorious success of 1940. The *Adlerhorst* was close to Ziegenberg on the east bank of the Rhine and so quite close to the western front. First of all, explained the now revitalised warlord, he would pull together all of his available forces, including his new super-tanks, the massive, 70-ton Tiger II, or *Königstiger* (King Tiger).

Then, he announced, he would send his best SS armoured brigades through the Ardennes Forest, just as he had done four years before in the triumphant defeat of France. From there he would slice through the

Allied armies and, like the curved blade of a scythe, sweep northwards to take the vital supply port of Antwerp.

This, he declared, would split the British and American armies and deprive the Allies of their key supply port. They would be caught off-guard by the aggressive, fast moving offensive by battle-hardened German troops, who would again be triumphant against the *'green... mongrel nation... with its strong ties to the Jews'* [7] as Hitler described all American troops.

This time, the plan was for his elite Panzers, led by *Generaloberst der Waffen-SS* Sepp Dietrich, to emerge from the forest and mountains of the Ardennes and perform the same *'sickle-cut'* manoeuvre that Rommel had done four years before. This would split the American and British armies in Belgium and his Panzers would quickly seize their primary objective, Antwerp.

Antwerp was the lifeline for supplies and fuel to the Allied advance and they would soon be calling for an armistice, Hitler confidently predicted. As he often did, Hitler invoked his all-time hero of German history, Frederick the Great.

Liking himself to the great ruler of the Seven Years War, Hitler used words to the effect that with the Führer's indefatigable will to win and the will of the German people to never accept defeat, they were bound to overcome whatever adversity was set before them. To Hitler's uncompromising mind, his plan was certain to succeed.

All he needed now was one million soldiers, a thousand tanks, two thousand fighter aircraft, and five hundred million litres of fuel!

The Ardennes Offensive began on 16 December 1944. Hitler had amassed around 450,000 troops and 1,500 tanks and assault guns. Army Group B, made up of the Fifth and Sixth Panzer Army and the Seventh Infantry Army, advanced through deep snow, using searchlights bouncing their beams off the clouds to light the way through the forest. Hitler had counted on bad weather keeping Allied fighter aircraft on the ground and that is what happened at the start. This gave the Panzers safe passage through the foggy passes of the Ardennes, and in the first few days the Germans made good progress.

A company of German soldiers wearing US Army uniforms was dropped behind enemy lines to add confusion by changing local road signs and directing traffic the wrong way.

In the French town of Malmedy, the Sixth SS Panzer Army was bogged down and short of fuel. Not for the first time, they took their frustrations out on some US Army prisoners, lining them up and executing one hundred by machine-gun.

On Christmas Eve, the weather conditions cleared. With the very low temperatures, the German tanks had been using more fuel than had been predicted and many had no option but to stop and wait for supplies. They had planned taking fuel from captured Allied fuel dumps, but none had been found.

When the skies cleared, the German tanks were stranded on the roads and the Americans were able to get their P-47 ground-attack Thunderbolts to pulverise the immobile Panzers with their new high velocity rockets.

By the turn of 1945, the British 21st Army, led by the redoubtable Field Marshal Bernard Montgomery, was attacking with full force from the north while General George S Patton had made a remarkable sharp turn in the south where his 3rd US Army was punching northwards. Both generals were determined to close the pincer behind the Germans.

The whole German advance was fast running out of petrol; an elementary mistake by Hitler, but fanatical Nazi Sepp Dietrich refused to change direction to try to find fuel because, he said, '*he had to obey Hitler's orders to the letter.*'

Commanders in the field could clearly see the whole operation was collapsing. Von Rundstedt, High Commander West, asked Hitler to call off the Ardennes Offensive so that he could reorientate Germany's armoured strength to the eastern front, but Hitler flatly refused. [134]

LESSONS FROM HISTORY – Moscow 1815 and 1941, Cannae 216 BC, The Bulge 1944

Hitler claimed he had studied and learned military tactics from the great commanders of history, but he had never undertaken officer training nor had he read serious history books on war strategy or battle tactics. His self-belief was based on his earlier aggressive and opportunistic attacks on poorly defended countries, overwhelming them using Blitzkrieg tactics that had been developed by his most talented generals, Guderian, Rundstedt and Rommel. Once Hitler took overall command, he had

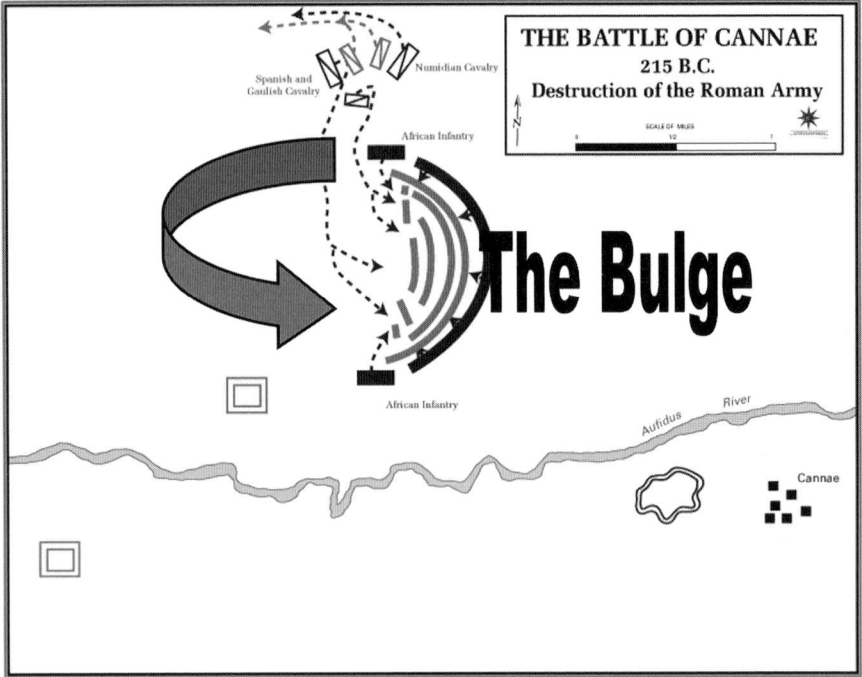

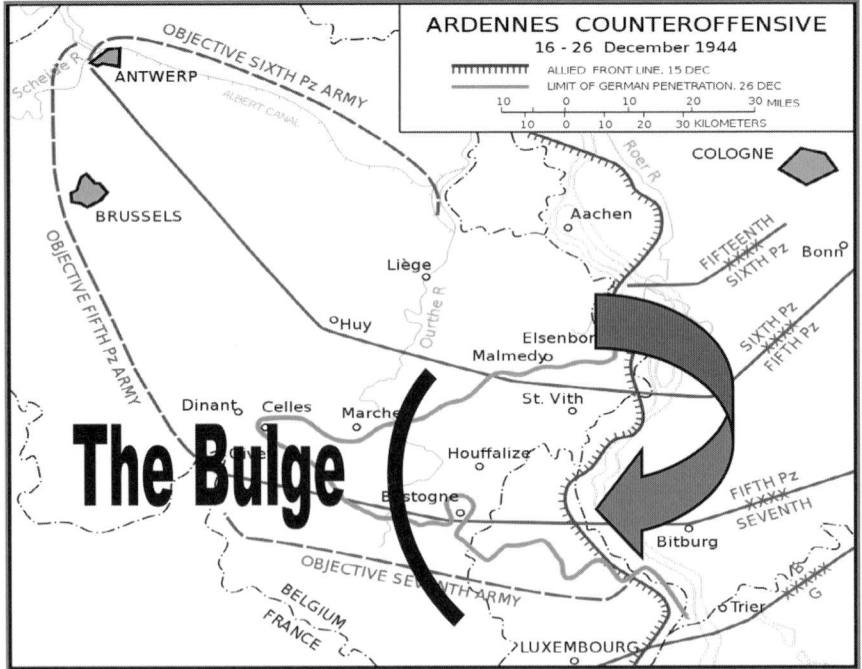

Hitler claimed he had studied and learned military tactics from the great commanders from history. In 1944, he ordered his Panzers to split the allied armies but they rolled into the same trap that Hannibal Barka had exploited two thousand years before at the Battle of Cannae in 216 BC – they allowed the attackers to create a bulge through the middle, then cut them off from behind.

neither the training nor knowledge nor the natural skills to fall back on and so made one military mistake after another.

In 1941 he had failed to heed the lessons of Napoleon's invasion of Russia and the inevitable dangers of a Russian winter.

In 1944 he then walked into a situation that Hannibal Barka had exploited two thousand years before at the Battle of Cannae – allow the attackers to push through the middle, then cut them off from behind.

Hitler's plan to split the Allied armies by using all his best forces to push through the enemy's centre was, in effect marching into Hannibal's classic pincer counter-attack.

It was Hitler's repeated weakness, demonstrated at Stalingrad and at many other scenarios (Ch.19), that he became obsessed with a particular theatre of war. His 'tunnel-vision' prevented him from looking at the wider picture, from listening to his experienced commanders, or from considering any option that even hinted of giving ground. He could never see the tactical advantages of retreating and regrouping until it was too late.

Field Marshal Otto 'Walter' Model, commander of Army Group B, an ardent Nazi and one of Hitler's most positive and able commanders told a senior officer just before the Ardennes attack started that the plan '*hasn't got a damned leg to stand on.*' [132]

Panzer General Baron von Manteuffel, leading the southern group, later said of Hitler, '*He was incapable of realising that he no longer commanded the army of 1940.*' [8]

Hitler's last big military mistake, commanding not on the field of battle but from his Headquarters in the *Wolfsschanze*, hundreds of miles from the front line, ended in the collapse of the great plan Hitler called the Rundstedt Offensive but Rundstedt disowned it saying the order had been sent to him, complete in every detail, with the handwritten warning in Hitler's own hand, '*Not to be Altered*'.

Relief of Bastogne

By 18 December 1944, the soldiers of the 101st Airborne Division were surrounded in the town of Bastogne. The Americans were outnumbered five to one, had little ammunition, barely any food, and most soldiers didn't have cold-weather gear.

On the face of it, the 101st were doomed. Brigadier General Anthony McAuliffe had his men form a 360-degree perimeter around the artillery guns. This tight circle of defence faced intense enemy fire but held. The German commander, General von Lüttwitz, seeing the American position as hopeless offered them honourable surrender on the 22nd. McAuliffe's now famous reply was curt. He wrote: '*To the German Commander. NUTS! The American Commander.*'

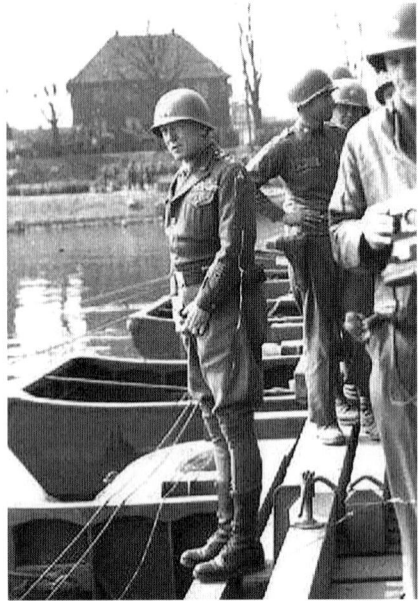

General George S. Patton, Jr. Taken just after urinating in the River Rhine as he crossed into the German heartland. (*Edited photograph by T/Sgt. Paul K. Dougherty from the Webmaster's collection*)

The next day, the fog lifted allowing reinforcements and supplies to be airdropped. Then the American P-47 Thunderbolts came to the rescue, relieving the artillery who had almost entirely run out of ammo. The Panzers, still painted green and brown for summertime, made clear targets against the white snow, and their narrow escape options sealed their fate.

Commander in Chief of all Allied forces, General Dwight D. Eisenhower, knew of the desperate situation at Bastogne and ordered General Patton to get there as quickly as possible. Patton had already anticipated this and astounded both Eisenhower and Churchill with his speed and efficiency in the enormous task of turning six divisions sharp left towards Bastogne. When Patton met the First US Army commander Omar Bradley on 21 December he famously said to him: '*Brad, this time the Kraut's stuck his head in the meat grinder, and I've got hold of the handle.*' [136] It was pure Patton. Five days later the 4th Armoured Division, part of his Third US Army, relieved the 101st Airborne Division at Bastogne and then pushed on to close the net behind the German armies now trapped in the '*Bulge*'.

Patton then led his army over the Siegfried Line after building a pontoon bridge across the Rhine on 22 March 1945. In true Patton style, he boasted later that he 'took a piss' in the river as he crossed into the German heartland.

Once again, Hitler's failings as a Supreme Commander were to cost Germany another major defeat at the Battle of the Bulge. As well as the 120,000 German casualties, the material loss of 600 tanks and 1,600 aircraft was immense, irreplaceable and all for nothing. The half a million soldiers and the thousands of tanks and assault guns that had been thrown into the Ardennes Offensive in a last hopeless attack plan, was entirely of Hitler's creation. It should and could have been used, not as an offensive force but in defence of the Fatherland. That would have been his best hope of possibly getting the Allies to the table for peace talks.

Instead, the mistakes he made in the Battle of the Bulge opened the way for the whole Allied force to cross the Rhine into the Fatherland. The weakening of the eastern front meant that the Soviet offensive happened sooner and met with considerably weaker German forces.

1944 had been even worse than 1943. From the moment Hitler had appointed himself Commander in Chief of the Wehrmacht, Germany had suffered more casualties than during the whole of the war up to the end of 1942 including Barbarossa and Stalingrad. Hitler had been personally responsible for the loss of 44 divisions and the blood of well over a million German soldiers. [10]

At no time since appointing himself as *Feldher* did Hitler find any fault in his own decisions, certainly none to which he ever admitted. On the contrary, his self-belief – usually an important quality of leadership – was, for him, actually a blind, egotistical trait that Hitler exhibited to Guderian, telling him '*There is no need for you to try to teach me. I have been commanding the Wehrmacht in the field for five years and during that time I've had more practical experience than any gentlemen of the General Staff could ever hope to have. I've studied Clausewitz and Moltke and read all the Schlieffen papers. I'm more in the picture than you are!*' [149]

But blame for all of the defeats, the setbacks, the lost ground and the collateral damage rests entirely at the feet of Adolf Hitler. The Ardennes Offensive or Battle of the Bulge was created and commanded by Hitler and it was the last big mistake that he would make on the field of battle as *Feldherr, Oberkommando der Wehrmacht*.

Chapter 19

Festungen – Fortified Localities – Stand or Die

'Sometimes we need to lose the small battle in order to win the war.'

Sun Tzu

Hitler's ideas on military strategy never got beyond attack with maximum force and speed – Blitzkrieg – then never concede territory or surrender – no matter the cost.

After taking a decision, never turn back, even if you get a thousand difficulties!!'

Adolf Hitler [160]

This strategy that Hitler called *Festungen*, or fortified localities, created an obvious quandary when his troops were faced with overwhelming forces. It meant they were not allowed to retreat and retrench to a more defendable position from which they could better counter-attack. His idea was that instead of retreating, his army, or a body of German troops, would take up a defensive stance in a strong position, such as a city or large town, and then allow themselves to become encircled. There they would remain as the front line, supplied, re-armed and reinforced by the Luftwaffe. [99]

His Führer-logic was based on his ideological image of medieval Germany, when a few knights could hold out for a long time in a huge stone castle against a besieging army equipped with horses, lances, arrows, wooden towers, and ballista.

Hitler believed the *Festung* offered two benefits;

1) It would tie-down large numbers of enemy as they spend time and resources besieging the *Festung*.
2) It would form the basis of any future counter-offensive.

Hitler never wavered from this belief despite many outcomes showing it to be disastrous.

Führer-logic was based on Hitler's ideological images of a medieval castle, or *Festung*, holding out for a long time against a besieging army armed with horses, lances, arrows, wooden towers and ballista.

Festung Europa – The Atlantic Wall

> '*He who defends everything defends nothing.*'
>
> Frederick the Great

The first time Hitler applied his *Festung* strategy was when he felt fear for the first time. By May 1940, the Blitzkrieg charge reached its first stopping point – Dunkirk. If Hitler had been a great commander – such as Julius Caesar – he would not have stopped on the beaches of northern France. While the impetus was with his forces, a Channel crossing would have caught the British on the back-foot, unprepared – but he did not, he stopped. He lost his nerve and backed off and then it was too late.

Having failed to dominate the skies over the English Channel, and being unsure of the counter-attacking strength of his enemy, Hitler's strategy then was to make the European mainland a massive *Festung*.

The Atlantic Wall was a project so colossal that had it ever been completed it would have been the largest, man-made structure ever built,

Atlantic Wall 1942-1944

Iceland
(Britain)

Faroe Islands
(Britain)

Sweden   Finlan

Norway

enmark

Ireland

Great
Britain
and North
Ireland

ather-
ands

German Empire

Belgium

Bohemia/
Moravia   Slovakia

Northern-France

Hun

Liechtenstein
Switzerland

Vichy France

Croatia

Monaco

Italy   Montenegro

Portugal   Spain

Alba

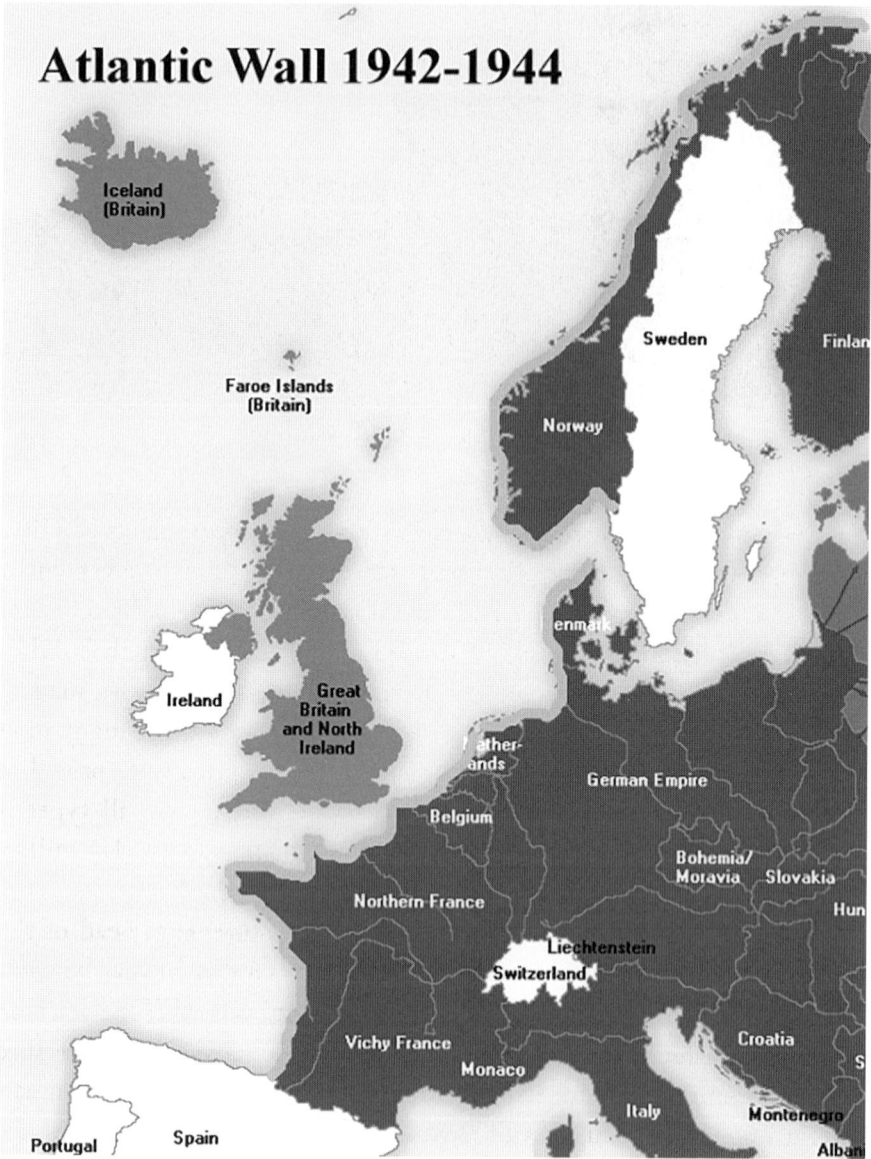

The *Atlantikwall* (yellow line) could have been the largest, single man-made structure ever built, greater even than the Great Wall of China.

greater even than the Great Wall of China. This herculean task was given to the best man available to Hitler – Fritz Todt, creator and head of *Organisation Todt*, OT.

Todt had extensive experience, as his organisation had built the *Westwall* or Siegfried Line along the French border and had built hundreds of

Massive gun emplacements over 'Gold' Beach, Normandy.

miles of autobahns in the pre-war years under the instructions of Hitler who had wanted a fast road system for the expeditious movement of troops across Germany. Todt had the knowledge, engineering skills and materials, but soon ran short of manpower when tasked with building the *Atlantikwall*, as it was called by the Germans. Nazi laws made it compulsory for German citizens to labour for the state, but many more hands were required and soon the concentration camps were providing the labour – slave labour. Most were Jews but there were all types of detainees, including prisoners-of war. By 1944, there were 1.4 million people working as slave-labour on the project.

By the end of 1941, Todt's successes and his position as head of this mighty engineering empire gave him the false impression that he could say what he wanted to Hitler. This was always a mistake in Nazi Germany and shortly after he told his boss that the war could never be won, he died mysteriously in a plane crash. Control of OT was given to the Minister for Armaments, Hitler's closest 'friend', Albert Speer (Ch.8).

Military control over the inspection, development and manning of the *Atlantikwall* was initially under *Generalfeldmarschall* von Rundstedt, commander in the west, but after the Allies raid on Dieppe in August 1942, Hitler became alarmed at the apparent weakness of the wall. His answer was then to make another mistake – he took Rommel, the great tank commander, away from the battlegrounds of North Africa, and then from his new command in the defence of northern Italy, and directed him to be General Inspector of the Western Defences. His orders were to make the fortified walls of *Festung Europa* that stretched all the way from Norway to Northern Spain, impenetrable – an impossible task, even for one as adaptable, skilful and resourceful as the 'Desert Fox' himself.

The first difficulty was, as ever, caused by the Führer himself. He confused the objective by dividing responsibility between Rommel and the aging and tired von Rundstedt. Both men had opposing ideas on how best it should be done. Rommel had been ordered by his Führer to create 3,800 kilometres of concrete walls, invasion-proof defences and gun emplacements to prevent any enemy gaining a foothold on the mainland of Europe. Rundstedt, on the other hand, was arguing that stationing large numbers of fast-moving Panzer groups in northern France, ready to race to any point of attack by road and rail, would have been a better strategy. Contradictory strategies were not unusual as Hitler often gave conflicting orders to parallel commanders, creating rivalry and causing confusion and wasted resources.

Neither of these plans could achieve Hitler's objective as it was physically impossible to man and gun every inch of coastline, and the roads and railways could never be relied upon due to constant sabotaging of the infrastructure by local resistance groups such as the *Maquis* (French Resistance).

So Hitler's *Festungen* theory failed. From the moment the Allies hit the Normandy beaches, the twentieth century version of medieval castle walls were quickly reduced to rubble. Bombardment from the massive guns of the 1,213 warships, the majority of which were Royal Navy battleships, cruisers and destroyers standing offshore, softened-up the *Atlantikwall* pill-boxes and gun emplacements perched on the sand dunes above the beaches of Sword, Gold, Utah and Omaha. Then the 4,000 landing craft, filled with the bravest of Allied soldiers, rushed the beaches. Despite taking high casualties at Omaha, the Allies soon broke through all the beach-lines and established toeholds on the mainland. By the end of June, just under one million Allied troops were firmly established in northern Normandy, well behind Hitler's *Festung* ramparts.

The D-Day invasion on 6 June 1944 clearly demonstrated that the *Festung Atlantikwall* had turned out to be a 2,400-mile-long failure. By the time the Allies had pushed all the German armies back across the Siegfried Line, it had cost Hitler around half a million men and thousands of tanks, guns and planes.

Hitler had made another big mistake, but not for the last time.

Festung – Moscow – Soviet Counter-Offensive

Hitler had failed to act decisively before. In late 1941 (Ch.16) he changed his original plan to take Moscow soon after the start of Operation Barbarossa. The German pincer attack had been thwarted because of the time this had given the Soviets to mount a massive counterattack on 5 December 1941 that resulted in the Chief of Staff of OKW, General Halder, and the gifted tank strategist, General Guderian, giving orders to withdraw to a more defendable line west of the Oka River. These orders were given without asking Hitler, so on 19 December Hitler appointed himself Supreme Commander of all German forces (Ch.18) and promptly rescinded the order. Hitler simply could not understand why it was, under any circumstances, better to withdraw to a defendable line, and his reaction to such a strategy was one of blind fury and obstinacy. Five years later at the Nuremberg trials Field Marshal Paul von Kleist described Hitler's mental state and his single-mindedness, telling the court it was -

> *'more of a problem for a psychiatrist than for a General…if you talked [to Hitler] for more than two hours and thought you had convinced him, he just began where you had started just as if you had never said a word.'* [8]

So, on 20 December 1941, in the midst of the most serious military setback so far in the war and against all the advice he was receiving from his most senior commanders, Hitler dismissed his commander-in-chief, von Brauchitsch, Panzer commanders von Bock, Hoepner and Strauss, and on Christmas Day, even his finest Panzer general, Guderian. They were all sent back to Berlin.

Now the Führer, as Supreme Commander was able to show his military *'genius'* without impediment. He ordered every soldier to *'stand or die'*, to hold his ground and to defend every patch by *'digging trenches with howitzer shells if needed'*. [98]

This was to be another *Festung*, despite the fact the ground was frozen, temperatures were well below freezing and that no winter supplies had been able to reach the front lines.

By 7 January 1942, the whole German army had been pushed back 100 miles from Moscow. It would cost Hitler a third of a million well-trained, battle-hardened troops and thousands of tanks, artillery guns, and fighter aircraft. Hitler's *Festung* policy had proved to be yet another big mistake.

Festung – Stalingrad – winter 1942–43

Perhaps Hitler's *Festungen* theory was reinforced in his mind when he witnessed the intransigence and resolve of the citizens of Leningrad that began when Army Group North attempted to take the city in September 1941. In what was to become one of the longest and most destructive sieges in history, the Russian people, held in contempt by Hitler as *untermensch*, finally defeated the Aryan soldier by holding out and suffering almost unimaginable deprivations for 872 days, until 27 January 1944 when they were relieved by a massive Red Army offensive.

But to put the *Festungen* theory into perspective – more citizens were killed in Leningrad than died in the combined bombing of Hamburg, Dresden, Hiroshima and Nagasaki. [92] Not that that statistic would have influenced Hitler, as he was never in any doubt that his military theories were infallible.

Five hundred miles south of Leningrad, in December 1942, the German Sixth Army had occupied 90 per cent of the near ruined city of Stalingrad, and then found themselves surrounded. To the great surprise of the Germans, the Soviets had amassed a new army under Zukhov – his masterplan for Operation Uranus was the complete encirclement of the city and simultaneous pincer attacks from the north and the south. The main defenders were not German but Romanian and Italian, and they were swiftly swept aside allowing the two points of the pincers to meet on 23 November at a place called Kalach. The German 275,000-strong Sixth Army was trapped in the city that Hitler had only just boasted to his nation that they had taken. [Ch.16]

At this moment, General Paulus knew the best course of action was to break out while there was still time. But Hitler refused his request saying *'whatever the circumstances, you must hold on to the Stalingrad position… everything that lies in my power is being done to help you in your heroic struggle.'* Hitler had ordered Manstein to ride to the rescue with his Army Group Don, which included two Panzer divisions and an infantry division. In addition, Hitler claimed, with the arrogant assurance of Göring, that his Luftwaffe would keep the Sixth Army supplied by air. Hitler again believed his blustering *Reichsmarschall* – despite his record of failures to supply troops in other *Festungen*.

Paulus knew he needed 750 tons of supplies every day – Göring promised 550 tons a day – but by January air-dropped less than 100 tons a day.

Despite Hitler's Chief of Staff, General Zeitzler, supporting Paulus's request, the Führer coldly ordered another *Festung,* telling him that losing Stalingrad was absolutely out of the question as the strategic effect would be a territorial loss that he knew Germany could never win back.

By Christmas, the situation was beyond hopeless, but Hitler and his propaganda minister – Goebbels – arranged a mocked-up radio message which sounded as if it was coming live from his troops in Stalingrad, to be broadcast to the German nation. In Stalingrad, the ground had frozen to minus 40C – too hard to dig and the men too weak to try, so frozen corpses were piled high to form protective barriers from the enemy. The ground was so hard that mortar shells bounced off and exploded in mid-air, causing terrible wounds. Russian snipers fired from the rubble of smashed buildings. The Volga had frozen over but for much of the past weeks it had been uncrossable due to chunks of floating ice.

By 16 December, Manstein's AGD were only 62 miles from Stalingrad, but Hitler again refused permission to Paulus to break out towards Manstein, and so Manstein, being a field marshal, ordered General Paulus to do so but it was to prove impossible as his men could hardly move due to exhaustion, lice infections, and frozen limbs. Daily rations were down to one small piece of frozen bread and watery soup with dead horses' bones in it.

There was almost no fuel either, so tanks were useless, and they probably would not have started anyway as the oil in their engines and gearboxes would have frozen too.

Those that could move tried desperately to get onboard one of the few aircraft that was able to make it out. Many were shot as they tried to board without permission and some men died as they fell from the tail-wings of the plane they had grabbed as it took off.

Paulus hand-wrote a pathetic letter to Manstein apologising that withdrawal could not be done; it began,

'Dear Field Marshal, in the circumstances I hope you will overlook the inadequacy of the paper and the fact that this letter is handwritten'. [8]

Stalingrad: Many soldiers froze to death where they lay.

Manstein's powerful AGD halted on 28 December, 35 miles from Stalingrad. It came under heavy attack from the south by Soviet forces, and Manstein knew he had no option but to withdraw before he too was cut-off. With the Sixth Army trapped in Stalingrad and AGD forced to turn back, this was the actual moment Stalingrad was lost without hope.

At the turn 1943, so many German soldiers were committing suicide that Paulus had to send a message to his men: '*suicide is forbidden as it is dishonourable.*' Most men's fingers were so badly swollen with frostbite anyway that they could not have pulled the trigger of a weapon.

One survivor, Colonel H.R. Dingler, later recalled: '*Everywhere lay the corpses of German soldiers… they had just died in the snow,*' but Hitler issued yet another order to Paulus: '*Surrender is forbidden… Sixth Army will hold their position to the last man and the last round….*'.

Hitler knew it was hopeless, but in his most desperate attempt to persuade Paulus to hold, he sent him a message promoting the general to field marshal. This was no honour, but a contemptuous way of telling him to shoot himself, as both men understood that no German field marshal had ever surrendered before.

It made no difference as at 7.35am on the morning of 31 January 1943, the new field marshal was captured in his bunker and soon surrendered the remains of his Sixth Army.

The Soviets took 91,000 prisoners, including 22 generals – the only survivors of the original 275,000. Only 9,000 ever returned to Germany years later, some not until 1955. It was victory for Russia but at the terrible cost of over a million casualties.

Hitler's largest *Festung* had cost both sides hugely in human lives, but crucially he had also lost 23 Axis divisions including 3 Panzer divisions, 13 infantry divisions and many other support troops. It was to have a decisive effect on the balance of power on the Eastern Front.

Far from admitting any error of judgement in demanding that Stalingrad become a *Festung*, Hitler issued a communiqué from OKH to the German people that the Sixth Army had '*fought shoulder to shoulder down to the last bullet…the sacrifice was not in vain.*' [103]

It may have been Hitler's biggest mistake of the whole war, but at exactly the same time as this failed *Festung*, Hitler had been demanding another one in the desert on the other side of the Mediterranean.

Festung – El Alamein, North Africa – November 1942

'*The Führer must be crazy!*' Field Marshal Rommel shouted to his Afrika Korps staff officer as he read the order he had just received from Hitler, 2,500 miles away, safe in his northern bunker, the *Wolfsschanze*. The Führer's order, or *Führerbefehl* of 3 November 1942, was unequivocal – '*Stand fast, yield not a yard of ground and throw every man and gun into the battle… victory or death.*' [100]

Rommel later wrote that the order was impossible and that he had, in fact, already begun withdrawing his Afrika Korps the night before. Rommel felt that such '*stand and die*' orders by the Führer were more to do with propaganda to the German public than with reality on the ground. At this stage, Rommel was a loyal and traditional German officer and would have found it difficult to disobey a directive from Hitler.

Twelve days before, Rommel's Afrika Korps had felt the first impact of General Montgomery's Eighth Army offensive that had, by November 1942, finally pushed the Germans into a position where they had to retreat or surrender.

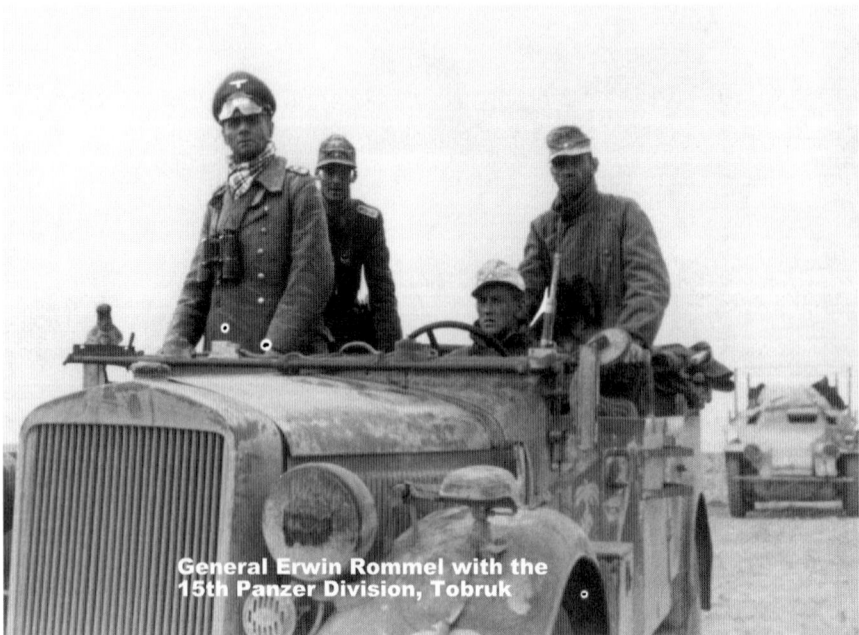

'*The Fuhrer must be crazy!*' Field Marshal Erwin Rommel shouted to his Afrika Korps Staff Officer as he read the order to '*stand and die*' that he had just received from Hitler. (*Shutterstock*)

General Montgomery's Eighth Army's resounding victory at El Alamein was recognised instantly by Churchill as a turning point of the war.

Rommel had lost 450 tanks and 1,000 guns during the Battle of El Alamein and the best he could do at this point was to withdraw what was left of his armour, fuel supply and field guns in as good order as possible.

This left him no choice but to leave behind 20,000 Italian troops and 10,000 German soldiers that included nine generals, almost a third of the Afrika Korps. [8]

The resounding victory for the Commonwealth soldiers of the Eighth Army at El Alamein was to become recognised as the turning point of the Western Allies' war against Nazi Germany.

Churchill, astute as ever, understood that very well. On 15 November, he ordered all church bells in Britain to ring out in celebration of the momentous occasion and he marked this turning-point moment of the war with his remarkably perceptive eloquence, telling the British people: '*This is not the end, nor is it the beginning of the end, but it may be the end of the beginning.*'

Rommel's army had already lost some 20,000 Axis troops killed or wounded in the battle but he knew he could retreat and still fight an effective rear-guard action along the 125 miles of North African coast road. On 8 November, the remnants of the Afrika Korps reached the first available port of Mersa Matruh, where Rommel was able to extricate only twenty tanks – all that was left of his hitherto all-conquering army of twelve Axis divisions. [101]

This was one big *Festung* mistake that Hitler may have ordered – but he did not get.

Festung Tunis 1943 – Hitler's '*fatally strategic blind spot*'.

Winston Churchill told the House of Commons in February 1943 that Hitler had a '*fatally strategic blind spot*'. By trying to hold on to the northern tip of Tunisia, '*It was*', said the prime minster, '*indeed, quite remarkable that he should be ready to run the risk and pay the price.*' Referring to Stalingrad and other hopelessly defended places he had observed in the recent past, Churchill said that he saw the same '*master's hand*' that had already '*brought upon the German armies, the greatest disaster they had ever suffered in all their military history*'. [8]

Churchill did not use the word *Festung*, but what he meant was that Hitler's narrow concept of defensive warfare was hinged on his *Festung* policy, and although this had been shown to be a very big mistake many times so far, Hitler was determined to apply it yet again to his quarter of a million beleaguered Afrika Korps trapped in northern Tunisia.

In the months after the battle of El-Alamein in October 1942, Rommel's Afrika Korps had been pushed steadily westwards, closely

Churchill, astute as ever, ordered all church bells in Britain to ring out in celebration of the momentous occasion, telling the British people 'This is not the end, nor is it the beginning of the end, but it may be the end of the beginning'.

pursued by Field Marshal Bernard Montgomery's Eighth Army, until they were squeezed into the northeast of Tunisia. The US First Army had also come a long way eastwards through Morocco from where they had landed in Operation Torch, and so the German army now found itself with its back to the Mediterranean at the port of Tunis in January 1943. German reinforcements had arrived there under the newly promoted General Hans von Arnim and many of them now bolstered Rommel's army too.

Rommel was able to make use of this new situation by applying his Napoleonic tactic of '*interior lines*'. Lines of movement and communication within an enclosed area are shorter and safer than those on the outside, hence as the area held by a defensive force shrinks, the interior line advantage held by that defensive force increases.

Rommel had earned the epithet the 'Desert Fox' from his earlier successes and he now intended utilizing his central position between the two converging Allied armies to strike and cripple them separately. Unfortunately, General Arnim was not made of such stuff as the brilliant, fast-thinking Rommel and there was a crucial delay of a couple of days, by which time Rommel had been ordered directly by Mussolini to attack northwards, not eastwards. Rommel objected, arguing that was '*bound to bring us up against strong enemy reserves*'. He was soon to be proved right.

On 19 February, Rommel sent his 10th and 21st Panzer Divisions, with their far superior Panzer IV and Tiger Tanks, to smash into the inexperienced American forces in the Kasserine Pass where they destroyed over 100 US M3 light tanks. The Americans retreated in disarray, but outright success was thwarted by von Arnim's reluctance to exploit the Allied confusion. Severe weather, difficult mountainous terrain and reorganised Allied resistance including an intense US air attack, forced Rommel to call off the attack and withdraw.

Meanwhile, the overall Allied commander, British Field Marshal Alexander had been fully informed of German plans thanks to the interceptions of *Ultra*, intelligence obtained by the code-breaking experts at the Government Code and Cypher School (GC&CS) at Bletchley Park.

By the time Rommel regrouped and made a fresh attack against Montgomery's army on 6 March, Monty had massively increased his strength with 400 tanks and 500 anti-tank guns in position, and the

Germans consequent loss of another 50 tanks was compounded by Rommel falling sick and being ordered to return to Berlin.

Shortly after this, General Patton took over as commander of the US II Corps and set off in attack of the Afrika Korps. With von Arnim now in overall command, misjudgements were made. Another attack by the British Eighth Army, in which the New Zealand Corps were supported by the 1st Armoured Division, led to the German troops being outflanked and forced back into the port of Tunis by 10 April 1943.

It was clear to all commanders that the Germans had only one way out – across the sea to Sicily or the Italian mainland. Rommel, though sick, went directly to ask the Führer personally to allow a withdrawal but, true to form, Hitler refused and once again issued a *stand or die* order. It was reported by Goebbels to the people of Germany that their hero-warrior Rommel was too sick to return to his beloved Afrika Korps but this was more likely used as a way of saving his reputation. [120]

For that short time, the conditions in Tunis had been perfect for rescuing around a third of a million Axis forces, for having them regroup in Italy and then being used effectively in the blocking of the imminent Allied invasion that OKW and its supreme commander, Adolf Hitler, knew was sure to happen soon.

Field Marshal Harold Alexander, commander in chief of all North African Forces, had used that short time well. Bringing to bear all his fighting forces that included American, French, New Zealand, Indian and British troops, and cleverly using an elaborate deception plan, he opened the final offensive on the Axis armies on 6 May with a massive artillery bombardment by more than 600 guns on a front less than two miles wide.

Supported by fighter bombers attacking their infantry and with their backs being shelled by Allied warships offshore, the enemy was paralyzed and demoralised. Within a week, the Axis forces had suffered 40,000 casualties before surrendering along with their commander General von Arnim. More than a quarter of a million of their bravest, experienced troops soon found themselves rounded up and spending the rest of the war in Allied PoW camps.

Over the three years, Hitler's North Africa campaign, launched in support of his friend and ally Mussolini, had resulted in a loss to the Axis of around one million men. The German army was now suffering from a manpower shortage that had come about primarily because of Hitler's insistence that *Festung* was always preferred to tactical withdrawal. Millions of his best troops had been lost needlessly and German replacements simply could not keep pace with such a rate of attrition.

Hitler's generals knew it was a big mistake, but few had the courage to mention it. Those who did were swiftly sacked or retired.

Festung Northern Italy; Monte Cassino and the Gustav Line

'Those indomitable parachute regiments that uselessly poured away their [German] blood at Cassino.'

Ronald Lewin, author. [10]

The staged German retreat northwards through Italy in 1944 was effectively one *Festung* after another. In fact, the whole of northern Italy, from September 1943, was for Hitler one massive *Festung*.

Following the great successes under Montgomery and Patton, when they swept the Germans and Italians out of North Africa, the Allied leaders met in Casablanca to discuss the way forward.

Stalin had declined the invitation to join Churchill, Roosevelt, de Gaulle and Giraud, so the conference went ahead without him. Churchill was adamant that the combined Allied armies in Tunisia should retain the initiative and move swiftly towards Italy, via Sicily; his view prevailed, and Operation Husky began on 10 July 1943.

Two weeks later, the buffoon dictator of Italy, Benito Mussolini was deposed and imprisoned. On 8 September, the new Italian government surrendered to the Allies, but in response Hitler immediately deployed sixteen new divisions into the Italian mainland, taking swift control of Rome and vowing to keep back the Allies as far south as possible.

For a moment, on 12 November, Hitler's optimism was refreshed when a crack SS paratrooper unit landed ten gliders on the top of the Abruzzi Mountain where Mussolini was being held captive. [115] In a daring mission, *Il Duce*, as Mussolini loved to be called, was rescued, and flown back to meet the Führer. But the Führer was taken aback when he saw him: gone was the arrogant, strutting dictator and in its place was a haggard and emotionally defeated former Fascist ally. Hitler said that he was *'extraordinarily disappointed'* seeing *Il Duce* in this state – a broken man. Soon after, Mussolini said, '*Seven years ago, I was an interesting person. Now, I am little more than a corpse… I am finished. My star has fallen. I have no fight left in me.*' [116]

Hitler then declared his relationship with Italy over, adding that Italians were all traitors and that German troops would make the mainland of Italy an impassable fortress, a *Festung* greater than any *Festung* ever seen.

Hitler's concept of a *Festung* was built on a romantic vision of the past in which he seemingly forgot that there were no massive artillery guns or bomber aircraft in medieval history.

The 'leg' of Italy, from the Tyrrhenian Sea to the Adriatic, was about 130 miles wide, but much of it was rugged mountains, sharp peaks, and fast-flowing rivers. Only a narrow strip of land ran along each coast, making the advancing armies slow and easy targets for the German guns placed on the higher ground. Adding to those difficulties was the dreadful weather over the winter of 1943/44 of heavy rain that created tracks of deep mud, and the expertly constructed defensive positions occupied by battle-hardened troops imbued with dogged determination to serve their – now quite mad – Führer to the bitter end.

The Germans were outstandingly good at rear guard actions that constantly delayed the attacking forces, and inflicted heavy tolls. The Allies had learned this during Rommel's retreat from El Alamein and were to experience it again in the weeks following the D-Day invasion as the Allies inched their way off the beaches and eastwards, yard by yard and lane by lane through the *bocage* (thick woodland and hedgerows) of Normandy.

Even as General Mark Clark led his Fifth US Army in Operation Avalanche across the sea from Messina to Salerno on 5 September 1943, and Montgomery led his British and Canadian Eighth Army over the Straits of Messina to Reggio in Operation Baytown, and the British 1st Airborne Division parachuted onto the mainland at Taranto in Operation Slapstick, the German commander for Italy, Field Marshal Albert Kesselring, had already withdrawn the bulk of his forces northwards to where he had created the first of three *Festung* lines of walls and battlements.

The key line was the Gustav Line. It stretched 100miles from Garigliano in the west to the Sangro in the east, across the Apennines, and hinged on the ancient Benedictine monastery of Monte Cassino. [117]

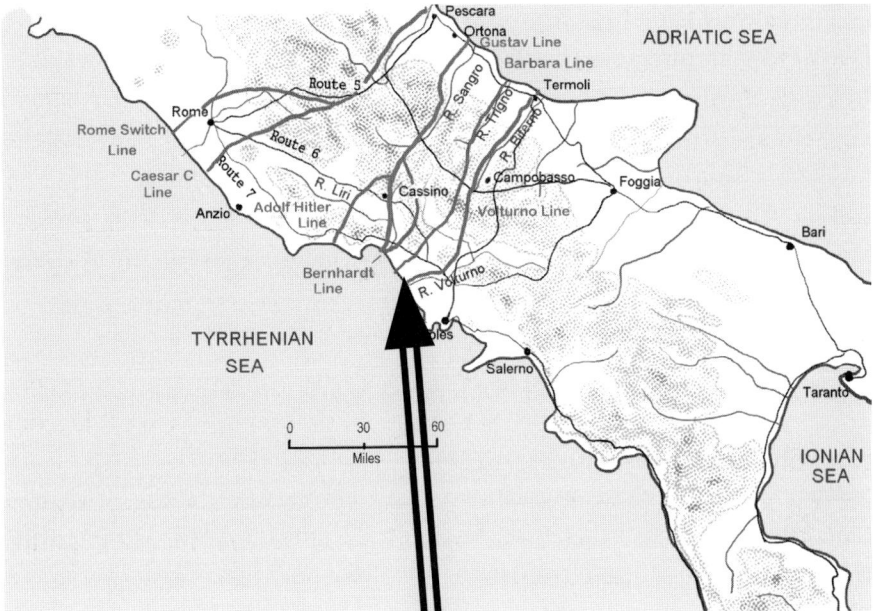

The Monte Cassino monastery was the hinge on the Gustav Line '*Festung*'. The Allies had to resort to bombing and reducing the magnificent, historic building to a pile of rubble.

The Gustav Line held out for over four months. Despite his instinctive love of fine architecture the reduction of a magnificent, historic building to a pile of rubble, was a price Hitler did not care about. Nor did he feel any remorse at the 20,000 of his own soldiers who lost their lives and the loss of his Tenth Army in what was another hopeless *Festung*.

The Allies were being delayed but were able to bypass this *Festung* by mounting a successful seaborne invasion, landing just south of Rome at Anzio.

Anzio – '*dig-in and wait*' – US General Mark Clark

The Germans were caught by surprise when 50,000 British and American troops, 5,000 vehicles that included heavy artillery, and lots of Sherman tanks landed on the beaches at Anzio on 22 January 1944. Despite this, the commander of the US Fifth Army, General Mark Clark, hesitated. He had been surprised at the recent Salerno invasion, where the Germans had responded swiftly and almost succeeded in throwing the Americans back into the sea. As a result, he had sent a message to his VI Corps commander Major General John Lucas to '*dig-in and wait… don't stick your neck out Johnny – I did at Salerno and got into trouble.*' [119] Both men now failed to recognise this key opportunity and decided instead to consolidate their positions. This really was a crucial, missed moment as the road to Rome was virtually open and it is very likely that another general, such as Patton, would not have hesitated. The experienced Kesselring moved fast, as always, and soon the Germans had set up a massive counter-offensive that effectively trapped the Allies on the Anzio coastline. By the end of January, the Germans had nearly 70,000 soldiers near Anzio with more speeding to the area. When Churchill received the report, he was both furious and frustrated, and he scathingly remarked to his chiefs of staff on 31 January '*I had hoped that we were hurling a wildcat onto the shore but all we got was a stranded whale!*' [8] Lucas, who one journalist described as having '*the round face and grey moustache of a kindly country solicitor*' had indeed failed to stick his neck out. He was immediately sacked and replaced by the starkly different, colourful and '*dashing*' Major General Lucian Truscott. [8]

The German recovery meant that some of the worst prolonged fighting of the Second World War ensued in what was reminiscent of First World

War trench warfare. The British called the trenches, wadis. Conditions were primitive, wet, and muddy. The Allies remained locked in at Anzio, unable to break out for four bitter months, and the casualty rate for both sides was truly terrible.

Meanwhile, the commander of British forces, General Alexander, made a third and remorseless attack to breakthrough from the west in support of the US Fifth Army. As the British 8th Army pushed up through the valley, outflanking the Monte Cassino defences, the Canadian Corps penetrated German defences in another valley, and on 17 May 1944, the Polish Corps made the final courageous assault that took the monastery and resulted in the collapse of the Gustav Line.

This was a second perfect opportunity for US General Mark Clark to advance swiftly and trap the still sizeable German army to prevent them retreating to a new *Festung*, known as the Gothic Line, north of Florence. Instead, Clark saw the glory in liberating Rome and that is what he did on 4 June 1944, leading a triumphal march into the capital. The Germans had, in fact, already moved out of the Eternal City so Clark's decision remains, to this day, one that raises heated debate. Churchill was once again furious, but Clark never got the glory for which he had hoped, as on the following day all eyes were on the D-Day landings in Normandy.

The Allied slog northwards continued slowly, with each hill, town and junction defended as fiercely as the one before. The northern Italy *Festung* held out over the long winter, but it was a never-ending mistake by Hitler as he was needlessly losing large numbers of manpower and equipment when the Allies were landing on the Normandy beaches and the Soviets were pressing remorselessly westwards. If Hitler had understood the art of warfare, he would never have allowed this to happen.

A bold plan months earlier could have created a position of strength from which he could have negotiated an armistice long before he lost half a million casualties in the Italian campaign, half a million in Operation Bagration (Ch.16) and another half a million or more after Operation Overlord (Ch.20). These repeated strategic mistakes all ended with the ruined city of Berlin being defended in April 1945 by old men and boys.

Festung Northern Italy was another big mistake.

Festungen on the Eastern Front

Operation Bagration 1944

Immediately after D-Day, Hitler failed to re-organise his Eastern Front by creating new, well entrenched, and realistically defendable lines. The German armies were spread out over a front of more than 1,500 miles. Even before the Soviet offensive known as Operation Bagration, Germany had already lost more than forty divisions that included almost one and a half million casualties.

Distracted by the events and deceptions of D-Day, Hitler was about to make one of his biggest military mistakes.

Fooled by Operations Bodyguard and Fortitude (Ch.20), he neglected to prepare for what he surely should have anticipated – Stalin's counterattack from the east in support of the D-Day invasion in the west. In fact, it was only sixteen days after the British, Canadian, and American forces landed on the beaches of Normandy that Soviet forces launched the even more massive Operation Bagration, named by Stalin in honour of the Russian Marshal of the 1812 campaign that pushed the million-strong French '*Grand Armee*' all the way back to Paris. Bagration would push the million-strong German army all the way back to Berlin.

Operation Bagration was on such a massive scale that it came as a great shock to Hitler and his generals as they could not believe that the Russians had been able to build-up such an immense force of men, weapons and equipment in such a short time. Of course, Stalin's men and women were recruited from a huge, seemingly infinite population, but his tanks, trucks, and many of his weapons had been built in Britain and America and shipped to the northerly Russian ports of Murmansk and Archangel. They had got there thanks mainly to the heroic Allied merchant seamen who risked their lives as they transported millions of tons of materiel through severe ice, storms, mines and U-boat attacks. By the summer of 1944, the Soviets had one and a half million guns, in a line, from Smolensk through Minsk to Moscow.

Stalin's first intention was to destroy German Army Group Centre, then advance straight to Berlin. To make this all the more possible, the Luftwaffe had been withdrawn to deal with the Allied troops invading Normandy, leaving the Soviets with full control of the sky.

On 24 June, the Third Panzer Army was wiped out as the First Belorussian Army emerged from the mist of the Pripet Marshes to start the monumental attack. Then the Soviet forces advanced over a front 250 miles wide and 100 miles deep.

Some large cities were recaptured instantly and hundreds of thousands of German troops were encircled, overwhelmed, and taken prisoner. They would then be sent on death-marches towards distant prisons in Siberia, and most would never see their Fatherland again.

At this point, the Germans should have had a Plan-B and made fast, strategic withdrawals to pre-designated defensive lines, but that option had

СТАЛИН
ВЕДЁТ НАС К ПОБЕДЕ!

Stalin told his generals to ignore Hitler's *Festungen* – leaving thousands of German troops isolated and trapped – only to be swept up later!

never been envisaged. Instead, Hitler's prescribed policy of 'no retreat – no surrender', known as *Festung* was the only option. He refused to listen to the pleas of his wiser, experienced commanders.

The Russians had a simple answer to Hitler's fortress cities, or *Festungen*, such as Mogilev and Bobruysk – they ignored them! Giving each a wide berth left thousands of German troops isolated and trapped, to be swept up at a later date. [8] The western territories of the Soviet Union were so vast that individual cities and towns became almost insignificant in the long-term strategy. What mattered was the recovery of thousands of square miles of the Motherland and the relentless push westwards. Within ten days, Army Group Centre had effectively ceased to exist, thereby creating a large gap between Army Group North and Army Group South, due entirely to the fortified localities demanded in Führer Order No.11. [8]

Not at any point did Hitler stop to ask his very experienced commanders what they thought. If he had visited the Eastern Front more often, rather than hunkering down in his *Wolfsschanze*, he may have seen for himself the endless failures of his idea – but he did not.

Operation Bagration Battleplan. At no point did Hitler stop to ask his very experienced commanders what they thought. His mistakes simply compounded and he just ranted and raved all the louder, sacking and replacing any General who lost ground, did not hold out his designated fortresses (*festungen*) or even suggest a tactical withdrawal. The effect was quick and clinical as the Soviets soon recognised the German weaknesses and over the next two months of Bagration, the Germans were to lose 11,000 men every day, killed, wounded or captured.

This was the antithesis to Churchill's command style. It is true that the great man often had a huge personal influence and, at times, could be fairly credited for creating, or promoting, new ideas to his generals. It is true he would have loved to have been leading the charge in every battle of the war – but when it came to strategy, he always came down on the side of his best advisers.

Hitler's incompetence as an army commander was not only recognised by his own commanders but also by the Soviet leadership and the British. Shortly after the start of Bagration, Churchill, as perceptive as ever, told the House of Commons -

'The Russian success has been somewhat aided by the strategy of Herr Hitler, or Corporal Hitler. Even military idiots find it difficult not to see faults in his actions.' [91]

A few weeks later, Churchill reassured his colleagues and the British public that Hitler was now an asset to Allied victory by twisting the knife of ridicule, when he said –

'We must not forget that we owe a great debt to the blunders – the extraordinary blunders – of the Germans. I hate to compare the... great Emperor and warrior Napoleon to Hitler... a squalid butcher... but both were temperamentally unable to give up the tiniest scrap of any territory... and by obstination at every point from Stalingrad, [Hitler] has stripped himself of the power to concentrate in main strength for the final struggle.' [91]

By August 1944, the Russians were undoing everything the Germans had done to them. Hitler had made many big *Festungen* mistakes, but many others were happening elsewhere.

Normandy and Falaise

In the six weeks following Operation Neptune, the D-Day landing on 6 June 1944, the Allies established their foothold in Normandy, taking the port of Cherbourg, in the Cotentin Peninsula. The German High Command had been expecting the invasion to land at Pas de Calais, falling for the elaborate deception plans over the previous months of Operation Fortitude (Ch.20). Hitler had been personally fooled. Indeed, so convinced was he that he had insisted his main forces, in particular his Panzer divisions, remain stationed in the far north-east of France, not to be moved without his explicit order. This mistake by Hitler had been a major factor in allowing the Allied forces the crucial time to gain control of the whole of Normandy by the middle of July 1944.

The German Seventh Army was responsible for holding northern France, and as they recovered from the shock of 6 June, were doing an impressive job holding the Allies' advance towards their prize target – Paris. As in every other theatre of war, the German forces showed remarkable skill and innovation in defence, and always seemed able to perform counter-attacks with precision and quality. This was the situation at the city of Caen, the gateway out of Normandy towards Paris.

After six weeks of fierce fighting, Montgomery's British and Canadian Second Army had tried in vain to push Rommel's forces out of the city, but finally the US First Army, under General Bradley, reached the south of Caen and the Allies were able to mount Operation Cobra on 25 July.

This situation had simultaneously compounded several crises for the German High Command. Hitler had many times shown his inability to cope with military setbacks, and his reaction was again true to form – sack the commander and order his army to '*stand and die*'. [8]

Before Hitler could sack him, however, General Dollman, commander of the Seventh Army, died or more likely shot himself. The Führer's most senior commander in the west, the 70-year-old but very experienced von Rundstedt, urged Hitler to allow him to make plans for a withdrawal from Normandy and set a prepared defensive line along the River Seine. Hitler would hear none of it, and immediately flew over to meet Rundstedt and Rommel at their command bunker in northern France. The two field marshals were blunt with their Führer, telling him massive reinforcements were needed, but as none were available, a rapid withdrawal to a strong defensive line was the only way to prevent defeat. Alternatively, they bravely told their Supreme Commander, he should look for a political solution to end the war, which Rommel told him bluntly was 'unwinnable'. [128]

Hitler ignored their advice, insisting upon a '*fanatical*' defence based on his own *festungen* strategy and which included counter-attacks with whatever was available. Rommel warned Hitler of the inevitable collapse of the German defences but was rebuffed. Soon after, Rundstedt and Rommel were summoned to Berchtesgaden. They were again rebuffed. On his return, Rundstedt allowed units of his forces to withdraw out of range of Allied naval gunfire that was decimating his forces. He notified OKW of this decision but his orders were instantly countermanded and Hitler relieved him of his command, replacing him with Field Marshal Gunther von Kluge. [129]

Kluge was a veteran commander from the Russian front and soon recognised the reality of the situation. There was nothing different he could do and shortly after the 20 July assassination attempt on Hitler's life he was viewed a suspect, although he had nothing to do with the conspiracy. At the beginning of August, he shot himself.

Hitler then moved his most successful general – Field Marshal Model – for the third time in 1944, to take command of AGB. Model had already earned the nickname of 'fireman' as he was now Hitler's first choice 'to the rescue' when one of the other generals – to his mind – failed. Hitler, as usual, replaced his commanders instead of discussing with his generals and looking at the real reasons behind his failings and setbacks.

The week before Operation Cobra began, Rommel was returning from Sepp Dietrich's I SS Panzer Corps command post to his headquarters at *La Roche-Guyon*. On the N179 his car was strafed with 20mm cannon shells by a Canadian pilot in a Spitfire from 412 Squadron. Rommel had been sitting in the front, by his driver, Daniel. In the back were staff members Captain Lang, Major Neuhaus and Feldwebel Hoike (who was there specifically as an aircraft lookout). The car crashed into a ditch, and Rommel smashed his head against the windscreen. His driver was killed, the others slightly injured. When Rommel returned to Berlin the bomb plot against Hitler on 20 July had just failed (Ch.11). Rommel had not been involved but his name was mentioned by others under torture by the Gestapo and the Führer ordered his erstwhile favourite and most successful general to end his own life. Hitler was so afraid of the demoralising effect this could have on the German peoples' folk-hero that he made sure Rommel was honoured with a state funeral and buried with full military honours.

Operation Cobra opened with a devastating air attack in clear conditions. Through the gap that had opened, sped the US First and Third Armies, the latter led by Patton, who then swung round and encircled the Germans in Normandy, from the rear.

Both the British and the Americans were then able to advance west out of Caen towards Falaise. By mid-August even Hitler could not fail to see the inevitable and he finally gave permission for a withdrawal from Normandy.

The only route of escape lay through a gap between the converging American and British spearheads at Falaise. Even in retreat, the Germans showed remarkable cool-headedness. Despite being under constant attack from the recently arrived Polish 1st Armoured Division, the remnants of the German Seventh Army and Fifth Panzer Army succeeded in breaking through to their next defensive line at the River Seine.

The cost of Hitler's *Festung* mistake this time was around half a million men [120] along with thousands of tanks, guns and aircraft abandoned or destroyed.

Festungen – in Eastern Europe

Greece 1944

Hitler greatly overestimated the likely resistance by the Greek forces in the spring of 1941 and sent in twenty-nine divisions that overwhelmed a weak enemy in short order. Greek resistance built up over subsequent years, but it had only small guerrilla-type victories due to their inability to unite the left- and right-wing groups of resistance fighters. There was no longer a Greek army, but in October 1944 Hitler had kept Army Group F in Greece instead of using them to defend Yugoslavia from the Soviet onslaught and their subsequent advance through Bulgaria and Romania during Operation Bagration.

As a result Greece was cut-off. Hitler had again ordered Greece to be a *Festung* and by the time a withdrawal was permitted Axis troops had lost around 30,000 casualties. Over the whole occupation, however, the Greek population shrank by almost a million, 400,000 of whom had starved due the resulting famine and 70,000 of whom were Jews who had been sent to concentration or death camps in Poland.

Budapest 1944–45

The siege began on 26 December 1944 when Budapest, capital city of Hungary, was occupied by 80,000 Axis troops, half of whom were Hungarian. During the siege, about 38,000 civilians died through starvation or military action. Hitler had declared Budapest a *Festung* and that it was, as always, to be defended *'to the last man'*. However, the Luftwaffe's glider flights that were bringing in some supplies had stopped and, after a failed attempt at a mass exodus of the city, the Axis commander unconditionally surrendered on 13 February 1945. Sadly, that was not the end, as the long siege of Budapest had so frustrated the Soviets that they took terrible revenge on the citizens with mass raping [93] and indiscriminate killing. Half a million Hungarians and German prisoners were transported to the gulags of distant Siberia, never to return.

Kurland Pocket 1944–45

The thirty-three German divisions of Army Group Kurland (formerly called Army Group North) were made up of the 200,000 troops of the Sixteenth and Eighteenth Army. As Soviet forces began to surround northwest Latvia, Chief of Staff Guderian urged Hitler to allow the evacuation of AGK, but he refused and another *Festung* was created. Hitler said he needed that part of the Baltic coast for imports of Swedish iron-ore, and it was also where one of his new 'wonder weapons' (Ch.21), the super-submarine Type XXI, was being tested. These were reasonable strategic arguments but they were belied by Hitler's fantasy that a well-equipped force was soon to be needed as a springboard for a new offensive. [94]

The Kurland pocket was then treated as a massive PoW camp by the Soviets right up to the end of the war. About 180,000 German troops, including 42 generals, were taken into captivity. Most were turned over to the NKVD and then disappeared to Russian prison camps in the Valdai Hills.

Breslau 1945

Breslau was then the capital city of Lower Silesia in Prussia (now in Poland). The German occupying forces prepared for a *Festung* siege by first sending out on foot all civilian women and children into the open countryside. It was January, the snow was deep, and the temperature at night was minus 20C. Few of the many thousands survived. The Germans, however, kept the local cigarette factory busy by producing more than half a million cigarettes every day. This was no doubt appreciated by the troops who were under constant fire from the Soviets, right up until the eventual surrender of Breslau on 06 May 1945.

The Final *Festung – Der Führerbunker* – April/May 1945

Hitler's Berlin Bunker, the *Führerbunker*, was no underground hotel. It was fifteen metres deep under the Old Chancellery, but it had no more than the most basic of utilities and comforts. Its greatest shortcomings were, of course, its mutual inaccessibility between the Supreme Command centre and the generals out in the fields of battle. Designed with the protection of the Führer as its principal objective, more priority had been given to the thickness of the concrete and supply of water and air than to the quality of the telecommunications with the Commanders of the remaining troops above ground.

As a *Festung* then, Hitler's Berlin Bunker could only partially fulfil its remit, as although it could certainly hold out for a time, it was a lost cause as a base for any future counter-offensive. As a fortress under attack, it was never going to be rescued by the Cavalry at the last minute, akin to Custer's Last Stand.

By the end of 1943, Hitler had very reluctantly accepted the loss of Stalingrad, the failure to take Moscow, and the huge tank losses at

Der Führerbunker was no underground hotel. It was fifteen metres deep under the Old Chancellery but it had no more than the most basic of utilities and comforts.

Designed with the protection of the Führer as its objective, more priority had been given to the thickness of the concrete and supply of water and air than to the quality of the telecommunications between the Commanders of the remaining troops above ground and the Führer deep below ground.

Kursk. Hitler had great difficulty believing that a battle was lost, only that it was a stumbling block and that his superior Aryan soldiers would ultimately prevail against the inferior Slav *untermensch*. It is surprising then that on 3 November, he issued Führer Directive No.51 [121] telling his senior generals that the 'east', by which he meant the vast area of land between Poland and Moscow, was so vast that Germany could afford to lose some of it without suffering a mortal blow – '*The threat from the East remains*' – he declared – '*but an even greater danger looms in the West: the Anglo-American landing!*' This reality had been driven home by the 'intelligence' OKW was receiving from their network of spies, some real but most 'fake' (Ch.20), convincing him of a massive build-up of Allied forces and materiel on the mainland of Britain and the imminent invasion of the European continent. '*If the enemy succeeds here,*' said the Führer, '*consequences of staggering proportions will follow immediately.*' He concluded, '*I can no longer justify weakening the West in favour of other theatres of war and have therefore decided to strengthen our defences in the West.*' [200]

In late 1943, Hitler wasted the proven battle skills of his most trusted commander, Field Marshal Rommel, when he gave him the job of overseeing the inspection and completion of the Atlantic Wall. Reich Minister Goebbels made great use of this propaganda opportunity by printing photographs in the press of massive concrete emplacements along the continental coastline, from where huge naval guns pointed out menacingly towards Britain.

Rommel, after a thorough inspection of the work that had been done over the previous two and more years, was appalled. He wrote in secret to a confidant that the '*The Wall*' was nothing more than '*a figment of Hitler's cloud-cuckoo-land…*'. [122]

The German public may have felt reassured but senior commanders such as General Hans von Salmuth of the Fifteenth Army in the Pas de Calais and Normandy knew better when he wrote to OKW in Berlin declaring, '*The Atlantic Wall… is like a thin and fragile cord.*'

Hitler clearly shared his generals' fears, although he would never allow them to express them, as he had already made sure that he would be the last one to die. There are very few credits that can be attributed to the Führer, but it is fair judgment to say that he was always prepared to 'go down with the ship' if all was lost. He despaired at any soldier who surrendered and considered all defeated, dead, or captured soldiers to be despicable cowards – a maxim he would apply to his own situation later in his *Führerbunker*. Nevertheless, he did all he could to have the final *Festung* built for what he clearly understood would one day be his 'last stand'.

Hitler had other bunker buildings during the war, the best known of which was the *Wolfsschanze*, or Wolf's Lair, in Poland; it was there, in July 1944, where Hitler came closest to being assassinated. It was mainly above ground and made of reinforced concrete which, ironically, would have actually caused his death by compression had the bomb gone off inside the bunker instead of in the temporary wooden hut nearby (Ch.11).

The Berlin bunker was built as a second-level air-raid shelter when Allied bombing increased over the capital. The upper bunker had been completed before the war started, but '*another deeper one was constructed in 1944, 28 feet below ground, directly under the Reich Chancellery, with the explicit purpose of keeping the Führer safe while still in control*'. [123]

The roof was ten feet thick, and all passageways from the thirty small rooms led to the main building with an emergency exit up to the Reich Chancellery garden. There were rooms for communications, conferences, guards and utilities, but Hitler had his own small suite of rooms, all modestly furnished, including a separate bedroom for Eva Braun. Of all his 'henchmen' (Ch.8) only his razor-sharp minded propaganda minister, Joseph Goebbels, and Hitler's closest, most sycophantic personal secretary, Martin Bormann, had their own dedicated rooms. There was, however, a special room for Hitler's doctor as, by this time, Hitler was a *'gibbering super-junky'*. [124] One entry in the diary of Dr. Morell reads, *'I cancelled [Hitler's] injections today, to give the previous puncture holes a chance to heal.'* [124]

Hitler had spent little time in the *Führerbunker* up until January 1945; after that, it became his 'home'. Except for some military meetings in an undamaged wing of the Chancellery, Hitler spent the rest of his time in the small, concrete walled rooms, deep below ground.

The erstwhile mighty *Führer, des Feldherr*, Leader of the Third Reich and acclaimed *'greatest Commander of all time'* [15] could do no more than rant to the backdrop of the constant hum of diesel generators, the buzz and clatter of the telex machine, the whiff of oil fumes and dampness, and the stale air of a basic air-conditioning system in which always hung the peculiar mixed smells of cooking, sanitation, and human bodies.

The other constant through April was the booming and tremor of bombs and artillery shells landing above the *Führerbunker*. As the ground shook, so did Hitler's left arm; not through fear but from his noticably deteriorated health. All news coming into the Bunker was bad, no forces were left for the omnipotent commander in chief to order into further destruction, and several generals were sacked or condemned as a traitor and shot. Somehow, in all this depressing pressure, Hitler was still rational enough to plan his own suicide. At the end of April 1945 Hitler dictated his last will to his typist-secretary, Traudl Junge. It contained no appeal for mercy; no hint of reproach; and no recognition of the hell, death, and destruction that he, personally, had brought upon the German people. He did not ask for forgiveness nor give any hint of atonement.

Instead, he claimed that he had neither wanted war, nor started it, and that all blame rested now, as in the beginning, with the Jews, with the Bolshevik traitors and, surprisingly, with his own generals who had failed him. As Führer of the German people, he would never flee Berlin and here he would make his final stand against those same enemies, taking his own life only at the final moment.

He began in a strangely reflective frame of mind. '*I die with a happy heart,*' he told his private secretary, '*and aware of the immeasurable deeds and achievements of our soldiers at the front, our women at home, the achievements of our farmers and workers and the work, unique in history, of our youth who bear my name.*'

Hitler then snapped out of this uncharacteristically romantic mood and back to business, as he then went on to '*expel the former Reichsmarschall Hermann Göring from the party and deprive him of all rights which he may enjoy… and I appoint in his place Grossadmiral Dönitz, President of the Reich and Supreme Commander of the Armed Forces… before my death I expel the former Reichsführer-SS and Minister of the Interior, Heinrich Himmler, from the party and from all offices of State*'. [125]

On 28 April, Hitler had received a letter from his Deputy Führer, Hermann Göring, offering to take over as leader and informing him that his erstwhile most dedicated henchman, Heinrich Himmler, had been in touch with the Allies offering to negotiate surrender terms. These betrayals were, to an already shattered Hitler, perhaps the last straws.

The actual Battle of Berlin had started on 16 April 1945 as Soviet forces gradually surrounded the capital city of Germany. The Führer's 56th birthday was four days later but he looked, physically and mentally, decades older. He was able to take a short walk to the Chancellery garden where he was filmed handing an Iron Cross medal to a boy aged about 12. This was a stark manifestation of the reality of what was now his last line of defence – boys, many from the Hitler Youth movement, and old men, the best of which were veterans of the First War. One armed with a *Panzerfaust* – a lightweight, single shot, anti-tank weapon – the rest had any weapon they could acquire – some had none. This was Hitler's last fortress of defence, his final *Festung*. Their duty now was to hold back over 2.5 million Soviet troops, equipped with 6,250 tanks and 40,000 artillery pieces that had all been assigned by Stalin to capture the city. [126]

Every day over the next two weeks bad news poured into the *Führerbunker*. Sometimes Hitler dismissed the reports with little thought, and at other times he ranted about the incompetence of his generals. On the afternoon of 29 April, he found out that his friend and ally – Benito

The ruined city of Berlin being defended in April 1945, street by street, by old men and boys.

Mussolini – had been executed by Italian partisans. Mussolini and his mistress Clara Petacci had been captured while trying to cross into Switzerland and summarily machine-gunned against a stone wall that surrounded a villa overlooking the beautiful Lake Como. Their bodies were driven to Milan where their corpses were abused by people who spat on them, fired shots at them, urinated on them and then hung them by their heels, upside down on a metal frame in front of a petrol station. The corpses were later cut down and thrown into the gutter, where they were further mocked and abused. [8] There can be little doubt that this deeply shocked Hitler; could the same fate await him and Eva Braun?

Hitler immediately ordered Dr Haase to test the cyanide capsules he had received from an SS physician. One capsule was given to Blondi, Hitler's much-loved Alsatian dog; she died instantly.

In the early hours of the following day, 30 April, the last line of German forces defending the outer city – the Twelfth Army, the Ninth Army, the LVI Panzer Corps, and the remnants of the Luftwaffe – each reported their failure to hold their lines and requested permission to break out as they would have exhausted their ammunition by midnight. For almost the first time in his life, Hitler did not refuse.

Just after 1 am, Adolf Hitler married Eva Braun in a small civil ceremony in the *Führerbunker*. There was a short celebration with champagne for the small wedding party, but not for Hitler who was strictly teetotal. He then went off and by 4 am he had finished dictating his will and testament to his secretary and all the documents were finally signed as witnesses by Goebbels and Bormann. [15] An exhausted Adolf and a tragically happy Eva then retired to bed as Herr and Frau Hitler.

The next morning, but still 30 April, Hitler emerged around 11 am to be told that Soviet forces were less than 500 metres from the bunker. After lunch the couple said goodbye to all the bunker staff, the secretaries, some officers and to Goebbels and Bormann. At 2.30 pm they went together into Hitler's personal study.

The new husband and wife sat quietly for almost an hour – Eva sat with her knees up on the sofa, Hitler beside her. She held a cyanide capsule between her teeth and Hitler did the same. Hitler had his own pistol, a Walther PPK, 7.65 in his right hand, and at 3.30 pm he placed the barrel to his right temple and they both bit into their capsules. At that same moment, Hitler pulled the trigger. Eva's head slumped over the left side

Mussolini and his mistress Clara Petacci were captured and summarily machine-gunned against a stone wall. Their corpses were abused by people who spat on them, fired shots at them, urinated on them and then hung them by their heels on a metal frame in front of a petrol station. Hitler was then convinced it would be his fate too, so he took his own life first, soon afterwards.

of the sofa; Hitler fell forward, his head falling onto the small table in front of him. The pistol dropped to the floor, by his feet.

Such was the final *Festung* of the Third Reich. A German Empire promised by Hitler was now in ruins, its enemies at the door.

Hitler's own words may haunt him: *Anyone can deal with victory; only the mighty can bear defeat… life doesn't forgive weakness… Germany will either be a world power or will not be at all.*'

Germany surrendered unconditionally on 2 May 1945. The '*Thousand Year Third Reich*' promised by Hitler had lasted just twelve years.

Now the extraordinarily lucky but fatally flawed leader was no more.

Chapter 20

Operation Bodyguard 1944

'There are two ways to be fooled; believe what isn't true or refuse to believe what is true.'

Kierkegaard, 1850

At a Führer conference in 1943, Hitler told his top generals and his henchmen *'If we are not deceived, the west is where the decisive landing battles will be fought.'* Later he told them, with absolute certainty that the Allied landings would be on the Pas de Calais beaches.

He then reminded them, with no hint of doubt in his own infallibility, *'Thank God I have a good nose for such things and can usually anticipate these developments beforehand.'*

It was not, however, his nose that was providing the predictions but the constant stream of what he was sure was top grade 'intelligence' passed to him by *Abwehr*, the military intelligence service of the Wehrmacht. Hitler had certainly got it right when he qualified his speech with the words, *'if we are not deceived'*, because that was exactly what he, his generals and, most of all, the *Abwehr* were being. They had been receiving from their network of spies in England some real, but mostly 'fake' information. In Operation Bodyguard, the most astonishing deception plan ever, Britain's MI5 had been feeding a network of 'turned' German spies carefully constructed information that assured German intelligence of imminent invasion at the Pas de Calais area.

Hitler then correctly prophesised *'If the enemy succeeds… consequences of staggering proportions will follow immediately.'* [200]

Deception

Deception is one of the oldest tactics in military history. In 530 BC, in his book on military strategy – *The Art of War* – Sun Tzu wrote – *'all warfare is based on deception.'* [111]

To carry it out successfully on a battlefield, during a battle, is in itself a very admirable act, but to make a deception plan that was to cover a large area of northern Europe, involve hundreds of thousands of troops, weapons, vehicles, boats and planes and then to maintain that deception from a well-placed, highly intelligent enemy for more than a year, has to be the most remarkable piece of military shenanigans ever performed.

A deception plan sets out to trick the enemy into believing what is not true so the first consideration is to ask – what is the enemy most likely to think you will do?

This was perhaps the easiest part of the trick because Hitler and his top Werhmacht commanders were already predisposed to believing the invasion would be at the Pas de Calais because, as Julius Caesar observed, *'Men in general are quick to believe that which they wish to be true.'* [110]

The Allied planners knew, from the start, that they would have to hold and control the enemy's attention and focus on that one piece of land that is the closest point from the southeast tip of England to the mainland of Europe.

So successful was the deception that, on the morning of 6 June 1944, as 150,000 British, Canadian, and American troops crossed the English Channel in Operation Overlord, heading for the Normandy coast, there was not one Luftwaffe plane in the skies, no German warships in the Channel and no U-boats lurking under the water. The vast bulk of the German army in the west was stationed 300 miles away in the Pas de Calais area. The north coast of France was manned mainly by coastal defence troops, thinly spread along the two hundred miles of beaches, bays and inlets.

At that very moment, Rommel, the man appointed by Hitler to oversee the building and security of a six-mile-deep defensive wall from Norway to the Bay of Biscay was in his home town in Germany, celebrating his wife's birthday whilst Adolf Hitler, the Commander-in-chief of all German forces, was having a lie-in, fast asleep in his bed in the Berghof on the southern Alps. None of his guards had the courage to wake him, as he had been up late the night before chatting about 'old-times' with Goebbels.

Operation Overlord, the Anglo-American plan to invade mainland Europe had, in principle, been the main point of discussion, and debate, between Britain and the USA since the latter committed to war in Europe in December 1941, three days after Pearl Harbor (Ch.17).

For Overlord to succeed it needed a number of factors to work together, one of which was a sub-plan named Operation Bodyguard. The Americans had initially called the deception plan '*Mespot*', but Churchill did not like it and insisted it be changed to '*Bodyguard*'. The name came from a point made by Churchill to Stalin at the Teheran Conference – '*In wartime, truth is so precious that she should always be attended by a bodyguard of lies.*'

Operation Bodyguard was the overarching deception plan made up of the various ways that the German high command could be misled into believing an Allied invasion would not be on the beaches of Normandy. This was to be achieved by three misdirections; making the Pas de Calais appear to be the main invasion target, keeping the real place and date of the invasion masked, and misleading the German high command into keeping as many of their forces in the Pas de Calais for as long as possible after the actual invasion in Normandy. The wide range of ideas for Bodyguard were worked on from the spring of 1943 by LCS (London Controlling Section) and a special section known as Ops(B) under the control of Eton-educated Colonel Harry Wild. Ops(B) was responsible for all material deceptions whereas LCS was responsible for the more clandestine use of diplomats and double agents.

Bodyguard planning was split into several operations, each one aimed at a different target but with same end objective – to fool the enemy. One was to create the notion that the Allies would invade from Scotland to Norway, another was an invasion in the Bay of Biscay, and another was that the Allied invasion would come from the Mediterranean area. But the most effective, as they were the most readily believed by the Germans, were known as Fortitude North and Fortitude South.

Fortitude North's aim, based in Edinburgh, was to allow enough communications to be intercepted by German radio operators to give the impression that large forces were being assembled and trained in Scotland and a fleet assembled to take them over to Norway. The primary medium used was wireless transmissions as it was generally believed that Luftwaffe reconnaissance was unlikely to be able to reach that far north.

It was very successful and it kept over 300,000 troops tied up along the long Scandinavian coastline.

Fortitude South's objective was to keep the German attention away from Normandy and fixed on the Pas de Calais. Their task was more exacting as the Luftwaffe could send air reconnaissance planes over the short distance from their bases in northern France and the lowlands. The planners would need to devise ways of physically deceiving those observers.

Fortitude South would also, with adroit guile and expertise, exploit the Allies' network of 'German' spies and double agents.

The first major deception was the creation of a massive, new 'ghost' army – the First US Army Group (FUSAG) to be commanded by the already famous and feared General Patton. His reputation had begun as soon as he had landed in North-west Africa in November 1942 as part of Operation Torch. Montgomery was pushing Rommel back from the east following his greatest victory at El Alamein and the two great Allied generals met at Tunisia in April 1943, taking the surrender of all German and Italian troops in North Africa. From there, two months later, they launched the massive joint invasion of Sicily (Operation Husky) and then of Italy.

Patton's reputation and status within Germany had grown to something akin to the way Rommel's name had in Britain two years before. Patton's aggressive, attacking, fast moving Seventh US Army, in particular his armoured corps, quickly earned him respect and praise from both sides. He was often seen leading a tank charge into battle and although that was regarded by some as reckless, to others it was glamorous, fearless and romantically gallant. Whatever the view, and Monty's was not one of admiration, the Germans saw Patton as America's top commander.

Patton, however, being the bullish, uncompromising character he was, made a bad mistake – twice in one week. While visiting field hospitals in Cyprus, he questioned one soldier who was suffering from 'battle fatigue'. Patton was not sympathetic to such 'modern' sicknesses, and accused the soldier of cowardice, slapped the humiliated private on the face and ordered him back to the front line and then did the same one week later. Both incidents were somehow reported back to the Supreme Allied Commander, General Eisenhower. For these actions, Patton faced his downfall. Eisenhower insisted that, at the very least, he had to personally apologise to the abused soldiers, the doctors and the medical staff present. But that did not save him as the press and media got wind of the story – and the American public turned on their erstwhile war hero. Patton now had to make a full public apology and then, as ordered by

Eisenhower, adopt a low profile and hope the issue would die-down. All this only enhanced his 'tough-guy' image in Germany.

Eleven months later, Patton was reprieved and given, with some irony, the command of an army that did not exist – the First US Army Group (FUSAG), ostensibly based in south-east England. Patton's command was seen as confirmation by the Germans that he would be leading the forthcoming invasion. Patton revelled in his fame and made the most of his image as a hard-man by being pictured toting two ivory-handled Colt 45s in holsters. Patton had become the first 'ace card' that the Allies could play in this very serious game of deception.

Next, Ops(B) looked at how they could persuade the Germans that this massive, new, fictitious army existed and that it was preparing for a full invasion at the Pas de Calais. The answer was to build hundreds of dummy tanks, lorries, trucks, and landing craft that would look real from the air when German reconnaissance planes flew over taking photographs. Newspaper reports and photographs of Patton touring FUSAG camps were also leaked.

London Controlling Section (LCS) aimed to convince Hitler and his OKW by means of counter-espionage, using methods more akin to spy fiction. In Operation Fortitude, however, fact would be stranger than fiction.

The *Abwehr* was celebrating the massive amount of information it was receiving from their network of spies based throughout mainland Britain. What Hitler had no idea of was that each and every one was now a double-agent, all working for British Intelligence.

Adolf Hitler and his top commanders were sure there would be a massive Allied invasion in 1944. Their problem was – when and, crucially, where? Scandinavia, Northern European coastline or in the south, from the Mediterranean? These doubts, the British planners of Operation Fortitude North and South were determined to exploit to the absolute maximum.

To do this, a range of sometimes outrageous plans were set in motion aimed at keeping the enemy's dwindling resources of men and machines spread out as thinly as possible over all fronts.

Hitler then made another big mistake. Certain as ever of his 'gifted talent' as a commander, and in no doubt the landing would be at the Pas de Calais, he insisted that all his best mechanised units, particularly his elite SS Panzer divisions, must remain in the Calais area and that none could be deployed without his personal approval. This was to prove an extremely opportune mistake when the Allies landed, 200 miles away along the coast.

Fortitude South had many sub-plans, each with a different number under the name Quicksilver. Quicksilver 1 was the core deception that FUSAG was based in south-east England, preparing to land in the Pas de Calais. Quicksilver 2 was radio deception; Quicksilver 3 was dummy tanks, trucks, and landing craft; Quicksilver 4 was bombing raids on railways and roads in the Calais area; Quicksilver 5 was increased activity around Dover; and Quicksilver 6 was the simulation of night-time activity.

Fake radio traffic was sent over the airwaves simulating the communications of FUSAG and detailing the Allies plan to advance on the Calais region sometime in mid-July 1944. Since the Allies had cracked the German Enigma code, they could monitor the success of the false information they were handing the enemy.

Hitler was taken in totally. All the elements of Operation Bodyguard and Operation Fortitude had served to reassure him of his own convictions and to stubbornly block out the many warnings given to him by some of his generals who suggested the invasion at the Pas de Calais may be an elaborate ruse, but Hitler told his generals, with absolute self-belief -

> *'I think that diversionary actions will take place in a number of places – against Norway, Denmark, the southern part of western France, and the French Mediterranean coast... I expect the Allies would then attack in force across the Strait of Dover.'* [108]

> *'The worst of all deceptions is self-deception.'* Plato

Agent Garbo

LCS was part of MI5 which, during the war years, had intercepted spies sent over from Germany and turned their allegiance to Britain. The most famous spy was the heroic Spaniard Juan Pujol Garcia, whose clandestine name was '*Garbo*'. Garcia had set out to be a double-agent while living in Lisbon. He began by sending regular pieces of convincing disinformation to the *Abwehr* who, once convinced of his usefulness, then sent him to Britain where he further convinced German Intelligence that he had created a network of twenty-seven sub-agents, spread around the British mainland.

In fact, what Garcia had done was to report to MI5 setting up this highly sophisticated fake spy-ring, and sending the best quality disinformation, supplied by MI5, to German Intelligence. So successful was he that Hitler had *'Garbo'* awarded the Iron Cross.

MI5 had a number of other brave and effective double-agents feeding the Germans what they wanted to hear. In France a Polish officer, Roman Czerniawaski, was running a spy-ring when he was captured by the Germans who then offered him a chance to work for them as a spy in Britain. He accepted their offer, but on his arrival in England, he went straight to work for British Intelligence under the name, *'Brutus'*.

Another double-agent was the flamboyant, handsome, Yugoslav-Serbian, Duško Popov. A highly intelligent lawyer, working through the Yugoslav government-in-exile in London, he had infiltrated the *Abwehr* and become one of their most valuable assets. His spy-name to MI5 was *'Tricycle'* because he was head of a group of three double-agents. Popov was known then for his many encounters with famous, beautiful women such as the French film actress Simone Simon. [112] He was the model on which author Ian Fleming based his James Bond, Agent 007 character. Popov was later awarded the OBE [113] but all these enigmatic and brave double-agents were hidden heroes of D-Day.

Only weeks before D-Day, another larger-than-life plot was hatched to deceive the Germans into thinking a major Allied attack from the south may be launched from the Mediterranean Sea.

Second Lieutenant M.E. Clifton James was acting in the Pay Corps Drama Group's amateur production as 'Monty', the well-recognised hero of El Alemein. James's physical likeness was so convincing that it caught the eye of Lieutenant Colonel Jervis-Reid who promptly suggested a most unusual idea to LCS.

Soon after, James was ordered to London and briefed on the plan, named Operation Copperhead. LCS wanted James to play a key part in a deception aimed at convincing the Germans that an invasion, called Operation Dragoon, would precede the main invasion in the Pas de Calais. James was asked to play the part of Monty again, but this time in a real situation. It was not a role he could possibly turn down and within days, James was standing by the great man himself, in an army base somewhere in the south of England. His brief was simple – watch, follow and emulate the Field Marshal's every step, habit, quirk and trait – become Montgomery. James did brilliantly well, even though it was not easy for him to give up smoking and drinking, as Monty did neither. Soon he was being flown to Gibraltar in Monty's plane, acting as the man himself. The likeness was remarkable and all who met him were taken in, including the watching eyes of the local German spies. Shortly after, James was in North Africa, talking to the Allied commander in Algiers and then in Cairo about a mysterious and secret 'Plan 303'. Again, reports were rushed back to the *Abwehr* that Monty was in the Mediterranean. No invasion could be imminent without the presence of Montgomery, so an Allied invasion from the Mediterranean was most likely in the near future, deduced the German high command.

Operation Copperhead was a notable success, confusing Hitler and his generals at the critical moment, only a week or so before Operation Overlord.

Operation Fortitude's success extended even further – on the eve of D-Day, Allied bombing of transport and communications areas around Calais was increased and metre high dummies nicknamed '*Ruperts*', that looked like soldiers parachuting from the sky, simulated a huge airborne

A   B   C

The most successful and sophisticated deception in history was MI5's Operation Bodyguard. The plan completely fooled Hitler and the Abwehr.

A. '*Garbo*' set up a highly sophisticated fake spy-ring in Britain and was totally trusted by German Intelligence. B. Another double-agent spy was the flamboyant, handsome Yugoslav/Serbian Duško Popov, whose promiscuous lifestyle and elaborate network was so fantastic, it is often seen as akin to a James Bond movie. C. Second Lieutenant M.E.Clifton James was an actor who portrayed General Montgomery so well in Gibraltar that German spies were convinced there was to be an invasion from the Mediterranean.

invasion. Large numbers of these fake paratroopers, accompanied by a company of genuine SAS soldiers operating loudspeakers that blasted out sounds of gunfire and shouting, were parachuted into several areas, miles to the east and the west of Normandy. For a critical period, this ruse successfully drew German strength away from the Normandy beaches.

All the extraordinary ideas infused into Operation Fortitude came together in near perfect harmony on 6 June 1944. It is clear that the D-Day invasion on to the Normandy beaches was a surprise to the Germans, as Rommel, the overall Commander in Normandy, had only the night before flown 750 miles to be at his wife's birthday celebrations at his home in Berlin. He had left his post, convinced that the weather forecast of a storm meant that no Channel crossing would be possible over the next few days.

Hitler had sat up till the early hours, talking excitedly to his Propaganda Minister, Joseph Goebbels (Ch.8). The Führer finally retired to his bed in the Berghof at 3 am – just before the first troops hit the beaches – but he was still fast asleep at 11 am, many hours after the German Commanders had first realised what was happening. So absolute was Hitler's power that no-one, not even his most senior army generals, had the courage to rouse their leader from his slumbers. It may seem astonishing, but those vital hours lost to the German high command had a very significant effect, as Hitler had previously ordered that none of his most prized SS Panzers – all stationed in and around Calais – could move without his personal command. Once Hitler was told, he dismissed it as a diversion and told his generals to wait for the real invasion, which Operation Bodyguard had convinced him would soon follow at the Pas de Calais.

Rapid deployment of those elite, battle-hardened tank divisions to the beaches of Normandy could have been disastrous for the Allies. It would have denied them the critical first hours after impact to establish a foothold on the high ground above the beaches and the crucial disembarking of essential vehicles, equipment, ammunition and reinforcements. But it was already too late.

Hitler refused to believe he had been duped and continued to hold fifteen divisions in the Calais region for many weeks afterwards. [114] This was a costly mistake by Hitler.

British Intelligence was able to judge the success of the many parts of Operation Fortitude South as they had been breaking and reading all German coded transmissions for years, thanks to a futuristic piece of equipment invented by the genius mathematician and codebreaker, Alan Turing. What he called the 'Bombe' was the first prototype computer and was based at British Intelligence's secret location in Bletchley Park, Buckinghamshire.

The many deceptions continued after D-Day. Another invention, known as 'window', was clouds of aluminium foil pieces dropped from aircraft on the air path towards Calais, fooling German radar into thinking a large force was on its way. For days after, Garcia continued to feed messages to the Germans, assuring them that Normandy was a diversion, and that Patton would soon be leading the main strike towards the Pas de Calais.

Operation Fortitude North also achieved its aims – Hitler retained twelve divisions with around 300,000 troops in Scandinavia.

There had been turning points in the past: Moscow, Stalingrad, Kursk, and then El Alemein when Churchill had rightly described the moment as *'the end of the beginning'*. Following the total deception of Operation Bodyguard and the success of D-Day, he would surely have believed that this was now *'the beginning of the end'*.

Hitler had made another very big mistake; he and most of his generals had fallen for the greatest military deception plan ever created and successfully executed in world history – Operation Bodyguard.

Chapter 21

Wonder Weapons – V1 to Nuclear Bomb

'False hopes are more dangerous than fears.'

J.R.R. Tolkien

Preamble: There are several excellent books written on the subject of the many *Wunderwaffen* that were either thought of, imagined, designed, built, succeeded or failed during Hitler's period as Führer of the Third Reich. For recommended reading on this subject please refer to the bibliography references. This chapter will be an overview of Hitler's attitude towards new weapons and his failures to take the opportunities some of them may have offered.

There were at least 124 wonder weapon projects created, developed or abandoned over the period between the end of the First World War and the end of the Second World War.

Below is a list of the main categories from which Hitler hoped to produce his war-winning *Wunderwaffen*:

1. Chemical and biological weapons
2. Artillery
3. Tanks
4. U-boats, aircraft carriers, battleships
5. Aircraft, jets, helicopters
6. Missiles, rockets, guided weapons
7. Nuclear
8. Unconfirmed projects – remote control, flying saucers, UFOs, Die Glocke, Sun Gun, laser, microwave and particles beams

Nazi ideology had no room for modernist ideas in culture, art, society, science, or engineering. Hitler's military experiences through the First War (Ch.1) kept his mind in a time capsule of foot soldiers and trenches. He had no time for naval weapons, other than his misassumption that the bigger a battleship was, the better it was and submarines had no place in his imagination. But all of this was about to change.

Joseph Goebbels, one of his most influential henchmen (Ch.8), was a forward-thinking modernist whose progressive ideas excited the Führer, opening his innately reactionary mind to consider radical ideas that, in the past, he would have dismissed out-of-hand. Having seen the light, there was no stopping his newfound desire for any idea that might glorify his Third Reich and feed his intense hunger for territorial expansion – he was soon allocating vast sums of the nation's money to each one.

Hitler was lucky to have around him so many willing and committed scientists, designers, and engineers, each one more eager to impress their Führer with their specialised ideas and inventions.

There were, however, a number of hurdles in the way of such ambitious dreams. First, there was a shortage of natural resources within the borders of Germany, particularly iron ore, fuel and rubber. Hitler ordered his scientists and engineers to create synthetic forms of these raw materials, known in German as 'ersatz', as quickly as possible. This put the Germans a long way ahead of the great western powers in such thinking.

The Germans had been able to produce a low-quality rubber called 'isoprene' during the First World War, but production ceased in 1918. Rubber was essential for electrical equipment and tyres so it was soon top of the Nazi list. The manufacture of isoprene required acetone and aluminium, both of which were also essential for other priorities such as explosives and aircraft motors. There is always a chain of ingredients needed for any synthetic product which creates its own raw material supply problem.

Germany had a huge natural supply of coal in the Ruhr Valley and this was used extensively from 1919 onwards to produce synthetic fuels. By 1938 scientists had refined this into producing petrol of a quality good enough for cars to run on.

Poison Gas, Nerve Agents

One of the saddest twists in the search for synthetic products was when the Nobel Prize winning chemist, Fritz Haber, who first created poison gas in the First World War, went on to make Zyklon B, the chemical agent used to kill so many Jews in the Nazi death camps. The dreadful paradox was that Haber was himself a Jew. [144]

Many other gases and drugs were created with all the resulting horrors that could be imagined and all these monstrous cocktails were tested on the helpless human guinea-pigs trapped in the many concentration camps.

German soldiers were given a form of amphetamine mixed with morphine and synthetic cocaine to enhance their performance. It was never withdrawn even after it was realised that many were soon addicted to it. The Nazi leadership considered individual soldiers expendable in the name of the expansion or defence of the Reich.

Although Hitler could not understand the science behind these experiments, he was fully aware of them and believed that chemical and biological warfare would be the super-weapons that could have a most devastating effect on his enemies.

Artillery

Simpler for Hitler to understand was the V-3 'super-cannon' with a range of up to 100 miles. It could be fired from the European mainland and hit London. An earlier version of this feasible weapon had been developed in the First World War by the German manufacturer Krupps. They had succeeded in building the 'Paris Gun' that could fire upon the French capital from the German border. It was famously named 'Big Bertha' (after Krupp's wife) by the Allies.

The French had begun designing an even bigger gun, but the war ended before it could be built. In 1940, however, when Paris was occupied by the Germans, the plans were discovered, and German engineers began working on the new 'super-cannon' or V-3. The technical problems mounted, and progress was slow, but Hitler easily understood the impact that such a gun, relentlessly firing 600 high explosives shells every hour on London, would surely have in bringing the British to heel.

A site was created near Calais with a network of tunnels and armoured doors, serviced by an underground railway. Fifty new guns were emplaced despite one of them bursting during the later tests. Locally based British spies worked out what was happening, and the genius design engineer, Barnes Wallis, was able to again resolve the physical problems presented in attacking such a well defended place. Wallis had been the inventor and designer of the 'bouncing bomb' used successfully in the *Dambusters*' raid on the three dams in the Ruhr valley, the year before. To overcome the

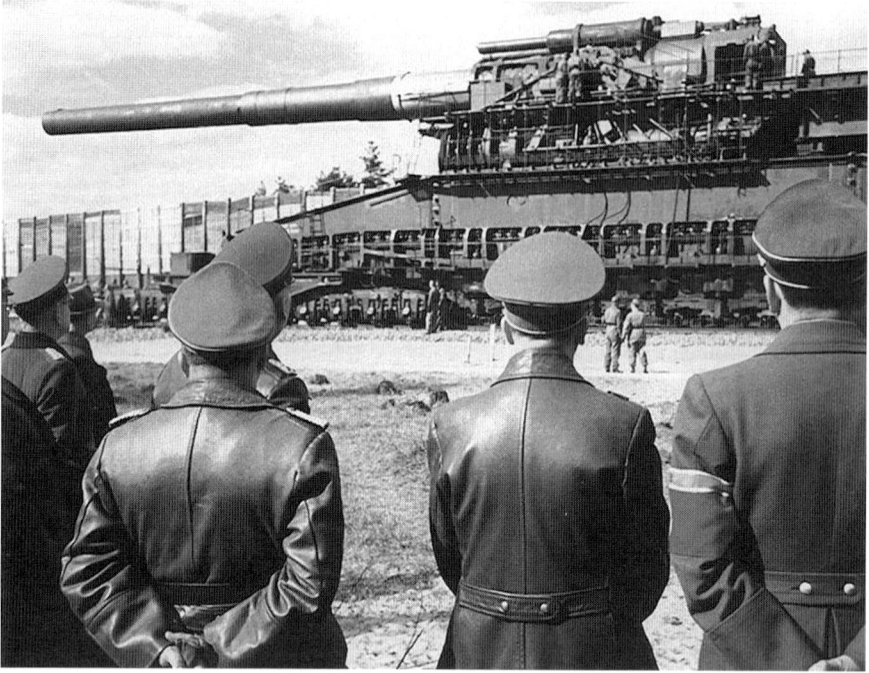

The K5 did succeed in firing a limited number of shells up to 70 miles.

The Porsche-built Panzer VIII Maus (Mouse) was huge at over 10 metres in length and made of 170 tons of thick steel but even more outrageous was the Landkreuzer P-100 Ratte (Rat).

problem of dropping a bomb on an underground factory, covered by up to 20 feet of reinforced concrete Wallis produced the '*Tallboy*'.

The same Lancaster bombers of 617 Squadron that had delivered the 'bouncing bomb' then dropped 35 tons of armour-piercing '*Tallboy*' bombs on the 'super-cannon' site and the V-3 was finished – never again to fire a shot.

Other giant artillery guns were built by Hitler's engineers including the spectacular 200-ton K5, the 300-ton K12 Railway guns, and the monstrous 1300-ton Gustav Gerat 'Dora'.

The K5 did succeed in firing a number of shells 70 miles, but all the giant guns were plagued by technical problems. Impressive though they looked, they never became the *Wunderwaffe* that Hitler was counting on to turn the tide of the war.

Hitler's mistake was that when told by his scientists and engineers that it would never be able to fire high explosive shells on London, he ignored them. The result was yet another colossal waste of time, money and valuable resources on wishful thinking by a dreamer, not a leader.

Tanks, Armoured Fighting Vehicles (AFVs), Self-Propelled Guns (SPGs)

It was also well within the Führer's intellect to see the value of tanks. He had personally witnessed the first British tank charges in the fields of Flanders near the end of the First War. Hitler was, in some ways, a bit of an expert on tanks or at least he prided himself in knowing detailed specifications of all the different models, often right down to the size or thread of a particular nut or bolt.

He was keen on spending vast sums of money on building bigger, faster, and more powerful tanks in vast numbers, convinced this was the simple key to success on the battlefield. He tended not to take account of the consequential extra weight and increased fuel consumption.

The Blitzkrieg successes between 1938 and 1940 were due in no small part to the number of state-of-the-art tanks and AFVs used by the German armies in Poland, France and, initially, in North Africa. Hitler's first realisation that all was not perfect followed the embarrassing retreat of Rommel's lightweight Panzer IIIs and IVs across the northern Sahara (Ch.14), pursued by the heavier Allied tanks. Hitler's immediate reaction was to order bigger tanks to be built urgently for use in Operation Barbarossa (Chs.10&16) – planned to start in mid-1941.

Dr. Ferdinand Porsche (grandfather of the man who designed the Volkswagen 'Beetle' and later the first Porsche 911 sports car) was ordered by Hitler to come up with new ideas and designs. He was in competition with Henschel & Son, a long-established manufacturer of heavy vehicles including AFVs. The outcome was the *Jagdpanzer Ferdinand* and the *Tiger*. The former was a formidable mobile anti-tank vehicle equipped with a devastating 88mm gun. Henschels' years of experience building the lighter Panzers no doubt helped them produce the soon to be ubiquitous, and very successful, Tiger tank, which would be continuously upgraded over the next three years.

Hitler was again taken by surprise during Operation Barbarossa, not only by the vast numbers of T34s that Stalin had been able to produce so quickly, but by their superior performance. The V12 engine was faster, the 76mm turret gun more powerful, the sloping armour more resistant, and the wider track better able to deal with the Russian terrain. Once again, Hitler's reaction was to order, as a matter of urgency, a bigger, heavier tank with sloping armour and fitted with the well-proven 88mm anti-tank gun. His enduring mistake was that he constantly interfered. No sooner was one design under way than he insisted on some modification – sometimes large, sometimes small – but every time it meant halting production and delaying delivery to the battle grounds.

Hitler began to explain the defeats in Russia (Ch.16) and Italy (Ch.19) by claiming that all would soon be reversed when the next improved versions of his Panzers were available. The final attempt at a super-tank was quite successful – the *Panzerkampfwagen Tiger Ausf. B* or *Königstiger* or King Tiger. It was bigger, heavier and had thicker armour but the Maybach petrol engine, re-used from earlier models, did not have the increased power to match the increased weight. Due mainly to Hitler's repeated interferences, it did not get into action until 1944 in Normandy and the numbers produced were severely limited by the huge increase and improved accuracy in the Allied bombing of the Henschel factories by the RAF and USAF.

Many other variants of tanks, AFVs and self-propelled guns were ordered, redesigned and rushed through production; so many, that this became part of the problem. Hitler's obsession with 'bigger means better' had a detrimental effect on the advantages his armies could have enjoyed had he kept focused on one improvement at a time.

One excellent development was the *Jagdtiger* (Hunting Tiger) project. This was to be the heaviest armoured vehicle used during the war, the final version being based on the Tiger II tank, heavily armoured with its 128mm Pak 44 L/55 gun that had a greater range and power than any Allied tank.

Delays again meant that only 88 ever got into battle over winter 1944/45 and at 78 tons there were a number of tactical and mobility shortcomings. Nevertheless, its accuracy on the battlefield was such that they were soon recognised as the deadliest opposition to any Allied tank. [144]

The *Jagdtiger* was still lightweight compared to Hitler's other ambitions. The Porsche-built *Panzer VIII Maus* (Mouse) was huge at over 10 metres in length and made of 170 tons of thick steel. But even more outrageous was the *Landkreuzer P-100 Ratte* (Rat). Hitler was most excited by this design and truly believed that the *Ratte* would win the war for him.

In reality, the proposed 1,000 ton, 35-metre-long goliath was to be five times heavier than the *Maus* which was already twice the size of a Soviet T-34. Few generals supported Hitler's dream 'tank' – Guderian, said, disparagingly, *'Hitler's fantasies sometimes shift into the gigantic.'* [149]

Not content with the *Ratte* notion, Hitler proved Guderian's observation accurate when he backed the idea for the appropriately named *Landkreuzer P.1500 Monster*. This was to be a self-propelled gun weighing more than 1,500 tons – 500 tons bigger than the *Ratte*. The *Maus* and the *Ratte* had already revealed the many problems of these gigantic steel machines – transportation was the first.

They could not be moved on rail or on road as they would be destroyed by the sheer weight, as would any bridges. If that could be overcome then they would also be so slow moving that they would be easy targets for enemy aircraft attack. After wasting so much time and money on Hitler's outrageous fantasies, his brilliant armaments minister, Albert Speer, (Ch.8) finally convinced Hitler to cancel the *Maus*, *Ratte* and *Monster* with not even a prototype of the latter being built.

All these ideas, projects and fantasies – and the resulting waste of vast sums of money, resources and production time – were wholly Hitler's responsibility. If he had focused on perfecting the *Jagdtiger*, then he might have had a super-weapon to improve his prospects of winning, or at least extending, the war.

The supply of raw materials was a never-ending difficulty. Hitler was forced to keep a third of a million troops in Norway, just to protect his only supply of iron-ore. Later he had to divert a large part of his Panzer armies invading Russia towards the oil fields of the Caucasus. Manufacturing so many different AFVs with so many different specifications meant logistical and delivery problems.

Just as serious was the issue of labour. German men were needed for the armed forces, and it was against Nazi ideology for women to go out to work. This was another of Hitler's mistakes, made despite the sound advice of Albert Speer who later wrote that '*it was quite extraordinary how adamantly he opposed this… Britain had fully mobilised. Putting women into factories and uniforms… it remained impossible to the end to persuade Hitler that in total war women had to work in war production.*' [144]

The rate of production in British factories was remarkable during the war years and much of that was credit to the workforce of women who were willingly trained on the types of work that had traditionally been done by men. There were few jobs that women could not master and that included the production of weapons, vehicles, ammunition and tanks. They were also invaluable members of the Armed Forces.

The answer to the labour problem for Hitler was slave labour.

To Hitler, all those held in concentration camps were *Untermensch* and so could be treated in any way. Prisoners were worked to their death, with little food, water, or sleep – it was ideological madness of the most extreme psychopathic kind. It was also a colossal waste of his most needed resource, labour.

U-boats Aircraft Carriers, Battleships

Adolf Hitler had no interest in, and even less knowledge of, naval warfare. He did not give any serious thought to the impact that the blockade of Germany by the Royal Navy after the Battle of Jutland in 1916 had, as it was, in the end, the real reason for Germany having to surrender in 1918. This was not entirely surprising as the First World War had been started very much as a consequence of the Kaiser's conviction that if he built battleships bigger and in larger numbers than the British, then Germany would control the oceans and so be masters of the sea and then the whole world. This was not quite as mad as it may seem today as the fact that *'Britannia ruled the waves'* was indeed the reason why Britain controlled the largest empire ever known in history.

The Treaty of Versailles, following Germany's defeat in 1918, forbade Germany from building warships bigger than 10,000 tons. After Hitler took power in 1935 he entered into an agreement with the British that allowed Germany to build a navy up to 35 per cent the size of the British surface fleet and, even more incredibly, up to 45 per cent of British submarine tonnage.

If Hitler had taken any tactical interest in this gift of an opportunity, he would have insisted his conservative admirals had used the 1938 Z-plan to spend the limit, or more, on U-boats. Instead, he allowed them to squander huge resources building, over the war years, four aircraft carriers, six H-class battleships, three O-class battlecruisers, and twenty-six other different types of cruisers and destroyers – but only 249 U-boats.

This was a big mistake. Had he noticed how successful those early U-boats were in their late quest to blockade British ports he would have had many more built in the 1930s. He may also have noticed that Germany was brought to its knees in 1918, not by the failure of the Ludendorff 'Spring' Offensive, or even by the Allied 'Hundred-Days' counter-offensive, but by the devastating effect that the Royal Navy blockade of German ports had on the civilian population and consequently on the politicians whose decision it was to surrender.

Hitler's military knowledge was based on ideological prejudices and not on educated military calculations. He knew no better than to dismiss the U-boats as peripheral and agree with the Admirals that they had to dominate the surface of the oceans which meant having capital ships bigger and better than Britain.

By 1936, the aircraft carrier *Graf Zeppelin* was under way, and soon after, the mighty *Bismarck, Scharnhorst* and *Tirpitz* were launched. These new battleships were indeed formidable and superior to their British counterparts. HMS *Hood,* for example, could hit targets up to 17 miles away – the Tirpitz had a killing range of 23mls – and the Scharnhorst could shell its enemies out of sight at 26mls. Nevertheless, *Bismarck* was sunk in 1941 by the British battleships *King George V* and *Rodney,* supported by several cruisers – with the death of 2,000 German seamen.

During the battle of Cape North in December 1943, the 32,000-ton *Scharnhorst* was badly damaged when the Royal Navy's *Duke of York* hit her with 13 salvos, but she was hard to sink, and it took a number of other destroyers with many torpedo hits to put her to the bottom of the sea. Another 2,000 German seamen died.

The *Tirpitz*, sister ship to the *Bismarck,* had to spend most of its five years afloat hiding from the British Navy, anchored deep inside the natural defences of a Norwegian fjord. All three H-class battleships, and a number of others, were considered a constant and serious threat to transatlantic convoys so they were all under constant watch.

The *Tirpitz* had been attacked on numerous occasions and in different ways over the years, including one raid by the brave men in the new X-craft mini-submarines armed with limpet mines in Operation Source in 1943. In other attempts, the RAF dropped bombs on her, but they were not powerful enough to seriously damage her hull, so they tried again using the Barnes Wallis '*Tallboy*' bombs that had been designed by him to penetrate the extra thick, reinforced concrete that had protected Hitler's V-3 underground sites in northern Europe. The first raid scored two direct hits, but the Tirpitz stayed afloat, and so on 12 November 1944, thirty-two Lancaster bombers from No.9 and No.617 Squadrons dropped twenty-nine *Tallboys* on the ship. Two again were direct hits and this time the ship began to capsize. A fire then caused the magazine to explode and blow the turret off into the sea. The ship rolled over and sunk to the bottom. Around half the ships complement, about 1,000 men, perished.

As in the First World War, the Kriegsmarine would eventually prove to be no match for the Royal Navy and the Royal Air Force, but by 1942 the British Merchant Navy was suffering a colossal loss of ships, materiel and lives to the U-boats. In November, a new high was reached when 119 ships were sunk in the Atlantic. This was a crucial moment for the Allies as the only way Britain could survive was with the vital supplies being shipped over the Atlantic Ocean from Canada and the USA.

Credit was rightly given by Hitler to the head of U-boats, Vice Admiral Karl Dönitz and he was promoted to be *Oberbefehlshaber der Kriegsmarine*, Grand Admiral of the German Navy. Dönitz was able to make Hitler see the huge waste of resources in steel, money and manpower that had been misplaced in the creation of a surface fleet and to recognise the potential the U-boat had to knock Britain out of the war by attrition.

His predecessor, Admiral Erich Raeder had failed to either recognise the U-boat as his most valuable weapon or, more likely, was part of the inherent snobbery the German navy surface fleet had for what were deemed inferior submariners. The result had been that no priority was given to the construction of U-boats ,which used so much less steel and fewer valuable materials than a massive capital ship and would prove to be – Reichmark for Reichmark – a far better return on the vast amounts of money spent on surface ships.

By the time Dönitz took charge in January 1943, the early successes of the U-boats, known by their crews as the *fröhliche zeit* or 'happy time', when hundreds of merchant ships were being torpedoed and sunk, had ended. The Allies were equally slow to remember those valuable lessons from the First World War, and it took some time to organise a convoy system that afforded the protection of a herd though it remained vulnerable to predators on the edges. More importantly, great strides had been made in the development of underwater radar known as ASDIC (Ch.15) and other anti-submarine detection methods.

Dönitz looked at the weaknesses of U-boat tactics during the First World War and introduced a much improved system called *Rudeltaktik*. U-boats – informed by transmitters from his headquarters in western France – would co-ordinate their positions by calling each other on what they were sure were secured radios. Once assembled in the North Atlantic near an Allied convoy, they would attack in numbers, like a wolf pack.

This was a successful tactic limited primarily by the fact that British Intelligence at Bletchley Park had broken the German *Enigma* code and was reading every message transmitted. Dönitz was surprised that the British seemed to be able to anticipate so many *Rudeltaktik* attacks so well and urged improved designs for his U-boat fleet. In May 1943, Dönitz's younger son, a U-boat Captain, was killed when his *U-954* was sunk. Dönitz then worked on his Führer, convincing him of the better use of, and the real need for, the building of large numbers of new U-boats and describing to Hitler some of the innovative ideas evolving for a super-U-boat. The Type XXI included greater use of power from electric motors combined with diesel engines and an increased number of batteries being recharged while submerged, via a snorkel. It was twice as fast as the old Type VIIs, and could travel submerged at 5mph for 75 hours before needing to re-charge. Instead of four torpedoes, it had automated loading of six that it could fire at the faster rate of one a minute. For the crew of fifty-seven men, it offered roomier berths and a freezer to prevent food spoiling.

Hitler was finally on-side with Dönitz and agreed to go ahead and create this new super-submarine. Special pens had to be built and tens of thousands of prisoners of war or concentration camp interns had to be found and utilised. The sites were gradually discovered and bombed by the Allies, with one site hit by 'earthquake' bombs and then abandoned completely.

By 1945, 118 Type XXIs had been assembled but only four were ready for combat and only two went on sea patrol, neither of them sinking any Allied ships.

It was, as ever with Hitler, hesitation, vacillation, and poor judgement – and all too late. It was a big mistake, right up to the last few months, that he frittered away money and steel on out-of-date surface warships rather than the potentially war-ending Type XXI Super-Submarine.

Jets

One of Hitler's most surprising mistakes was his negligent dissipation of his country's wealth. He more or less threw money, manpower and his scarcest resources at almost every project shown to him – providing he was told it was yet another 'silver-bullet' that would outclass the enemy and bring him glory and victory in short order.

Reichsmarschall Herman Göring was in the modernist camp (Ch.8). He liked nothing more than the latest fashion and this applied to all areas of his ever more exotic lifestyle. He loved being one of the Nazi elite and revelled in being a confidant of his Führer. He was just as keen to look to ever more futuristic notions in aviation, as he saw them as a further enhancement of his larger-than-life ego.

Göring had been made *Oberkommando der Luftwaffe* in 1935 and was not slow in claiming much of the credit, willingly showered upon him by Hitler, for the crucial role played by the Luftwaffe in the defeat of Poland and France. His boast to his Führer to leave the defeat of Britain to him and his Luftwaffe had backfired somewhat by the end of 1940 but it in no way diminished his, or his Führer's, enthusiasm for faster fighter planes and heavier bombers. Hitler was fascinated by the promise of a much faster power source – the jet engine.

In 1928 a young British engineer, Frank Whittle, joined the RAF college in Cranwell and immediately recognised a radical improvement to the internal combustion engine used to power all aircraft since the Wright Brothers. He drew plans, wrote theses and explained his idea of a jet engine to whoever would listen. That proved to be difficult, and one Air Ministry 'bod', incapable of understanding Whittle's discovery, handed back his proposition, telling him it was '*impractical.*' [150] Undaunted, Whittle went on to register a patent for the turbojet engine in 1930. He was 23 at the time, but he would not see his design in flight for more than a decade of reluctant and hesitant official support. A year after the Second World War began, the Air Ministry finally awarded joint contracts to Vauxhall and Rover to build Whittle's new turbojet engine – but only Rover took it forward, albeit very slowly. So slowly that Whittle decided to cobble together his own engine and create an experimental aircraft himself that did fly several short hops in April 1941. In May, the Gloster E.28/39 took off at Cranwell in Lincoln and flew for 17 minutes, reaching a top speed of 370mph, faster than the Spitfire. At the end of the flight, test pilot Pat Johnson said to him, '*Frank, it flies.*' And Whittle replied, with true British modesty, '*Well, that's what it was bloody well designed to do, wasn't it?*' [151] A few months later Whittle suffered a nervous breakdown. But he was promoted to acting Air Commodore in 1944, knighted in 1948, and was later also awarded the Order of Merit.

WHAT WOULD IT HAVE BEEN LIKE FOR THE FIRST TEST PILOT OF A TURBOJET AEROPLANE?

RAF Test Pilot John Grierson (later Wing Commander) put it like this after flying the Gloster E. 28/39, fitted with a Rover W2B#110 turbo-jet engine on 1 March 1943:

'*The main impressions of my first jet-propelled flight were first of the simplicity of operation. The throttle was the only engine control; there were no mixture or propeller levers, supercharger or cooling-gill controls and the fuel system had simply one low-pressure valve between the tank and the engine pump, and one high-pressure valve between the pump and the engine. There was no electric booster pump. Secondly the absence of vibration or the sensation of effort being transmitted to the pilot's seat was outstanding.*' [153]

In Germany, they were not so slow. At first consideration, Hitler approved any idea of a super-fast aircraft although he was not able to understand the science and engineering behind the theory of jet propulsion put forward by Hans von Ohain, a German physicist at *Heinkel Flugzeugwerke*, the aircraft manufacturer. Ohain had also started working on the idea of a turbojet in 1936. He received substantially more support from the *Reichsluftfahrtministerium* (German Air Ministry) and by August 1939 had built the world's first jet-powered aircraft. However, Ohain's design was flawed, and a more efficient version was made by Anselm Franz, an Austrian engineer at Junkers Aircraft Manufacturers, and Ohain's engines became obsolete. Franz's design changed the compressor type to an axial design, and it successfully powered the world's first operational jet fighter, the Messerschmitt Bf110 on 15 March 1942. But it was not until 18 July that the Prototype Me-262 A-1a *Schwalbe* ('Swallow') flew and satisfied all the requirements placed upon the programme. The test flight preceded the Gloster Meteor by nine months.

The Germans had a significant time advantage, but Hitler's interferences again delayed – and to some extent jeopardised – the speedy development of this genuinely revolutionary and potentially war-winning *Wunderwaff*. So impressed was the Führer when this ground-breaking new jet-fighter was demonstrated to him in November 1943, that he demanded it be redesigned as a jet-bomber, later to be designated the *Sturmvogel* (Storm Bird). Hitler was still convinced he could bomb Britain into submission. He had already said as much in his speech to the Reichstag on 4 September 1940:

> *'If the British Air Force drops two, three or four thousand kilos of bombs, then we will drop 150,000, 180,000, 230,000, 300,000 or 400,000 kilos, or more, in one night. If they declare that they will attack our cities on a large scale, we will erase theirs!'*

Hitler's belief that bombing would bring Britain to its knees was wrong. He should have learned that from the failure of the Blitz on London and on other cities such as Coventry, Manchester, and Sheffield, and on the ports of Portsmouth, Plymouth, Glasgow, and Belfast.

All these air raids had done was to add resolve to the British people to take what was thrown at them and to trust in Churchill and the British armed forces to fight back because, as Churchill had subsequently and so emotionally said in the House of Commons, '*We shall never surrender!*'

Hitler's demand to use the jet engine in a new bomber was a ludicrous mistake. It meant the resources and production time wasted on his change of plans had again delayed the real advantage this could have given Germany. More bombing by faster jet planes would offer no real advantage, yet a large number of high-speed jet fighters could have gained control of the skies. That was where modern warfare was to be won or lost. General Adolf Galland – widely regarded as Hitler's greatest fighter ace (he had survived being shot down four times and was credited with 104 aerial victories) – was also Hitler's chief adviser on aircraft, and he wrote in 1944, after a number of test flights, '*I would rather have one Me262 in action than five 109s.*'

The jet fighter was not the only one of Hitler's wonder-aircraft conceived, planned, designed, built, and occasionally flown. There was the first jet-powered bomber, the two-engine Arado Ar-234 B-2 '*Blitz*', built in 1944.

Another, probably the most exotic and futuristic looking was the Horten Ho IX/Gotha Go-229 'flying wing' fighter-bomber. The Go-229 was a response to Hitler's insistence for a light, jet-powered bomber capable of carrying a payload of 2 tons – only 20 were made.

Among the many other jets that never got much past the drawing board were the:

- Messerschmitt Me-329 Zerstörer heavy fighter
- Gotha Go P.60A day fighter/interceptor 'flying wing'
- Blohm und Voss Bv P.210 fighter bomber, a stubby, swept-wing, tailless plane
- Focke-Wulf Triebflügel vertical takeoff and landing (VTOL) fighter
- Focke-Wulf Ta 283 interceptor

Every jet-plane needed a specially trained pilot, and this was one resource that Hitler found constantly in short supply. By the last weeks of the war there were very few pilots able to fly the 250 jet aircraft that had been transported to the front line. Allied fighters countered their speed deficit by changing tactics and, most effectively, by identifying bases and destroying many on the ground.

The most exotic and futuristic looking prototype was the Horten Ho IX/Gotha Go-229 'flying wing' fighter-bomber. Only 20 were ever made.

Of the 200 or so Me262s that went into combat, only 100 remained in May 1945.

After the war, the Allies captured the remaining Me262s, reverse engineered them and used many of the ideas in the development of the Lockheed P-80 Shooting Star, the North American F-86 Sabre jet, and the Soviet MiG-15.

Once again, Hitler's *Wunderwaffen* advantage in aircraft design was to be lost because of his misjudgements and his interference in science and engineering well beyond his intellect and understanding.

Helicopters

Research and development programmes into rotary wing aircraft were already well on the way as demonstrated by a Focke-Wulf Fw61 at the 1938 Berlin Motor Show.

By 1940, there was a small fleet of Flettner Fl282 *Kolibri* (Hummingbird) flying off a heli-pad on the cruiser *Köln* and – later – another group serving *Kriegsmarine* units in the Baltic, all used successfully for reconnaissance.

The first flight in 1940 of the Fa223 *Drache,* or Dragon, impressed the Air Ministry so much that they immediately ordered five variants to be built, but there was still a way to go on development before it could be used for military purposes.

Rotary wing aircraft were already well on the road as demonstrated by a Focke-Wulf Fw61 during the 1938 Berlin Motor Show.

As soon as production was underway, the factory was badly damaged by Allied bombers, and despite changing locations twice more, the same happened again. By 1943, a much-improved design had been built, named the V3 prototype, a larger four-rotor version.

This was followed by further Vs up to a V18, but so many delays, variants and design changes, combined with repeated air attacks, meant the helicopter was never able to be exploited in action; and it would have been very unlikely to have changed the outcome of the war, had it been so.

Missiles and Rockets

Of all the 'nearly-weapons' built, part-built, designed or just thought-of, the one area the Germans really were on the edge of winning the war with was in what is today called ICBMs, or Intercontinental Ballistic Missiles. Although the atomic bomb would have probably done the same, advancement in nuclear science still had a way to go, so that cannot be regarded as an imminent likelihood in 1944 or 1945.

Missile and rocket weaponry were futuristic concepts at the start of the war, and yet as early as 1939, Hitler had boasted in a speech, '*The moment might very quickly come for us to use a weapon with which we could not ourselves be attacked.'* [144] In response, the expert adviser to the British government, R.V. Jones, concluded, *'There are a number of weapons… which must be considered seriously… [they] include gliding bombs, aerial torpedoes and pilotless aircraft'.* [154]

The failure of the Luftwaffe to conquer the skies over Britain in 1940 revitalised the earlier research done on unmanned flying bombs. A crude creation named the FZG76 was soon improved, and by the end of 1942 the first missile was successfully launched from a Fw200 Condor. Six months later a ground-based launch catapult system had been devised and an early gyrocompass fitted to give a basic auto-pilot mechanism.

The Argus-built pulsejet engine pulsed fifty times per second giving it the distinctive buzzing sound that the people of England soon nicknamed *'buzz-bomb'* or *'doodlebug'*. The warhead was triggered when the wind-driven odometer reached its pre-set mileage, up to a maximum of 149 miles, at which point the flying-bomb instantly dropped to earth. It was named by Hitler the V-1, V for *Vergeltungswaffe* or 'Vengeance-weapon', and although not very accurate, it was more than good enough to be fired in large numbers from several bases in northern France, the first exploding in the south of England on 9 June 1944 in Hitler's knee-jerk reaction to the D-Day landings three days earlier. [145]

Mass destruction but more than 400 V-1s were fired in the first three months, most hitting London but some Portsmouth and Southampton. A few V-1s crashed soon after launch, 25 were destroyed by Anti-Aircraft fire and 7 were shot down by Allied fighters (a dangerous practice as the 830 kg warhead's high explosive burst often came close to the aircraft that had destroyed it). The initial impact was upsetting for citizens, but the V-1 was never going to turn the tide of the war on its own.

Much more likely to achieve that objective was the first, truly futuristic weapon; the rocket powered suborbital spaceflight missile, the V-2. It was silent and travelled at five times the speed of sound for more than 225 miles. Its immensity was not lost on its creators at its first test launch on 3 October 1942. Team leader General Walter Dornberger turned to his number two, Werner von Braun, and said, *'Today… is the first day of a new age… today space travel was born.'*

The site at which Dorenberger's team of rocket scientists worked was on an island off the Baltic coast in north-east Germany, called Peenemünde. It had only recently been completed due to a lack of early commitment and funding from Hitler. Despite the remarkable achievements of 3 October, Hitler was not convinced until six months later when Dornberger and Braun flew to the *Wolfsschanze*. On 8 July 1943 they showed film of the successful V-2 test launch to the Führer. Hitler suddenly realised what he had not properly understood up to that point and immediately authorised the rocket programme be given top priority.

But it was already too late as British Intelligence had been receiving detailed reports from Polish agents that rocket development was probably going on in Peenemünde.

RAF reconnaissance photographs had substantiated the suspicions and six weeks after the *Wolfsschanze* meeting, Peenemünde, lying 800 miles due east of London, was attacked in Operation

On 8 July 1943, Hitler saw a film of the successful V-2 test launch and immediately authorised the rocket programme to be given top priority. (*Shutterstock*)

Hydra by 596 RAF heavy bombers. The research centre was damaged and whilst several top scientists and engineers were killed, collateral damage included enslaved workers and several hundred prisoners. Another raid, carried out by the USAF, put the V-weapons programme back by some months. The Allies paid a high cost too – 215 aircrew in 40 bombers were lost. [156]

The V-2 programme recovered at a new site in Poland, much of the work being done underground in the Hartz Mountains. The Germans also developed a mobile launch system, making them less vulnerable to attacks and giving them more flexible options for firing positions. Many further modifications were needed as the development was dogged by technical problems. One test launch, which crashed in Sweden, allowed Allied engineers to gain valuable knowledge from the wreckage, including that liquid oxygen was used as a fuel.

Nevertheless, by September 1944, the Germans had built more than 3,000 V-2s, a quite remarkable achievement given the difficulties of obtaining sufficient amounts of scare materials and fuel. Most were

launched against Paris, London and Antwerp with much damage, widespread panic and the death of over 9,000 civilians. Had Hitler been able to follow this up with a constant barrage of V-2s, including targets in Russia, there may have been a very different outcome to the war.

Realising the huge mistake that he had made three years earlier, Hitler, possibly for only the second time ever in his life, said to Dornberger, '*I have had to apologize only to two men in my whole life. The first was Field Marshal von Brauchitsch. I did not listen to him when he told me again and again how important your research was. The second man is yourself, General Dornberger, I never believed that your work would be successful.*' [155]

Not only was Hitler apologising to a General but more significantly, he was realising that he had had before him, as early as 1942, the very *Wunderwaffe* that could have turned the war in his favour and perhaps even forced the surrender of both Britain and Russia. Hitler admitted it this time; he had made a very big mistake.

Guided Missiles

The Fritz-X was the first ever precision guided missile used in combat. It was used to attack Allied ships on numerous occasions in September 1943 but the Allies soon found ways of blocking the signals used to guide the weapon using electronic counter measure (ECM). It was yet another innovation that should have received more backing than it did.

The Fritz-X was the first ever precision guided missile used in combat. It was invented and first used by the Germans to attack allied ships on a number of occasions in September 1943.

Atomic Bomb

The one truly super super-weapon that would have surely won the war for Germany was effectively prevented from evolving by Hitler because of his most extreme ideological obsession – his hatred of Jews.

At the start of the war, Hitler gave the go-ahead to a group of chemists and physicists after they published a report claiming they were able to split the uranium nucleus. The project was named the *'uranium project'* but to Hitler it looked more like science-fiction, so he did not give it any priority over the long list of other, what seemed to him, far more likely *Wunderwaffen* projects that he had before him.

As big as the mistake proved to be, it could perhaps be excused. Few non-scientists would have made a different decision as nuclear physics was a science for only the most brilliant minds. Many of those brilliant minds were German Jewish scientists, and because they did understand the implications of this discovery, they most certainly did not want such a mega-power to end up in the hands of Hitler. They all departed to the USA as quickly as they could. Among them were Albert Einstein, Edward Teller, Otto Frisch, Hans Bethe, Rudolf Peierls, John von Neumann and the turncoat, Klaus Fuchs. [144]

Consequently, those who did pursue the *'uranium project'* made slow progress, while the physicists who had been welcomed to America with open arms were working rapidly towards the final outcome of the *'Manhattan Project'*. The German scientists were also hindered by the Allies awareness of what was going on and their constant efforts to prevent its progress, whenever possible. This was well depicted in the 1965 Hollywood film, *The Heroes of Telemark,* in which a number of brave Norwegian resistance members sabotaged the Norsk Hydro plant in Nazi-occupied Norway where the crucial component deuterium oxide, better known as 'heavy water', was being produced.

The German atom bomb project failed, not so much because Hitler did not appreciate its war-winning potential but because he allowed his warped anti-Semitic ideology to blind his judgement.

Silver Bullet

As Hitler's early luck faded, he began to look for other ways to win the war, and nothing was more appealing than *Wunderwaffen*. The list of failed and uncompleted *Wunderwaffen* is a surprisingly long one and includes many that were way ahead of their time. More than 75 years later, many have been created and most have surpassed even the boldest dreams of their originators. Chemical and biological weapons; artillery and missiles that can be computer guided onto any target; submarines that can travel round the globe without surfacing, able to fire intercontinental ballistic missiles; supersonic aircraft; helicopters that can go almost anywhere and lift tremendous weights; space travel and satellites; cruise missiles and armed drones that are guided by satellite navigation.

All of these, and more, are a legacy of the race led by Hitler's desperate desire to negate the dreadful mistakes he had made and to find the war-winning 'silver bullet' – his elusive *Wunderwaffen*.

Epilogue

I

As the flames leapt high above the shallow pit at 6pm on the last day of April 1945 in the Reich Chancellery garden, just a few metres from the only exit of Hitler's *Führerbunker*, eight Nazis, including Bormann and Goebbels, stood staring at the blazing inferno with their right arms held rigidly straight out in a most macabre salute. The corpses of Adolf Hitler, Führer and Chancellor of the Third German Reich and his new wife of only forty hours, Eva Anna Paula Hitler nee Braun, were being reduced to cinders in the flaming pyre.

At 1am earlier that same morning, Adolf and Eva had been married. At 2.30pm, later that day, the couple had retired to Hitler's private room, deep down underground in the Bunker that had been built for him only the year before and in which he and Eva had been confined since 15 January 1945 (Ch.19).

Now nothing but a pile of white ash and a few bones remained of either of them. Hitler was dead but the war was not over. The Grand Admiral Karl Dönitz, Head of the *Kriegsmarine,* as a most loyal Nazi and dedicated supporter, had been appointed by Hitler in his last will and testament to be the new Head of State, the President of Germany. The problem was he was not in or near the Bunker on 30 April and others, like Bormann and Goebbels, were not in any hurry to pass on the message to Dönitz who remained unaware of his Führer's death. The two former henchmen (Ch.8) wanted some time to consider their own best options at that moment.

The first plan was to negotiate. They sent General Krebs, the former Attaché to Moscow, to the Russians under a white flag, to hand a letter signed by them to Marshal Zhukov. When Krebs returned in the early hours of 1 May it was only to tell them that the Soviets would not negotiate and that they demanded unconditional surrender by 4pm that day. After further discussion and with no alternatives, Goebbels finally sent a telegram to Dönitz informing him of the situation that afternoon. It was not till late that evening the German people heard the news, broadcast on German radio. But they were not told the truth; they were led to believe that their 'beloved Führer' had died that day, not the previous day, on the frontline '*fighting to his last breath against Bolshevism… a heroic death… at the head of the heroic defenders of the Reich capital*'. [15]

Not everyone was convinced. Some commanders were quick to tell their men that Hitler had taken his own life and thereby abandoned those who had sworn him loyalty. Those commanders then concluded that the war was over and ordered their men to end the fighting immediately.

Joseph Goebbels, Reichsminister for Propaganda and Hitler's most loyal, faithful and devoted henchman was not about to betray his master, even now. His wife, Magda, was with him in the bunker, along with their six innocent children, aged from 4 to 12. Magda was equally dedicated to her Führer and she and her husband decided upon the most bizarre, even horrific, act based on some perverted sense of devotion to him. They gave each child a shot of morphine and then broke a phial of prussic acid, also known as cyanide, into each child's mouth while they slept in their bunk beds. Shortly after, Goebbels gave his adjutant his framed photograph of Hitler and ordered him to make sure his and his wife's body were properly burned. Mr and Mrs Goebbels then led each other up the concrete stairs and stepped out into the Reich Chancellery garden. Together they bit into their own cyanide capsule and collapsed to the ground. The same adjutant then fired two shots into the back of each head, as he had been instructed to do earlier.

All that was left for everyone else to do, trapped in the *Führerbunker*, was to attempt a break out. The Soviets were only a few hundred yards to the east of the city and the British a little further to the west. They all were aiming to get to the British lines – some did, others did not.

II

Dönitz, meanwhile, 250 miles north in Flensburg on the Danish border, tried his luck to conserve some hope and dignity in the terms of surrender. Not that he, nor the Nazi armies and their commanders, deserved any, he nevertheless offered a partial capitulation to the western Allies, along with a desperate hope that they might unite into a common front against Bolshevism.

He formed a cabinet that he believed reflected a less fanatically Nazi impression, and ruled the Nazi salute and *'Heil Hitler'* greeting into history. This created enough of a delay in the fighting to allow almost two million German soldiers time to avoid incarceration by the Russians by surrendering first to the British and American forces. Alas, Dönitz's offer held no water for General Eisenhower, the Supreme Commander of the Allied forces.

The German delegate to the American headquarters, Field Marshal Jodl, was instead given only a few hours to sign the unconditional surrender. Events had taken some days to reach this point, so it was not until the early hours of 7 May that the full, official capitulation was signed, in which it was stated that all German military engagements must end by the end of the next day, 9 May 1945.

III

The war that had been deliberately started by Adolf Hitler on 1 September 1938 was over and now the cost was about to be measured and those still around who were culpable, would soon have their day of reckoning.

Millions of people had been killed or died as a consequence of the First World War but many more had done so as a result of the Second. The cost in lives, property and materials, and the sheer moral degradation, were immeasurable, but something had to done. The total number of deaths over the whole period of the Second World War has been researched intrinsically but to this day the final numbers remain a best-estimate. Of the 70 to 80 million who died, around 50 million are attributed to direct military actions and 20 million from consequential diseases and famine. [83]

In the early part of 1945, discussions were being held within the British Cabinet as to how they would best deal with Hitler and all the senior Nazis on their anticipated surrender. Churchill had no doubt that they should all be shot, or at least executed without trial as soon as possible after the end of the war. The Americans and, for their own reasons, the Soviets, wanted a trial. Churchill was finally persuaded that such an end to Hitler would only be likely to result in him being remembered as a martyr, and he agreed instead to the joint establishment of an International Military Tribunal. Within a few months, the Allies had set up an international court of Justice in the place where the most ostentatiously brazen Nazi rallies had taken place every year – Nuremberg.

For those senior Nazi politicians and officers who had survived to this point, their time had finally come. Many had not got this far, some dying in battle and some, like Hitler, at the end of their own pistol or by swallowing cyanide. Below is a brief description of how many of the remaining senior Nazis and henchmen mentioned within this book ended their time on earth.

Not every Nazi supporter was punished, particularly non-military ones such as the leaders of giant industrial companies and big businesses. Many of those involved had benefited hugely and soon were able to turn their expertise, garnered wealth, factories, and key workers on to the new post-war demands. As previously shown (Ch.8) Hugo Boss soon changed from making Nazi uniforms to becoming what the company still is today, a tailor of fine menswear. Mercedes continues to produce some of the very best quality cars and road vehicles, as do Volkswagen, Audi and Porsche. Many other major companies continue today to grow and prosper, such as Siemens, Kodak, Adidas, Barclays Bank and Deutsche Bank, to name only a few. Germany may not have become the greatest military power in mainland Europe, but it has certainly developed into the strongest economically.

IV

Adolf Hitler, however, remains to this day, the most recognised and the most universally despised person in history. His legacy left many Germans of the new post-war generation deeply ashamed and consumed by regret and remorse. Endless discussions, debates, books, films, and television programmes have been made about him. Some simply condemn him, while others try to analyse his actions, including psychoanalysing his mind, in which they attempt to argue that he was mad, a psychopath, the epitome of evil – nay, evil itself.

Evil is a concept that can be difficult to define and is indeed a matter for individual moral judgement. For Adolf Hitler, it is a word that may even seem inadequate, not only for the quantity of human beings who paid the ultimate price with their lives but also for the inhuman extremes of perverse pain and terrible suffering he caused them. Admittedly, his cruelty was exercised indirectly since he was never known to have personally killed another human and he made sure that he was never seen with blood on his hands. It cannot be countered, however, that Hitler was solely responsible for the start of the Second World War. He had deliberately pursued Socialist economic policies since gaining control of the German economy and, thereafter, had little option but to take over other neighbouring countries to avoid national bankruptcy, beginning with his personally planned and ordered invasion of Poland on 1 September 1939. Everything that followed was as a direct consequence of that order.

Before that fateful day, Hitler had already predicted that:

'Whoever lights the torch of war in Europe can wish for nothing but chaos'. [162]

V

It was other people, ordinary people and events, unpredictable events that had carried Hitler to the top. He started with no more than a cause and a hypnotic oratory so how was it he so quickly became the widely adored and most powerful man in Europe?

It's not that Hitler had no leadership qualities for he was an inspirational Party Leader, attracting genuinely talented individuals, or henchmen to his side (Ch.8), and he was a very tough, shrewd, single-minded politician whose steely determination was tempered just enough with patience to allow him to wait for the right moment before striking. Hitler also had a tremendous memory that he used, often for the most trivial details, that could give him the edge over others, like his Generals who he would often mock or deride as he impressed those present with his pernickety knowledge of the specifications of military equipment. The artistic elements in his character also made him understand and appreciate the real value of image and spectacle that appealed to a very wide audience. It was no accident that he had the most recognisable personal features and that the flag and the Nazi uniforms and insignia were so bold, even terrifying. All had been the vision of Adolf Hitler and all of it had made a massive contribution to the broad public appeal of the Nazi Party and, in particular, of its seemingly charismatic leader.

All these qualities, however, were able to be used only because of the one outstanding natural gift he possessed – the power of his oratory. His speeches always included his gratitude to his audience, his empathy for their concerns and difficulties, the simplified reasons for Germany's problems and then the pointing to those specific people who were to blame. This was not unique in public and political speeches but what was unique in Hitler's speeches were his resolutions. He offered a vision, a clear way forward to a better place. Perhaps the greatest quality of leadership is just that; creating the big picture and showing the audience the clear road towards that great vision.

Hitler was certainly carried to the top by providence and transported by the most incredible run of good luck. When the luck ran out, he did not then have the military skills or leadership needed, and he soon began his fall the long way back down the slope to ruin and death, caused entirely by the big mistakes that he and he alone had made.

VI

Could there ever be another Hitler?
Yes! History is made up of the unexpected, the unplanned and the unpredictable so it is not unreasonable to imagine that a random juxtaposition of unforeseeable events could conspire again, at any time, to produce another enigmatic leader with the mystical powers to beguile a people, a country or to even turn the whole world into some dreadful dystopian abyss.

END

What Happened to Each Character

Beck, General Ludwig: suicide following the failure of 20 July plot to assassinate Hitler

Blomberg, Werner von: died of cancer in Nuremberg, March 1946

Bock, Field Marshal Fedor von: killed on 3 May 1945 by an Allied fighter plane strafing his staff car

Bormann, Martin: sentenced in his absence to hang at Nuremberg, October 1946 but remains found in December 1972 showed he had committed suicide by biting into a cyanide phial, probably on 2 May 1945

Brauchitsch, Field Marshal Walther von: arrested on charges of war crimes but died of pneumonia in 1948 before trial

Bussche, General Axel von dem: avoided execution after the 20 July plot to assassinate Hitler. Studied Law post-war then was headmaster of a German boarding school. Died January 1993

Canaris, Admiral Wilhelm: hanged at Flossenbürg Concentration Camp 1945

Dönitz, Karl: sentenced to 10 years, released on 1 October 1956. Died of a heart attack in December 1980

Dornberger, General Walter: Engineer and rocket scientist who escaped to the USA. Died in Germany in 1980

Eckart, Dietrich: heart attack in Berchtesgaden on 26 December 1923

Fritsch, General Werner von: the second German general to be killed in combat in Poland, September 1938

Fromm, General Friedrich: discharged from Army in the post-20 July purge then executed by firing squad for cowardice in March 1945

Goebbels, Joseph and Magda: suicide together by biting into cyanide phials in the garden of the Reich chancellery on 1 May 1945

Göring, Hermann: suicide by biting into a cyanide phial on 15 October 1946, the day before he was due to be hanged at Nuremberg

Guderian, Field Marshal Heinz: released without trial in 1948. Died on 14 May 1954

Haeften, Lieutenant Werner von: Stauffenberg's adjutant: shot by German firing squad on 21 July 1944

Halder, General Franz: found not guilty in civilian trial then worked with the USA. Died naturally in 1972

Hanfstaengl, Ernst 'Putzi': defected to the USA in 1937, died in Munich in 1975

Hess, Rudolf: suicide by hanging in Spandau Prison in August 1987 aged 93

Heydrich, Reinhard: assassinated in Prague by two SOE-trained Czechs on 27 May 1942

Himmler, Heinrich: suicide by biting into a cyanide phial on 23 May while disguised as an Army Sergeant

Hindenburg, Paul von: died of lung cancer 2 August 1934

Hitler, Adolf: suicide by biting into a cyanide phial and simultaneously shooting himself in the right temple with his own Browning pistol in his private room in *Führerbunker* on 30 April 1945

Hitler, Eva, née Braun: suicide by biting into a cyanide phial alongside her new husband, Adolf Hitler

Jodl, General Alfred: hanged at Nuremberg 16 October 1946

Keitel, Field Marshal Wilhelm: hanged at Nuremberg 16 October 1946

Kempf, General: imprisoned for only two years then died naturally in 1964

Kesselring, Field Marshal Albert: sentenced to hang at Nuremberg but sentence commuted. In prison until October 1952. Died after a heart-attack in July 1960

Kleist, General Paul von: sentenced by the Russians to 25 years in Vladimir Central Prison. Died of heart failure in November 1954

Kluge, Field Marshal Günther Adolf Ferdinand von: implicated in 20 July plot and committed suicide with cyanide on 19 August 1944

Küchler, Field Marshal Georg von: sentenced to 20 years' imprisonment then reduced to 12 years in 1951. Released 1953 and died 25 May 1968

Leeb, General Wilhelm Ritter von: released after Nuremberg trial then died in Bavaria from a heart attack in 1956

Manstein, Field Marshal Erich von: sentenced to 18 years imprisonment. Died of a stroke on 9 June 1973

Manteuffel, General Baron Hasso von: released in 1946, became a German politician then a lecturer in the USA. Died 1978

Model, Field Marshal Walter: shot himself in a German forest on 21 April 1945

Morell, Dr Theodor: arrested but never charged. Grossly obese and suffering from poor health, he died in a German hospital on 26 May 1948

Ohain, Hans von: joined the USA space rocket science project. Died in Florida in 1998

Olbricht, General Friedrich: shot by German firing squad 21 July 1944

Paulus, Field Marshal Friedrich: captured at Stalingrad, acted as a witness for the prosecution at Nuremberg, died of MND in Dresden on 1 February 1957

Popitz, Finance Minister Johannes: a conservative and monarchist, was involved in the 20 July plot and hanged on 2 February 1945

Reichenau, Field Marshal Walter von: after a stroke in January 1942 he suffered head injuries in the ambulance plane when it crashed and he then died

Ribbentrop, Joachim von: hanged on 16 October 1946 at Nuremberg

Röhm, Ernst: murdered by SS guards in June 1934

Rommel, Field Marshal Ernst: suicide in October 1944 after being arrested for involvement in 20 July plot to assassinate Hitler

Rosenberg, Alfred: hanged at Nuremberg

Schlabrendorff, General Fabian von: sentenced to death by Hitler's decree after 20 July plot but avoided execution, worked for USA Secret Service then a judge in Germany. Died on 3 September 1980

Speer, Albert: sentenced to 20 years imprisonment at Nuremberg on 1 October 1946. Died from a stroke on 1 September 1981 in London

Stauffenberg, Colonel Claus von: shot by German firing squad, 21 July 1944

Strauss, General Adolf: died in Germany in March 1973

Thomas, General Georg: sent to Dachau after 20 July plot, died in Allied custody in 1946

Tresckow, General Henning von: suicide by hand grenade, 21 July 1944

Udet, Ernst: suicide by shooting himself in the head while on the phone to his girlfriend, November 1941

Warlimont, General Walter: sentenced to life at Nuremberg but released in 1954, died in Germany 1962

Glossary

Abwehr: German military intelligence service for the Reichswehr and Wehrmacht from 1920 to 1945 commanded by Wilhelm Canaris

Adlerangriff: or 'Eagle Attack'. Large number of Heinkel He 111 bombed the UK on 13 August 1940

Adlerhorst: or 'Eagle's Eyrie'. Hitler's bunker below Kransberg Castle in the Taunus Mountains, Hesse

Afrika Korps: *or German Africa Corps; Deutsches Afrikakorps*, DAK. German expeditionary force commanded by Field Marshal Erwin Rommel during the North African Campaign until its surrender in May 1943

Anglo-Saxons: people from tribes such as Angles, Saxons and Jutes from the area of Europe known by the Romans as *Germania* who invaded and settled in Britain around 500–1000 AD

Appeasement: was Britain's policy in the 1930s of allowing Hitler to expand German territory unchecked

Army Ranks: see table below

Aryan: a race of people that Nazi mythology claimed was pure and perfect and from whom the German people were descended

ASDIC or SONAR used radio waves to detect submerged U-boats, making them much less effective and shortening the Battle of the Atlantic

Axis Forces: name for all German Forces and their Allies

Bagration, Operation: codename for the Soviet Belorussian Strategic Offensive 1944 in the Eastern Front

Barbarossa, Operation: codename for the invasion of the Soviet Union by Nazi Germany and some of its Axis Allies, which started on Sunday, 22 June 1941

BEF: British Expeditionary Force the British Army sent to France in 1939 after Britain and France declared war on Nazi Germany on 3 September

Berghof: Adolf Hitler's home in the Obersalzberg of the Bavarian Alps near Berchtesgaden in Bavaria

Bletchley Park: Mansion house in Berkshire where the British Government Code & Cypher School (GC&CS) deciphered enemy messages

Blitz: German bombing campaign against the United Kingdom in 1940 and 1941

Blitzkrieg: German term meaning 'lightning war' where the attacker spearheads an offensive using rapid and overwhelming combined forces of dive bombers, armoured units and motorised or mechanised infantry formations

bocage: the thick shrubbery and woodlands that lined the roads of Normandy and gave excellent cover to the occupying German troops and armour

Bormann, Martin: head of the Nazi Party Chancellery and personal private secretary to Hitler with immense power to control access to the Führer

Boss, Hugo: founder of the fashion house Hugo Boss AG. He designed and manufactured most German military uniforms and was an active member of the Nazi Party from 1931 to 1948

Braun, Eva: the long time companion of Adolf Hitler and, for less than 40 hours, his wife. She met Hitler in Munich when she was a 17-year-old photographer's assistant and model

Brutus: Polish officer, Roman Czerniawaski was a double-agent spy who worked for British Intelligence under the spy-name 'Brutus'

Canaris: Vice Admiral Wilhelm, Head of *Abwer*

Capital ships: are a Navy's biggest and most important warships.

Chamberlain, Neville: Prime Minister of the United Kingdom from 1937–1940

Churchill, Winston S: Prime Minister of the United Kingdom from 1940–1945 and 1951–55

Commando Order: or *Kommandobefehl* was issued by Adolf Hitler on 18 October 1942 stating that all Allied commandos encountered by German forces in Europe and Africa should be killed immediately without trial, even in proper uniforms or if they attempted to surrender

Dachau: German concentration camp near Munich, opened in 1933 for political prisoners

Directive, Führer or *Führerbefehl:* instructions and strategic plans issued by Adolf Hitler himself that were binding and above all laws, covering a range of subjects from Operational orders to the governance of occupied territories and their populations

Division: see Table of Officer Ranks

Dönitz, Grand Admiral Karl: head of the German navy, including its U-boats and briefly succeeded Adolf Hitler as the German head of state in 1945

Eckart, Dietrich: founder of the NAZI Party

Einsatzgruppen: *Schutzstaffel* (SS) paramilitary death squads of Nazi Germany that were responsible for mass killings

Elser, Georg: constructed and placed a bomb near the platform from which Hitler was to deliver a speech on 8 November 1939 at the Bürgerbräukeller in Munich

Enabling Act: law passed on 23 March 1933 to allow Reich government to pass laws without parliament's consent

Ersatzheer: German Reserve Army

Felder: OKW *Oberkommando der Wehrmacht* Supreme Commander of the Army

Final Solution: a Nazi plan for the genocide of Jews

Focke-Wulf: German manufacturer of civil and military aircraft. Most successful were variants of the Fw 190

Franco: Francisco Bahamonde, *Generalissimo,* a Spanish general who led the Nationalist forces during the Spanish Civil War and then ruled Spain from 1939 to 1975 as a dictator, assuming the title Caudillo

Freikorps: right wing nationalist paramilitary groups in Weimar Germany between the world wars

Führer: German word for Leader. Title used by Adolf Hitler to define his role of absolute authority in Germany's Third Reich (1933–45). In *Mein Kampf* (1925–27) he asserted that such a dictatorship would be extended to the coming Third Reich

FUSAG: fictitious First US Army Group, ostensibly based in south-east England in order to deceive the German High Command the invasion of Europe was going to land at the Pas d'Calais

Gabčik, Jozef: a Czech hero, along with Jan Kubiš was parachuted into Czechoslovakia to assassinate Reinhard Heydrich on 27 May 1942

Garbo: Agent Spaniard Juan Pujol Garcia set out to be a double-agent and set up a highly sophisticated fake spy-ring. The German Intelligence trusted him so implicitly that Hitler awarded him the Iron Cross

Gauführer: a *Schutzstaffel* (SS) rank translated as 'SS-region leader'

Gauleiters: German State Governors appointed by the Nazi Party

Gefreiter: the second rank or grade to which an enlisted soldier could be promoted, Lance Corporal

Gestapo: or *Geheime Staatspolizei*, official secret police of Nazi *Schutzstaffel* (SS) created by Hermann Göring in 1933

Gloster Meteor: the first and only British and Allied jet aircraft to achieve combat operations during WW2

Goebbels, Joseph: Hitler's Reich Minister for Propaganda

Göring, Hermann: Created the Gestapo in 1934, Commander-in-Chief of the Luftwaffe, responsible for the war economy, appointed *Reichsmarschall*, Hitler's successor and deputy. Became very wealthy from artwork and property stolen from Jewish victims of the Holocaust. Addicted to morphine. In 1945 Hitler accused him of treason and ordered his arrest. He committed suicide the day before he was to be hanged

Great Depression: a worldwide economic depression that began in the United States along with the Wall Street Crash in 1929

Gustav Line: German defensive line across the Apennines and hinged on the ancient Benedictine monastery of Monte Cassino

H-class ships: All German battleships, cruisers & destroyers over 50,000 tons such as *Graf Zepplin, Bismarck, Scharnhorst, Tirpitz*

Hawker Hurricane: British single-seat fighter aircraft designed by Sydney Cam in 1935

Heinkel: *Flugzeugwerke* a German aircraft manufacturing company founded by Ernst Heinkel in 1922

Hess Rudolf: Deputy Führer to Hitler 1933–41. Imprisoned by Allies till death in 1987

Heydrich, Reinhard: chief of the Reich Main Security Office (including the Gestapo, Kripo, and SD). Also Reich-Protector of Bohemia and Moravia. and chaired 1942 Wannsee Conference which formalised plans for the 'Final Solution'. Assassinated 27 May 1942 in Prague by Czech patriots

Hindenburg, Paul von: a German general who led the Imperial German Army during World War I and later became President of Germany from 1925 until his death in 1934

Holodomor: Ukrainian word for famine created by Stalin's *collectivisation* policies in the 1930s

HMS *Hood, Duke of York, King George V, Rodney*: Capital class battleships of the Royal Navy

Iron Cross: 2nd Class and 1st Class. German military awards for bravery

James, M.E. Clifton: An amateur actor and Second Lieutenant in the British Army Pay Corps who was an close lookalike of Field Marshal Montgomery

Junge, Traudl: Hitler's personal Typist Secretary

Ilyushin: Russian aircraft manufacturer of a range of ground-attack fighter planes including jets

Katyusha: Russian multiple rocket launcher artillery weapon used from 15 July 1940

Kehlsteinhaus: or Eagle's Nest chalet used occasionally by Hitler at the very top of the escarpment that overlooked the Berghof, his house at the foot of the Alpine mountain near Berchtesgaden, Obersalzberg

Kriegsmarine: the navy of Nazi Germany from 1935 to 1945

Kripo: an acronym for *Kriminalpolizei*, the Nazi detective police force

Kristallnacht: or the Night of Broken Glass was a pogrom against Jews carried out by SA paramilitary forces and civilians in Nazi Germany on the night of 9 November 1938

Krupp Company: Nazi supporting family business, steel producer and manufacturer of many weapons

Kubiš, Jan: a Czech hero, along with Jozef Gabčík was parachuted into Czechoslovakia to assassinate Reinhardt Heydrich on 27 May 1942

Lancaster: British heavy bomber designed by Roy Chadwick CBE and manufactured by Avro in 1941

League of Nations: the first worldwide intergovernmental organisation whose principal mission was to maintain world peace. Founded on 10 January 1920 by US President Woodrow Wilson

Liberator B-47: Aircraft had the ability to undertake surprise air attacks against surfaced German U-boats in winning the Battle of the Atlantic.

The Very Long Range (VLR) Liberators vastly increased range closed the Mid Atlantic Gap [167]

Lucy Spy-ring: an anti-Nazi spy operation of German officers that was headquartered in Switzerland. It was run by Rudolf Roessler, a refugee with a radio and an Enigma machine and masquerading as a German military station (call-signed RAHS) so he could openly transmit their information to him through normal channels

Ludendorff, Erich: a popular, eccentric First World War General. Early member of the Nazi Party but hated Hitler, saying 'I solemnly prophesy that this accursed man will cast our Reich into the abyss and bring our nation to inconceivable misery. Future generations will damn you in your grave for what you have done.' [6]

Lufthansa: was a German airline in Nazi Germany that had close links to the Nazi Party

Luftwaffe: Military Airforce of the Wehrmacht 1933–45

Maquis: the French Resistance movement

Marxism: a social, political, and economic philosophy named after the German Karl Marx that argues for a worker revolution to overturn capitalism in favour of communism

Mein Kampf: a 1925 autobiographical manifesto by Nazi Party leader Adolf Hitler that outlines his political ideology and future plans for Germany. Published 1925 and 1926

   Mein Kampf extracts
   - The English could supply the merchants, the Germans the administrative officials
   - The English nation will have to be considered the most valuable ally in the world as long as its leadership and the spirit of its broad masses justify us in expecting that brutality and perseverance which is determined to fight a battle once begun to a victorious end
   - England would fight to the death to retain her Indian empire, and Germans had learned how hard it was to beat England
   - Germany should not try to take advantage of turbulence in the British Empire, and link its destiny with racially inferior oppressed peoples
   - France, in occupying the Ruhr, had alienated England, and this represented an opportunity for Germany

Mercedes: cars favoured by Hitler and manufactured by Daimler-Benz Company that also built a range of vehicles and weapons for Nazi Germany

Messerschmitt: named after its chief designer Willy Messerschmitt from 1938 and known for its Second World War fighter aircraft, in particular the Bf 109, Me Bf 110 and Me 262 A 1a Schwalbe

MI5: British Military Intelligence department led after 1942 by Sir David Petrie. Its main wartime success was taking the lead role in the now celebrated 'Double Cross System', which fed disinformation to Germany through turned German agents

Molotov, Vyacheslav: Soviet Minister of Foreign Affairs from 1939 to 1949. Signed the notorious 'pakt' with German Foreign Minister Joachim von Ribbentrop in August 1939

Morell, Theo: Hitler's personal physician from 1936–45. Himmler and Göring stated he was a 'quack' doctor with bad hygiene and body odour. He gave Hitler a range of barbiturates, heroin, cocaine and other stimulants [168]

Mussolini, Benito: Fascist Dictator of Italy and Axis ally of Germany. Popular in the 1930s but murdered by an Italian mob in 1945

National Socialist Party: actually the National Socialist German Workers' Party (NSDAP), commonly known as the Nazi Party, in Germany between 1920 and 1945 and ruled under Hitler as Führer, 1933 to 1945

Nero Decree: was issued by Adolf Hitler on 19 March 1945, ordering the destruction of key German infrastructure to prevent their use by Allied forces. It was officially titled *Demolitions on Reich Territory Decree*. It was countermanded by among others, Albert Speer, who wanted to preserve as much as possible for Germany following her defeat in 1945

NKVD: The Soviet Russian People's Commissariat for Internal Affairs. Later the KGB

Nuremberg: central city of the Reich where huge Nazi Party rallies were held every year. From 1945–49 Nazi war criminals were tried there and many executed

OKW: *Oberkommando der Wehrmacht*, the high command of Nazi Germany's armed forces

Panzer IV: German medium tank, 25 tons, 75mm gun used from 1939–45. Variants developed included assault guns, tank destroyers, anti-aircraft guns and self-propelled guns

Panzerfaust: a lightweight, single shot, anti-tank weapon

Panther Tank: It is considered one of the best tanks of the Second World War from 1943 for its excellent firepower and protection. Although less reliable, at 49 tons, it was lighter and faster than the Tiger I

Popov: British spy known for his promiscuous lifestyle and his many encounters with famous, beautiful women and was, in fact, the model that author Ian Fleming later used for Agent 007. Popov was later awarded the OBE (Order of the British Empire) [112]

Porsche: Ferdinand, Dr. Germen Engineer designed and built Jagdpanzer Ferdinand, Jagdtiger, Maus, Ratte

Putsch: from the Swiss to overthrow or rebel, or a *coup d'etat*

Radfahrer: Cyclist messenger

RAF: Royal Air Force

rasputitsa: deep thick, sticky mud caused by seasonal heavy rain in Soviet Union. Germans also called it 'schwarze erde' (black earth)

Rattenkreig: 'rat-war' was how the German soldiers in Stalingrad 1942–43 described the type of warfare being conducted among the cellars, sewers and building rubble

RDF: Range and Detection Finding. Radar to detect and find range of enemy aircraft or vessels

Reichsleiter: deputy Führer. In May 1941, Hitler appointed Martin Bormann to replace Rudolf Hess so as Head of the Nazi Party, Bormann controlled all its finances and became the Führer's right-hand man and no-one could get to see Hitler without first going through him

Reichstag: Berlin building that was the seat of the German government from 1894 till it was destroyed by a fire in 1933, then bombed and shelled in the 1940s

Ribbentrop, Joachim von: Minister of Foreign Affairs of Nazi Germany from 1938 to 1945. Signed the notorious 'pakt' with Soviet Foreign Minister Vyacheslav Molotov

Röhm, Ernst: founder of the *Sturmabteilung* (SA, 'Storm Battalion'), the Nazi Party's militia, and later was its commander but Hitler ordered his execution during the Night of the Long Knives

Roosevelt, Franklin D.: The only US President elected to the office four times, led America through the Great Depression and the Second World War. A great ally of Britain and Churchill

Ruperts: dummies dropped over Northern France on the eve of D-Day to look like Allied paratroopers and confuse the enemy

SA Sturmabteilung: (Storm Detachment) Paramilitary Nazis aka 'Brownshirts' led by Ernst Röhm

SAS: Special Air Service. Special Forces unit of the British Army

Schlieffen Plan: German First World War plan to attack France 1914

SD: *Sicherheitsdienst.* Security Service of the SS aka the Gestapo

Sealion: *Unternehmen Seelöwe.* German plan to invade Britain July 1940

Siegfried Line: known in German as the Westwall, a 390 mile defensive line built during the 1930s opposite the French Maginot Line

Social Democratic Party (German): the centre-left party of the Weimar outlawed by Hitler in 1933

SOE: British Special Operations Executive was a secret British Second World War organisation. It was officially formed on 22 July 1940. Its purpose was to conduct espionage, sabotage and reconnaissance in occupied Europe (and later, also in occupied Southeast Asia) against the Axis powers, and to aid local resistance movements

Soviet Union: the Union of Soviet Socialist Republics (USSR) existed from 1922 to 1991. Its government and economy were highly centralized until its final years. It was a one-party state prior to 1990 governed by the Communist Party

Speer, Albert: one of Hitler's closest friends. Served as his Architect and then Minister for Armaments and War

Spitfire, Supermarine: British single-seat fighter aircraft designed by R.J.Mitchell. Many variants were built, using several different wing configurations, 1936–48

SS, *Schutzstaffel*: Developed by Heinrich Himmler in 1925. *Allgemeine* or General-SS were responsible for enforcing Nazi racial policy, the *SS-Totenkopfverbände* ran the Death Camps and the Waffen-SS were elite combat units of the Army

Stalin, Joseph Vissarionovich: a Georgian revolutionary and the ruler of the Soviet Union from 1927 until 1953. He ultimately consolidated power to become the Soviet Union's de facto dictator by the 1930s. Formalised a a Marxism–Leninist communist ideology into a policy of his own known as Stalinism

Stauffenberg, Claus von: Aristocratic German officer organised the assassination attempt on Hitler on 22 July 1944 known as Operation Valkyrie

Sten sub-machine gun: British sub-machine gun from 1941–1960, chambered in 9x19mm, rate of fire 500 rounds per minute

Stormtroopers: elite German troops in the First World War then specialist troops in the Second World War

Strasser, Gregor: a leading Nazi in 1920s that became too powerful so was murdered in the 'Night of the Long Knives' in 1934

Stuka Junkers Ju 87: German dive-bomber and ground-attack plane, 1935–1945

T34 Tank: Soviet built medium tank 26 ton, introduced in 1940. Its 76.2 mm (3 in) gun was more powerful than its contemporaries while its 60 degree sloped armour provided good protection against anti-tank weapons

Tandy, Henry: VC, DCM, MM. First World War veteran who had Hitler in his rifle sights in 1918 but did not shoot as Hitler appeared to be injured. Hitler later confirmed the story

Thomas, General George: a senior Nazi planner of Operation Barbarossa who failed to warn Hitler of the likely economic and logistical problems. He later had a role in plotting against Hitler

Third Reich: Hitler's name for the Third German Empire he was creating, the second having been in 1871 and the first, the Holy Roman Empire from 800–1806

Thunderbolt P-47: US fighter plane made by Republic Aviation from 1941–66. A very successful, rugged ground-attack plane with rockets and bombs

Tiger Tank: main German battle tank from 1942. Made by Henschel, 60 tons, 88mm gun, V12 Maybach engine. Developed to Tiger II, King Tiger or *Königstiger*

Totenkopf: death's-head or skull was the insignia of all SS units and Panzer forces of the Nazi Army and units of the Luftwaffe

Treaty of Versailles: Six months after the Armistice ended the fighting of the First World War and the Allies had decided the fate of Germany at the Paris Peace Conference, the treaty was registered by the Secretariat of the League of Nations on 21 October 1919

Tricycle: Yugoslav/Serbian Duško Popov was a double-agent spy and head of a group of three double-agents. Likened to James Bond as Popov was known then for his promiscuous lifestyle and beautiful women. He was the model that author Ian Fleming later used for Agent 007. Popov was later awarded the OBE

Turing, Alan: OBE, FRS. English mathematician, computer scientist, logician and cryptanalyst who invented the 'Bombe' machine which can be considered a forerunner of the modern computer. Responsible for breaking the German Enigma codes in Bletchley Park, 1941. Seen now as the father of theoretical computer science and artificial intelligence [169]

Übermensch: the Nazi concept of the superior man or super-man first philosophised by Friedrich Nietzsche that became central to Hitler's ideology. The German or Aryan race was *Übermensch* so all others were…

Untermensch: the Nazi concept of people who were identified as racially, socially and culturally inferior to the German or Aryan race such as Jews, Roma and Slavs

U-boat: *Unterseeboot*, German word for a submarine

ULTRA: intelligence obtained by GC&CS at Bletchley Park

Valkyrie: Plot to assassinate Hitler on 20 July 1944

Wall Street Crash: a major American stock market crash that occurred in the autumn of 1929 and caused the Great Depression of the early 1930s

Wehrmacht: was the unified armed forces of Nazi Germany from 1935 to 1945, consisting of the *Heer* (army), the *Kriegsmarine* (navy) and the *Luftwaffe* (air force). The Nazis used the designation to replace the previously-used term *Reichswehr*

Whittle, Sir Frank: OM, KBE, CB, FRS, FRAeS. RAF officer who invented the turbojet engine in 1936

Wolfsschanze: Wolf's Lair, Hitler's Headquarters in East Prussia, (now Poland) near Rastenburg where he spent a lot of his time after Barbarossa

Bibliography

[0] Joseph Goebbels, "Der Führer als Redner," *Adolf Hitler. Bilder aus dem Leben des Führers* (Hamburg: Cigaretten/Bilderdienst Hamburg/Bahrenfeld, 1936, pp. 27-34.

[1] https://www.warhistoryonline.com/instant-articles/hitler-key-mistakes.html [David Baker]

[2] https://www.youtube.com/watch?v=5agLW7fTzBc [Dr Andrew Roberts lecture in USA "*Why Hitler Lost the War*"]

[3] https://io9.gizmodo.com/the-8-worst-mistakes-made-by-the-axis-during-world-war-1514922468 [George Dvorsky 1914]

[4] https://best-quotations.com/authquotes.php?auth=1 [Best quotations]

[5] Ryback, *Hitler's Private Library.* pp. 169-72

[6] Kershaw, Ian *Hitler 1889–1936 Hubris*, W. W. Norton, New York, 1998

[7] Kershaw, Ian "'*Working Towards the Führer*' Reflections on the Nature of the Hitler Dictatorship" pp. 231–252 from *The Third Reich* edited by Christian Leitz, London: Blackwill, 1999 p. 243

[8] Roberts, Andrew, *The Storm of War* 2010

[9] Wilde, Robert. "*Understanding the Nazi Idea of Volksgemeinschaft.*" Thought Co, Feb. 11, 2020. https://www.thoughtco.com/what-was-volksgemeinschaft-1221370

[10] Lewin, Ronald, *Hitler's Mistakes* 1984

[11] https://www.britannica.com/topic/Mein-Kampf

[12] https://www.britannica.com/event/Dunkirk-evacuation/The-miracle-of-Dunkirk

[13] https://www.history.com/this-day-in-history/hitler-becomes-nazi-party-leader

[14] https://en.wikipedia.org/wiki/Military_career_of_Adolf_Hitler

[15] Kershaw, Ian, *Hitler 1936-1945 Nemesis* 2001

[16] https://en.wikipedia.org/wiki/Adolf_Hitler#Appointment_as_chancellor

[17] Strobl, Gerwin *The Germanic Isle*, Cambridge University Press: Cambridge, UK, 2000 p. 91

[18] Encyclopædia Britannica. "Franz von Papen". *Britannica.com*.

[19] Joachim C. Fest (1 February 2013). *Hitler*. Houghton Mifflin Harcourt. p. 216. ISBN 0-544-19554-X.

[20] Gooden Philip, Lewis Peter. *The Word at War: World War Two in 100 Phrases.* (2014)

[21] Bouverie, Tim *Appeasing Hitler: Chamberlain, Churchill and the Road to War* Bodley Head, London, 2019

[22] https://www.historylearningsite.co.uk/nazi-germany/

[23] *Albert Speer: His Battle with the Truth*, Gitta Sereny, p.218

[24] Shepherd, Ben (2016). *Hitler's Soldiers: The German Army in the Third Reich*. Yale University Press. ISBN 9780300179033. p. 29

[25] Stahel, David (2009). *Operation Barbarossa and Germany's Defeat in the East.* Cambridge, UK: Cambridge University Press. ISBN 978-0-521-76847-4. P86

[26] Robert Gerwarth, in "The Vanquished: Why the First World War Failed to End" (Farrar, Straus & Giroux),

[27] Thomas Weber, now written "Becoming Hitler: The Making of a Nazi" (Basic),

[28] Thomas Mann's startling essay "Bruder Hitler," in *Esquire* in 1939, under the title "That Man Is My Brother."

[29]   Volker Ullrich, "Hitler: Ascent 1889–1939," was published by Knopf in 2016
[30]   Ron Rosenbaum, in his 1998 book "Explaining Hitler,"
[31]   https://www.mtholyoke.edu/acad/intrel/WorldWar2/arsenal.htm
[32]   Jonathan Dimbleby, The Battle of the Atlantic: How the Allies Won the War, Oxford University Press, 2016
[33]   https://en.wikipedia.org/wiki/Battle_of_the_Atlantic
[34]   Guderian, pp. 354–55.
[35]   ed, Trevor-Roper, Hitler's Table Talk, p. 629
[36]   https://dailyhistory.org/Why_did_the_Germans_suffer_a_defeat_at_Kursk_in_1943%3F
[37]   David Eddings, Sorceress of Darshiva, 1991.p223.
[38]   https://en.wikipedia.org/wiki/Battle_of_Kursk#Termination_of_Operation_Citadel
[39]   Clark, Lloyd (2012). Kursk: The Greatest Battle: Eastern Front 1943. London: Headline Publishing Group. ISBN 978-0-7553-3639-5.
[40]   Bergström, Christer (2007). Kursk — The Air Battle: July 1943. Hersham: Chevron/Ian Allan. ISBN 978-1-903223-88-8.
[41]   Sir Winston Churchill's Fighting Speech to U.S. Congress (1943) | British Pathé
[42]   https://www.historyplace.com/worldwar2/riseofhitler/warone.htm
[43]   https://en.wikipedia.org/wiki/German_iolvement_in_the_Spanish_Civil_War
[44]   https://www.britannica.com/biography/John-Churchill-1st-duke-of-Marlborough
[45]   Hitler—The Missing Years: London: Eyre & Spottiwdoode, 1957, 184
[46]   Churchill's Wartime Speeches – A Total and Unmitigated Defeat. The Churchill Society, London. Retrieved 3 May 2019.
[47]   Motl, Stanislav (2007), Kam zmizel zlatý poklad republiky (2nd ed.), Prague: Rybka publishers
[48]   Olson, Lynne (2008) Troublesome Young Men: The Rebels Who Brought Churchill to Power and Helped Save England New York: Farrar, Straus and Giroux. pp. 120–22]
[49]   Moorhouse, Roger. The devils' alliance : Hitler's pact with Stalin, 1939-41. London. ISBN 9780099571896. OCLC 934937192
[50]   https://en.wikipedia.org/wiki/Anglo-Polish_military_alliance
[51]   Hitler, Adolf (1988). Hitler's Table Talk, 1941–1944. Oxford; New York: Oxford University Press. ISBN 978-0-19-285180-2.
[52]   Dederichs, Mario R. (2009) [2005]. Heydrich: The Face of Evil. Drexel Hill, PA: Casemate. ISBN 978-1-935149-12-5.
[53]   https://encyclopedia.ushmm.org/content/en/article/freemasonry-under-the-nazi-regime
[54]   Zeller Jr., Tom (17 January 2007). "The Nuremberg Hangings — Not So Smooth Either". New York Times. Retrieved 15 October 2019.
[55]   Kitchen, Martin (2015). Speer: Hitler's Architect. Yale University Press. ISBN 978-0-300-19044-1.
[56]   https://uboat.net/technical/shipyards/
[57]   Hugh R. Trevor Roper (ed). Blitzkrieg to Defeat: Hitler's War Directives 1939–1945 (NY: Holt Rinehart and Winston, 1971) pp. 206–207
[58]   Seelow, A. (2018), Demystifying Hitler's Favorite Architect. Review of: Magnus Brechtken, Albert Speer. Eine deutsche Karriere Architectural Histories, 6(1): 1-11, Germany, doi:10.5334/ah.334
[59]   https://en.wikipedia.org/wiki/Order_of_battle_for_Operation_Barbarossa
[60]   https://en.wikipedia.org/wiki/Battle_of_the_Atlantic
[61]   Bellamy, Chris. Absolute War: Soviet Russia in the Second World War : a Modern History
[62]   Hellmut G. Haasis. Bombing Hitler: The Story of the Man Who Almost Assassinated the Fuhrer. Translated by William Odom. Skyhorse Publishing Company, Incorporated. ISBN 978-1-62087-954-2.

[63]   https://www.military-history.org/fact-file/hitler-facts-10-little-known-facts.htm

[64]   Geoffrey Blainey; *A Short History of Christianity*; Viking; 2011; pp. 495–496

[65]   Peter Longerich; *Heinrich Himmler*; Translated by Jeremy Noakes and Lesley Sharpe; Oxford University Press; 2012

[66]   https://www.thevintagenews.com/2016/09/23/126133-2/

[67]   https://brooksysociety.com/2020/03/24/winston-churchills-reaction-to-pearl-harbor/

[68]   https://www.goodreads.com/author/quotes/14033.Winston_S_Churchill

[69]   Bullock, Alan (1962) *Hitler: A Study in Tyranny*. London: Penguin. pp.661-64. ISBN 0-14-013564-2

[70]   Below, Nicolas von(2001) At *Hitler's Side* (ISBN 1-85367-468-0

[71]   Mawdsley, Evan (2011). *December 1941: Twelve Days that Began a World War* (PDF). New Haven, Connecticut: Yale University Press. ISBN 978-0300154450.

[72]   Bullock, Alan (1962) *Hitler: A Study in Tyranny*. London: Penguin. pp.661-64. ISBN 0-14-013564-2

[73]   https://www.boredpanda.com/country-size-compared-to-usa-north-america/?utm_source=google&utm_medium=organic&utm_campaign=organic

[74]   https://spartacus-educational.com/Operation_Valkyrie.htm

[75]   Gill, Anton, *An Honourable Defeat: A History of German Resistance to Hitler* (1994)

[76]   Louis L. Snyder, *Encyclopedia of the Third Reich* (1998) page 332

[77]   Joachim Fest, Plotting Hitler's Death (1997) page 180

[78]   20 July 1944 Der Anschlag". The Spiegel. 20 July 2004. Retrieved 23 June 2018.

[79]   https://www.youtube.com/watch?v=pPNXKI2XUsM

[80]   Mitcham, Samuel W., *Hitler's Commanders: Officers of the Wehrmacht, the Luftwaffe, the Kriegsmarine, and the Waffen-SS* (page 31). Rowman & Littlefield, 2012

[81]   Hoffmann, Peter (1996). *The History of the German Resistance, 1933–1945*. Montreal: McGill-Queen's University Press. ISBN 978-0-7735-1531-4.

[82]   Fest, Joachim (1997). *Plotting Hitler's Death*. London: Phoenix House. ISBN 978-1-85799-917-4.

[83]   https://en.wikipedia.org/wiki/World_War_II_casualties

[84]   https://www.youtube.com/watch?v=1tQWj3ggfUI

[85]   *Dalton, Hugh (1986). The Second World War Diary of Hugh Dalton 1940–45. Jonathan Cape. pp. 62. ISBN 022402065X.*

[86]   https://www.youtube.com/watch?v=TBWETZYPa5A

[87]   Moorhouse, Roger (2006) *Killing Hitler*. Jonathan Cape, Random House, London p223

[88]   Speer, Albert. *Inside the Third Reich* London 1970. *Op.cit, p575*

[89]   https://www.youtube.com/watch?v=86kp10cboOQ

[90]   Roberts, Andrew (2019) *Leadership in War*. Allen Lane, London.

[91]   https://api.parliament.uk/historic-hansard/commons/1944/sep/28/war-and-international-situation and Churchill, *Dawn of Liberation*, pp 155/188

[92]   Walzer, Michael (1977). *Just and Unjust Wars*. Pp160

[93]   Ungvary, Krisztian; Ladislaus Lob; John Lukacs (April 11, 2005). *The siege of Budapest: One Hundred Days in World War II*. Yale University Press. p. 512. ISBN 0-300-10468-5.

[94]   https://en.wikipedia.org/wiki/Army_Group_Courland

[95]   *The Decline and Fall of Nazi Germany and Imperial Japan* - Hans Dollinger, Library of Congress Catalogue Card Number 67-27047, Page 278

[96]   http://commons.wikimedia.org/wiki/Commons:Bundesarchiv

[97]   https://www.operationbarbarossa.net/hitlers-directive-no-33/

[98]   Guderian, Heinz (Memoirs of a soldier), Smolensk, Rusich, 1999 (Russian translation of *Guderian, Heinz (1951)*

[99]   Carruthers and Erickson, *Russian Front 1941-45*, pp. 158-9

[100]   ed.Tsouras, Greenhill Dictionary of Military Quotations, p.246

[101]   ed. Young, Peter, *Decisive Battles of the Second World War*,1967 p.182

[102]   eds Heiber, Helmut and Glantz, David M., Hitler and his Generals: Military Conferences 1942-1945 2002

[103]   Domarus, Max, *The Essential Hitler: Speeches and Commentray* 2007

[104]   https://en.wikipedia.org/wiki/Operation_Avalanche

[105]   https://en.wikipedia.org/wiki/Operation_Slapstick

[106]   Leon Goldensohn, Robert Gellately, *The Nuremberg Interviews* by - History – 2004

[107]   Fleming, Gerald, *Hitler and the Final Solution* pg. 17 Statement to Josef Heil, 1922

[108]   Holt, Thaddeus, *The Deceivers: Allied Military Deception in the Second World War* (Scribner, New York, 2004) p565

[109]   https://www.brainyquote.com/quotes/julius_caesar_156555

[110]   https://www.quotes.net/quote/49527

[111]   Sun Tzu, *The Art of War*, Benediction Classics, Oxford. ISBN 9781789430059. Page 2 para 18.

[112]   By RKO - eBayFront and back, Public Domain, https://commons.wikimedia.org/w/index.php?curid=84068857

[113]   https://en.wikipedia.org/wiki/Du%C5%A1ko_Popov

[114]   Moore, Alan T. (2009-12-01). «The Principles Of Military Deception And Operation Quicksilver».2013-04-16.

[115]   https://www.history.co.uk/article/operation-eiche-the-rescue-of-benito-mussolini

[116]   https://www.history.co.uk/article/operation-eiche-the-rescue-of-benito-mussolini

[117]   https://www.roughguides.com/liberation-route-europe/italy/monte-cassino-gustav-line/

[118]   Butler, John, *The Golden Revolution*, Goldmoney Press (10 Mar. 2019)

[119]   https://www.historynet.com/mark-w-clark-a-general-reappraisal.htm

[120]   https://military-history.fandom.com/wiki/German_casualties_in_World_War_II

[121]   https://www.combinedops.com/Western%20Front%20Order.htm

[122]   https://warfarehistorynetwork.com/2019/01/17/smashing-hitlers-atlantic-wall/

[123]   Lehrer, Steven *(2006). The Reich Chancellery and Führerbunker Complex. An Illustrated History of the Seat of the Nazi Regime. Jefferson, NC: McFarland. ISBN 978-0-7864-2393-4.*

[124]   Ohler, Norman (2017), *Blitzed: Drugs in Nazi Germany. Penguin.* ISBN-10 : 0141983167

[125]   https://www.historylearningsite.co.uk/world-war-two/world-war-two-and-eastern-europe/the-final-political-testament-of-adolf-hitler/

[126]   Beevor, Antony *(2002). Berlin: The Downfall 1945. London: Viking–Penguin Books. ISBN 978-0-670-03041-5.*

[127]   Wilmot, Chester (1952). *The Struggle for Europe.* Collins. OCLC 838157.

[128]   *Lieb, Peter (2014). "Rommel in Normandy". In I. F. W. Beckett (ed.). Rommel Reconsidered. Mechanicsburg, PA: Stackpole Books. ISBN 9780811714624.*

[129]   *Messenger, Charles (2011). The Last Prussian: A Biography of Field Marshal Gerd von Rundstedt 1875–1953. Pen & Sword. ISBN 978-1-84884-662-3.*

[130]   Giangreco, Dennis; Moore, Kathryn; Polmar, Norman *(2004). Eyewitness D-Day: Firsthand Accounts from the Landing at Normandy to the Liberation of Paris. New York: Barnes & Noble. ISBN 978-0-7607-5045-2.*

[131]   Rundstedt Testimony, *Trial of the Major War Criminals Before the International Military Tribunal* (Nuremberg, 12 August 1946) vol. XXXI, p 29.

[132]   Interv, Luttichau with Metzsch, 14-19 Mar 52.

[133]   *Reynolds, Michael (2002). Sons of the Reich: II SS Panzer Corps. Havertown, PA: Casemate. ISBN 0-9711709-3-2.*

[134]   *Cooper, Matthew (1978). The German Army 1933–1945. Lanham, Maryland: Scarborough House. ISBN 0-8128-8519-8.*

[135] https://histdoc.net/history/NaSo1940-12-18.html Fuhrer Directive 21

[136] McNeese, Tim (2003), *Great Battles through the Ages: Battle of the Bulge*, New York City: Chelsea House Publications,

[137] *Good, Jack; Michie, Donald; Timms, Geoffrey (1945), General Report on Tunny: With Emphasis on Statistical Methods, UK Public Record Office HW 25/4 and HW 25/5, archived from the original on 17 September 2010, retrieved 15 September 2010* That version is a facsimile copy, but there is a transcript of much of this document in '.pdf' format at: *Sale, Tony (2001), Part of the "General Report on Tunny", the Newmanry History, formatted by Tony Sale (PDF), retrieved 20 September 2010*, and a web transcript of Part 1 at: *Ellsbury, Graham, General Report on Tunny With Emphasis on Statistical Methods, retrieved 3 November 2010*

[138] https://www.britannica.com/biography/Heinz-Guderian

[139] Keegan, John *The Second World War*, p458

[140] https://www.history.com/topics/world-war-ii/battle-of-kursk

[141] Murray, Williamson; Millett, Allan R. (2000). *A War To Be Won: Fighting the Second World War. Cambridge, MA*

[142] *Keegan, John (1989). The Second World War. New York: Viking.ISBN 978-0-67082-359-8.*

[143] Le Tissier, *Zhukov at the Oder*, p20

[144] Fitzgerald, Michael (2019), *Hitler's Secret Weapons of Mass Destruction*. Arctucus Publishing. London

[145] Porter, David, *Hitler's Secret Weapons*. Amber Books Ltd (2018)

[146] https://warfarehistorynetwork.com/2020/04/07/hitlers-wonder-weapons/

[147] Wunderwaffen: Nazi Wonder Weapons (skeptoid.com)

[148] McNab, Chris, *Hitler's Armies A History of the German War Machine*.Osprey Publishing. Oxford (2011)

[149] Guderian, Heinz, *Panzer Leader*, Penguin, 2009 (first published 1950)

[150] *Sir Frank Whittle Archived 7 February 2013 at the Wayback Machine*, The Daily Telegraph, Obituaries, 10 August 1996

[151] Frank Whittle: A Daredevil Who Built Jets, *Bloomberg BusinessWeek*

[152] Air Warfare: an International Encyclopedia: A-L ", Walter J. Boyne. ABC-CLIO, 2002. p. 234, 235. ISBN 1-57607-3459

[153] Flight International 13 May 1971, pp.678-678a

[154] Jones, R.V, *Most Secret War: British Scientific Intelligence 1939-1945*, Hamish Hamilton, 1978

[155] Piszkiewicz, Dennis (2006). *The Nazi Rocketeers: Dreams of Space and Crimes of War.* Mechanicsburg, Pennsylvania: Stackpol Books. P.94. ISBN 978081173387.

[156] https://www.youtube.com/watch?v=fIwB6rwzXsI

[157] Dietrich Dörner & C. Dominik Guess, *Summa Confidentia et Nimius Metus: A Psychological Analysis of Adolf Hitler's Decision Making as Commander in Chief.* Otto-Friedrich Universita"t Bamberg, University of North Florida, 2011

[158] https://www.phrases.org.uk/meanings/clutch-at-a-straw.html

[159] https://www.airforcemag.com/article/0911keeperfile/ *They sowed the wind and now they are going to reap the whirlwind.* Air Marshall Arthur T Harris, RAF Command, 1942

[160] https://www.goodreads.com/author/quotes/228523.Trevor_Ravenscroft

[161] https://www.britannica.com/topic/Mein-Kampf

[162] https://www.brainyquote.com/authors/adolf-hitler-quotes

[163] https://encyclopedia.1914-1918-online.net/article/war_losses_germany

[164] Solleder, Fridolin (1932). *Vier Jahre Westfront. Geschichte des Regiments List R. J. R. 16.* München: Verlag Max Schrift.

[165] https://hushkit.net/2018/04/17/spitfire-versus-messerschmitt-bf-109

[166] https://www.youtube.com/watch?v=EQKM5b1SoS0 TIK, Lewis

[167] Green, William. *Famous Bombers of the Second World War.* Garden City, New York: Doubleday & Company, 1975. ISBN 0-385-12467-8.

[168] https://en.wikipedia.org/wiki/Theodor_Morell#Hitler's_physician

[169] *Beavers, Anthony (2013). "Alan Turing: Mathematical Mechanist". In Cooper, S. Barry; van Leeuwen, Jan (eds.). Alan Turing: His Work and Impact. Waltham: Elsevier. pp. 481–485. ISBN 978-0-12-386980-7.*

[170] http://www.alternatewars.com/WW2/WW2_Documents/Fuhrer_Directives/FD_18.htm *Directive No.18, Gibraltar*

[171] *Geyer, Michael; Edele, Mike (2009). Geyer, Michael; Fitzpatrick, Sheila (eds.). Beyond Totalitarianism: Stalinism and Nazism compared. Cambridge University Press. ISBN 978-0-521-89796-9.*

[172] ICRC. "Convention for the Amelioration of the Condition of the Wounded and Sick in Armies in the Field. Geneva, 27 July 1929". Retrieved 5 March 2017.

[173] Hale, Oron James. *"Adolf Hitler As Feldherr." The Virginia Quarterly Review,* vol. 24, no. 2, 1948, pp. 198–213. *JSTOR,* www.jstor.org/stable/26439867. Accessed 27 Apr. 2021.

[174] Hayman, Ronald. *Hitler & Geli (1997).* Bloomsbury Publishing plc. London ISBN O 7475 2723 7

[175] Shirer, William R. *Berlin Diary,* New York 1941

[176] Nicolson, Harold. *Diaries & Letters Vol.2: The War Years 1939-45.* New York 1967

[177] Rauschning, Hermann. *Hitler Speaks: a Series of Political Conversations with Adolf Hitler on his Real Ams.* London 1940

[178] Waite, Robert G L, *The Psychopathic God Adolf Hitler,* New York, 1977

[179] https://spartacus-educational.com/GERraubal.htm OSS

[180] Fromm, Erich. *The Anatomy of Human Destructiveness,* London, 1974 p409-411

[181] Gun, Nerin E., *Eva Braun: Hitler's Mistress,* London, 1969 p77

[182] Hoffman, Heinrich, *Hitler was my Friend,* London 1955

[183] Wollstein, Hans J. *Renate Muller.* Retrieved 4 April 2009

[184] Hancock, Ian (2005), "True Romanies and the Holocaust: A Re-evaluation and an overview", *The Historiography of the Holocaust,* Palgrave Macmillan, pp. 383–396, ISBN 978-1-4039-9927-6, archived on September 28, 2011

[185] Chase, Jefferson (26 January 2017). "Remembering the 'forgotten victims' of Nazi 'euthanasia' murders". DeutscheWelle.

[186] *Schirach, H.von, Der Preis der Herrlichkeit-Erlebte Zeitgeschichte, Munich 1975*

[187] Hanfstaengl, Ernst, *Hitler:The Missing Years.* London 1957

[188] Waite, Robert G.L., *The Psychopathic God, Adolf Hitler,* New York 1977

[189] Lambert, Angela. *The Lost Life of Eva Braun* (2006) p103

[190] Goebbels, Joseph. *Unpublished diary for 30 March 1928,* quoted in Irving, *Goebbels,* p553

[191] Schroeder, Christa, *He was my Chief:the Memoirs of Adolf Hitler's Secretary* (1985)p213

[192] Toland, John, *Adolf Hitler,* New York, 1976

[193] Gun, Nerin E., *Eva Braun: Hitler's Mistress,* London 1969

[194] Bullock, Alan. *Hitler: A Study in Tyranny.* (1962)

[195] Schirach, Henriette von, *Frauen un Hitler. Nach Materialen von Henriette von Schirach,* Munich 1983

[196] The History Place - Rise of Hitler: Hitler in World War I

[197] http://www.nommeraadio.ee/meedia/pdf/RRS/Adolf%20Hitler%20-%20Collection%20of%20Speeches%20-%201922-1945.pdf

[198] https://historycollection.com/these-famous-historical-figures-suffered-from-unique-phobias/3/

[199] https://www.warhistoryonline.com/war-articles/top-10-unknown-facts-about-adolf-hitler.html

[200] https://ww2db.com/doc.php?q=331 – Fuhrer Directive 51

PHOTOGRAPHS AND IMAGES

[a] *Photo: Bundesarchiv, Bild 146-1989-089-00 / CC-BY-SA 3.0.*
[b] Public Domain File:Bill Clinton and Monica Lewinsky on February 28, 1997 A3e06420664168d9466c84c3e31ccc2f.jpg Created: between 1995 and 1997 date QS:P,+1995-00-00T00:00:00Z/8,P1319,+1995-00-00T00:00:00Z/9,P1326,+1997-00-00T00:00:00Z/9

OTHER SOURCES USED

Radio 4 – *In Our Time,* Melvyn Bragg. https://www.bbc.co.uk/sounds/search?q=in+our+time+hitler&page=1

https://www.youtube.com/watch?v=RpJxMGweNZQ *the Rise of Hitler 1929-1934*

https://histclo.com/bio/c/ind/ch/chamb/app/appi-anti.html *Names of all pre-war Anti-appeasers*

https://www.newyorker.com/magazine/2018/04/30/how-american-racism-influenced-hitler his character, personality

https://www.youtube.com/watch?v=aiIsGxgzkn4 *5 Worst Military Blunders:*

https://www.youtube.com/watch?v=uK3BeR3bzlM

https://ww2gravestone.com/84-german-generals-were-executed-by-hitler/

https://www.youtube.com/watch?v=p-_mav0kw44

https://en.wikipedia.org/wiki/Schutzstaffel

https://www.youtube.com/watch?v=GK419Nlp8eU&t=51s *Top 10 Mistakes by Hitler Proving he was an idiot*

RECOMMENDED FURTHER READING ON THE SUBJECT

There are many books available on the topic of Adolf Hitler, with authors approaching the subject from various angles.

The Storm of War by Andrew Roberts
Leadership in War by Andrew Roberts
Masters & Commanders by Andrew Roberts
Churchill: Walking with Destiny by Andrew Roberts
Hitler vols 1&2 by Ian Kershaw
Appeasing Hitler, by Tim Bouverie
Hitler & Geli by Ronald Hayman
The Lost Life of Eva Braun by Angela Lambert
Eva Braun: Hitler's Mistress by Nerin E Gun
Hitler's Secret Weapons by David Porter
Plotting Hitler's Death by Joachim Fest
Killing Hitler by Roger Moorehouse
Hitler's Armies by Chris McNab
Hitler's Mistakes by Ronald Lewin
Hitler & Stalin by Laurence Rees

The full list of references used in the research for this book is printed in the Bibliography.

Paul Ballard-Whyte

Index